THE HOUSE OF YAN

The House of Yan

A FAMILY AT THE HEART OF A CENTURY IN CHINESE HISTORY

LAN YAN

TRANSLATED FROM THE FRENCH BY SAM TAYLOR

HARPER

NEW YORK · LONDON · TORONTO · SYDNEY

HARPER

Photographs courtesy of the author.

Originally published as *Chez Les Yan* in
France in 2017 by Allary Éditions.

HarperCollins books may be purchased for educational, business, or sales promotional use. For information, please email the
Special Markets Department at SPsales@harpercollins.com.

First U.S. edition published 2020.

Designed by Jen Overstreet

Library of Congress Cataloging-in-
Publication Data has been applied for.

ISBN 978-0-06-289981-1

20 21 22 23 24   LSC   10 9 8 7 6 5 4 3 2 1

For my mother, always my role model.
For my father, always my hero.

The Yan Family Tree

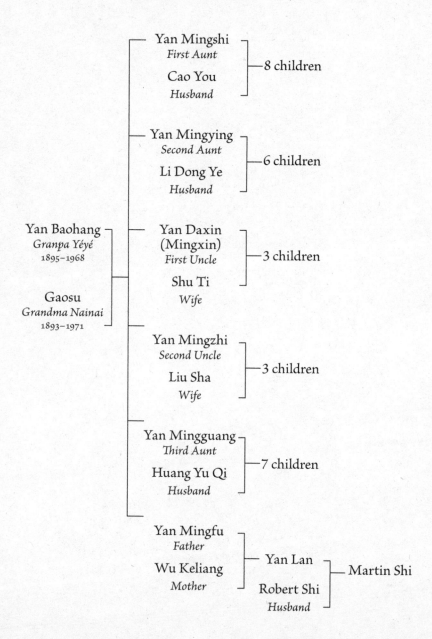

Yan Baohang
Granpa Yéyé
1895–1968

Gaosu
Grandma Nainai
1893–1971

Yan Mingshi
First Aunt

Cao You
Husband

—8 children

Yan Mingying
Second Aunt

Li Dong Ye
Husband

—6 children

Yan Daxin
(Mingxin)
First Uncle

Shu Ti
Wife

—3 children

Yan Mingzhi
Second Uncle

Liu Sha
Wife

—3 children

Yan Mingguang
Third Aunt

Huang Yu Qi
Husband

—7 children

Yan Mingfu
Father

Wu Keliang
Mother

Yan Lan

Robert Shi
Husband

—Martin Shi

Preface

On January 1, 2016, I was in Sanya, on the tropical island of Hainan in the south of China, to celebrate the New Year with my father.

I told him I was thinking of writing about the history of the Yan family. Despite his eighty-four years and fragile health, my father leaped up and squeezed my hands with all his strength, as if he wanted to impart all the energy inside his body.

Not only is that an excellent idea, he told me, but you should make it your priority for the coming year.

I didn't say this to him, but his reaction reassured me in the decision I had made.

During all the years I spent in France, whenever my French

friends asked me about my family or the history of China, I could tell how astonished they were when I told them what we had lived through. They had very little conception of what had happened during the Cultural Revolution or the period that preceded it.

One day, my closest friends, Catherine and Bertrand Julien-Laferrière—Bertrand is my son's godfather, and I am the godmother of one of their Chinese daughters—encouraged me to tell the story of my family, which was, in microcosm, the history of modern China. That was ten years ago, and their words have continued to echo within me, along with the famous adage that, for an accomplished life, one must plant a tree, have a child, write a book.

My son is twenty now; how will he ever know his family's history if not through books? Biographies of my grandfather have already been published in China. My father completed his memoirs after ten years of writing and research in Beijing and Moscow. My mother, too, wrote the history of her family for me. I am grateful to her for that and I feel honor-bound to continue this tradition.

What I have seen, heard, experienced was so intense that I must take my turn to bear witness to it.

Yan Lan[*]

---

[*] In China, my name is Yan Lan. The family name always appears before the given name in China, as you will notice throughout the book.

Prologue

I was four months old when my parents entrusted me to the care of my paternal grandparents. Mama was about to leave for Rome, before joining the Chinese embassy in Bern, where she was posted during one year. And with my father being a Russian interpreter for many high-placed Chinese dignitaries, among them the supreme leader Mao Zedong, he did not have time to look after me either.

So it was that the faces of Nainai, my grandmother, and Yeye, my grandfather—along with the face of the ayi, my nanny—became more familiar to me than those of my diplomat parents; more familiar and, if I am honest, more tender and kindly toward their little Nan-nan (their nickname for me), and considerably less severe than my mother's.

In her memoirs, my mother writes that she left her baby at the State Council's residence in the center of Beijing, where my paternal grandparents had, for years, lived in a staff apartment on the third floor, right-hand door, of Building 10.

That was the address where I lived, where I had my bedroom, where my grandfather's chauffeur took us when Yeye came to fetch me for the weekend from the entrance to the garden of the boarding school where I was placed at the age of three.

So it was unusual, that day when my mother came to pick me up from a primary school. To be enrolled there, I had to pass an exam. And on the solemn occasion of my application to join the first-grade class of this prestigious establishment, my mother had made herself available, eager as she was to find out how her daughter had fared in that oral exam.

I have good reasons to remember that day. The test—as my mother called it—was this: I was shown the picture of a cat climbing the trunk of a tree where a small bird was perched on a branch. The teacher asked me to tell her what I thought would happen next.

"And what did you say?" my mother asked me.

I explained that the cat was climbing up to the bird so he could become its friend.

"That's completely wrong," my mother replied, instantly irritated. "What you should have said is that the cat was about to eat the bird."

Needless to say, I was not accepted. That was the first and the last time that I failed an exam.

It was summer 1964. I was seven years old.

1

A revolution is not a dinner party, or writing an
essay, or painting a picture, or doing embroidery;
it cannot be so refined, so leisurely and gentle,
so temperate, kind, courteous, restrained and
magnanimous. A revolution is an insurrection, an act
of violence by which one class overthrows another.

—Mao Zedong, the Little Red Book, 1966

There are seven or eight of them.

Seven or eight men, heels hammering up the three flights of
stairs in Apartment Building 10 of the State Council's residence.

Their fists pound on the door.

Seven or eight caps, uniforms, armbands rush into the apartment.

"Yan Baohang!" the caps bark.

This is not the name of the woman in the kitchen, our ayi, who is making dinner, and who cries out in fear.

It is not the name of my grandmother—I shove my face into her soft fleece blouse, and her hands cover my ears to protect them from the shouting.

Yan Baohang, the name they are barking all over our apartment, is my grandfather's name. The name of the man I call Yeye.

I am crying because I am not used to all this yelling, all these staircase stampedes, all this banging on doors.

Despite my grandmother's hands, which tremble as they stroke my hair, despite the downy warmth of her blouse, where I have cocooned my fear, the barking of those seven or eight tense jaws terrifies me.

"Yan Baohang!"

My grandfather's name.

Yan Baohang does not hide. He has come out of his office. He stands there calmly. "Yes, that's me. Who are you? What do you want?"

One of the caps turns to me then and says, "No need to cry, little girl. He is just coming with us so we can talk. It's very simple." The cap adds, "He will come with us for a few hours. Or a few days. To talk with us. And when he has said everything he has to say, your grandfather will come home. So there's nothing to cry about!"

My grandfather does not say: "That's right, Nan-nan, don't be scared!" My grandfather Yan Baohang, who does not look angry or upset (have I ever seen Yeye angry or upset?), who does not even seem worried, merely serious, replies in the cool, composed voice that he always uses in solemn moments. "In that case, gentlemen, in order for me to comply with your request—namely, that I follow you so that we can 'talk'—I must see some official papers, an arrest warrant, something that proves..."

Papers? But how could a few pieces of paper prevent my grandfather from eating dinner with us, as he does every evening? How could a few pieces of paper deprive me of my grandfather's palm placed ritually on my head as he says in his gentle, tender voice: "Come on, Nan-nan, it's time for bed now."

But as I peek sideways from my grandmother's blouse, just to check that such papers do not exist, I see them being taken from the pocket of a uniform jacket and held in front of my grandfather's face. With one hand he adjusts his glasses; with the other he signals the men to go through into his office. And he says: "The only radio in the apartment is in there. Please, gentlemen, examine it to ensure that it is not, as you claim, a telegraph transceiver. You are still suspicious? Very well, gentlemen, then please take this radio, have it examined. Let us be done with this."

Forty minutes passed. The three of us did not move. Did not speak. The ayi stood in the kitchen doorway, while Nainai and I sat in the dining room. Other than the pounding of my grandmother's heart, which I could feel through the fabric of her blouse, other than my grandfather's dry cough, reaching us from his office where he was locked in with those soldiers, not a single sound was audible in the dark apartment building. The night held its breath.

Suddenly, from behind Yeye's office door, I hear a loud burst of words.

"COUNTERREVOLUTIONARY! BOURGEOIS! REVISIONIST! SPY!"

I do not know what those words mean. All I hear is, "BAD! WRONG! LIAR! TRAITOR!"

My grandmother touches her hand to my forehead and realizes that those yelled insults have triggered a fever. I am scared of losing Yeye, and my heart is gripped by the feeling that something terrible is about to happen.

It all happens in a fraction of a second. "Don't be afraid," my grandfather says as he comes out of his office and walks, flanked by soldiers, toward the front door. That is his only concern at this moment, as he prepares to leave his home, his wife, the mother of his seven children, as he prepares to leave his granddaughter, the only child of his youngest son, as he prepares to leave the ayi who has served his family for ten years: that we not be afraid. And, most of all, that we do not insult him by awaiting his return before we eat dinner. He says all of this while the seven or eight tense jaws under caps mass around his tall and noble figure.

We stayed outside the door for a long time. In shock.

Not the front door. No, we stood outside the wide-open door of his office for a long time before we dared go in. Something of him remained there, in his office, and it was with that something that we tried to find consolation.

Nainai went in first and I followed her, refusing to let go of her hand. Then came our dear ayi. She had been living with us in Beijing for ten years, having come from her native Hebei province to help my grandmother look after me. Her gentle face was more familiar to me than the face of my own mother. I thought I had seen every possible emotion on that face of hers, depending on whether I was docile, obedient, conscientious, lazy, careless, or bad-tempered. But never had I seen her cry before.

On my grandfather's desk there were pages from the *People's Daily*, the *People's Liberation Army Daily*, and the *Red Flag*, annotated in the margins in his handwriting.

"Lan, come and help me," he would say, gesturing with his chin at the ink stone, the rice paper, the calligraphy brush: the treasures of a Chinese man of letters. He watched my clumsy hand movements, guiding them until the ink came from the stone onto the lashes of the brush. He was as skilled at Chinese calligraphy as he was at writing with a fountain pen or even a ballpoint pen, which was the only way that we knew how to write. Everybody agreed that Yeye was an excellent calligrapher. And connoisseurs praised the quality of his poems in the ancient style.

Yeye knew the classic texts, too, the stories of the ancient dynasties that were no longer taught in schools: the *Great Learning*, the *Doctrine of the Mean*, the *Analects* of Confucius, and the *Mencius*, the "Four Books" that all honest men were supposed to possess. The spidery handwriting that covered the newspapers and magazines that he read also demonstrated a perfect understanding of English.

The only thing missing from his office was the large radio on which, every morning at 7:30, even on weekends, he would listen to the news. But that radio was not his. My father had lent it to him the previous year because my grandfather's radio had died.

Nainai was right. I remember it all the more since, soon after that date, instead of telling me that my father was under house arrest in his office, they simply announced that, because he was "very busy at the moment," he would only be able to come and see me occasionally. Nainai, who was used to reading my thoughts and emotions in my face, must have guessed what was on my mind: "Don't worry, Nan-nan," she said, "you'll see, by January or February everything will be back to normal and Mingfu will be with us again . . ." I noticed that she was loath to add the name of another beloved person—my grandfather—to this sentence, and I realized that was because adding just one more name would mean starting a list. I understood that many people who were dear to me, family members whom I saw less and less often, remained in suspense, waiting to find out if their name would lengthen a dark list that was at that moment being formed in the deranged minds of the list makers, who wanted to bring together every member of each family: aunts, uncles, even in-laws. As I looked at the beautiful portrait that I had always seen above my grandfather's desk, I noticed for the first time how curious that picture was: a black-and-white photograph, a face in profile, in a marble frame that made the image appear three-dimensional. My grandfather had told me the name of that person several times. He had even told me that I had met him. But he knew so many people—so many people wanted to shake his hand—that it was hard for me to recall one particular name . . . Except that not everybody had the privilege of having their framed portrait hung above his desk! And as I was trying to remember that name, it suddenly came to me, brought to mind by my grandfather's last words . . . On the doorstep, surrounded by the seven or eight Red Guards, he had started coughing. My grandmother had run to fetch him a coat and while she handed it to him, Yan Baohang had said: "No need to worry, my dear Gaosu, it's nothing serious . . . just tell the prime minister about it. Yes, that's right, nothing serious, but let Zhou Enlai know about it."

It was fall in Beijing. On that night—November 6, 1967—it was cold in the apartment, since the official date for the use of heating had not yet been issued, but my grandmother and I did not sleep. We stood by her bedroom window and watched the Milky Way throw its luminous net across the sky. Below, the maples in the garden were blood-red.

2

Although t tree may grow a thousand meters high,
its leaves fall back always to its roots.

—Chinese proverb

From time to time, Nainai would take me to visit some old
friends. The esteem that my grandparents had felt for them
since the 1930s meant that I had to call them Grandpa Wang and
Grandma Wang, just as Nainai called them Big Brother Wang
and Sister-in-Law Wang, in accordance with Chinese tradition.

I have forgotten the name of the alley—the *hutong*—where
they lived. Banchang Hutong? Lumicang Hutong? But I will
never forget the tiny room where the Wangs lived, a combination
bedroom, kitchen, and living room. Somehow in that minuscule
space where the whole family was crammed, we, too, were welcomed and would drink tea with them, even if I could not under-

stand how such a thing was possible, even if drinking tea in that room, which opened directly onto the street, was, for me, just like drinking tea on the street. Anyway, drinking tea was one thing, but beyond that, I had no idea how they managed to sleep with the minimum of decency required by a family that, clearly, did not lack decency.

I did not ask questions, so I could not know what connected my grandparents to these people who were slightly younger than they (they were in their sixties at the time), though obviously they must have been close friends because the Wangs were invited, in return, to drink tea in Building 10, in Xibianmen: a neighborhood of a much higher standing. I was surprised that they did not seem to resent us for living in a large apartment where each person had his own room, a spacious and light-filled apartment with large bay windows that did not look out on another building, a dining room and a living room where two or three dozen people—family or friends—were often gathered. When my cousins visited, they were jealous because, unlike them, I was able to live there. And while it is true that they received just as much affection as I did from our grandparents, I was lucky enough to share a home with them. As for my grandparents, I thought it remarkable how naturally and gracefully they accepted their situation.

And yet there was, in that impoverished *hutong* whose name I have forgotten, at least one element that ought to have given me a clue to understanding what brought people from such opposed ways of life into a happy and harmonious unity. Those people were Dongbei Ren.

And what does this mean, "to be Dongbei Ren"? To answer that crucial question, I had only to remember what my grandfather would say whenever he was asked: "Where are you from?" This question was always posed by people from Beijing to any other Chinese person—at least those whose accent did not betray their origins. It was important to know where one was from, so that one did not "feel like a duckweed without roots," as the proverb puts it. All you need do is look at a map and compare the scope of China to that of any European nation in order to understand that this question has a meaning beyond any sense of misplaced nationalism. When two Chinese people meet for the first time, the question "Where are you from?" is one of the most common. And if by chance you meet a native of the same region or province where you grew up, that person instantly becomes your compatriot, as if being Chinese were not quite enough. And when that happens, the distance between the two of you vanishes immediately.

"I am Dongbei Ren," Yeye would always answer when someone asked him that question. This meant: "I come from Dongbei, in the northeast of China. I come from the former Manchuria, even though I am not a Manchu—the minority that, throughout the last dynasty, ruled over China from 1644 to 1912, and under this dynasty I was born. I am not Manchurian; I am Han. All the same, I cannot deny that my homeland is there, in the northeast. And, of the three provinces (Heilongjiang, Jilin, and Liaoning) that comprise that region—to my eyes the most beautiful region of China—I am from Liaoning. I come from the forest, the land of tall tree trunks; I come from the snow and the cold. I come from that world of evergreens: the pine and the thuja, the giant juniper and the silver birch. I belong not to the China of rice and tea because, as you know, that China begins below the Yellow River, well south of Beijing; no, I belong to the China of wheat and sorghum, the China of dumplings and galettes, the China of the best tobacco, which can be burned in a water pipe. And without wishing to insult those of my compatriots who were not lucky enough to have been born there, I come from that region so fiercely torn from Japanese hands that we know the price, the terrible price paid in blood."

But my grandfather would not deliver this tirade in the *hutong*, for the simple reason that the Wangs were from the same land; they already knew all of this without having to be told. But how did I know they were Dongbei Ren? Well, as they did not belong to that section of Chinese people who had been to London or Edinburgh, as Mrs. Chiang Kai-shek once said, not only had they kept something in their mannerisms of their original peasant coarseness, but also the intonations of Beijing—urban, standardized, excessively civilized—had not worn away the rough edges of their accent. So, when they sang together, always the same song, "On the Songhua River," it was their big, warm, powerful voices that let it be known: "My house is in Dongbei, by the river Songhua . . ."

My parents, too, lived in a *hutong*. Despite being diplomats, they did not belong to the regime's "normal" cadre class. They had to walk through a courtyard to go to the toilet, although they did have a pair of two-bedroom apartments, converted into a traditional house—a little *siheyuan* built around a square court-yard, where four other families lived; and in China, back then, this was already evidence of privilege, since the paradox in this continent-sized country is that each individual has always had to fight over his own little living space. But my parents were most often in Europe: Paris or Rome, or Switzerland for my mother; "Eastern Europe," as it was called at the time (Moscow, Warsaw, Bucharest), for my father.

At eight or nine, having never traveled and without any-thing to compare it to, I was not aware of the similarity between certain buildings in Switzerland, Holland, or Denmark and the architecture of the State Council's residence: 1950s architec-ture, solid and sober, with a concern for its residents' well-being; intelligent enough to include some domesticated nature in the form of gardens of pagoda trees and jujube trees, weeping wil-lows and persimmon trees. The only thing I was able to say about our residence—and you will gauge from this how spoiled I was as a child—was that the third floor of Building 10 had a balcony (which, of course, did not overlook another building!) where I was allowed to keep chicks, bought one memorably happy day at the market, on a whim. Those chicks grew up into hens, and one of them—a particularly fat one—tried to escape once, launching itself off the balcony and flying, or rather falling with style, from the third floor down to the flower beds below. So it was that the other residents stared in stupefaction at my grandfather running after the hen in his bathrobe and slippers.

"I'm telling you, it was Mr. Yan Baohang!"

"Yan Baohang? The minister?"

"I don't know if he's a minister. I thought he was head of protocol."

"Head of protocol? Yeah, maybe . . . but he's a senator anyway, as you know. Or, rather, he was a permanent member of the Political Consultative Conference . . . He was even governor of Liaobei in his day, back when the communists first won those provinces in the north."

"Okay, but so what? The residence is full of big cheeses like that . . ."

"Well, at eight o'clock on Saturday morning, watched by his granddaughter, little Lan, who was yelling at him, 'Yeye! Please catch her!' Mr. Yan Baohang was running around the gardens in his slippers and his bathrobe trying to grab hold of a hen so he could take it back to the little girl!"

As is true all over the world, there were magical words—often place-names—that allowed you to identify yourself instantly.

If, for example, I said that I lived in Xibianmen, the person I was talking to would immediately think of the State Council's residence and ask: "Isn't that where the former Chinese vice president used to live, back in the Kuomintang days? Isn't that where the Huangs live—the family of Huang Yanpei! Isn't that home to Yan Baohang, the former governor of Liaobei, the senator?"

"That's Yeye," I would reply, unable to conceal my pride.

And if the other person then said: "Might I ask Miss Lan if her papa is also a member of the People's Consultative Conference?" I knew that they were likely to be impressed if I replied:

"No, Papa works at the Zhongnanhai [the central government headquarters]." But I would not tell them that I sometimes ate lunch with my father at the Zhongnanhai, because I was not trying to impress them, and because at the time I was not aware of what a privilege this was. Bragging was frowned upon in our family, so I did my best not to brag about anything at all, and in any case it did not seem such a big deal when I went to eat there: I presented myself to the guards on duty, trying not to be intimidated by the stiffness of their bearing; then one of them would call over another employee whose job was to walk with me to my father—that was it. Nor did I tell anyone that I had once been invited to watch a private showing in the cinema room of Mao Zedong's residence, simply because I did not realize how extraordinary that was.

But to return to the subject of Xibianmen: quite simply, everyone who had mattered before the New China, before 1949 and beyond, lived there, in one of those bourgeois, Western-style family apartments, two on each landing, in three-story buildings surrounded by trees. There were many former generals there, dignitaries of the *ancien régime*, a number of people in honorary positions, members of the People's Consultative Conference and the National People's Congress, etc.

In our building there were also some celebrities without any connection to politics. People came from all over the country, if they were lucky enough to be given an appointment, to see Dr. Ye, who lived on the first floor of Building 10. And even though nothing in the construction of the residence's buildings—the layout of the rooms, the arrangement of furniture—had been designed with any regard to geomancy or other precepts from ancient China, Dr. Ye practiced traditional Chinese medicine. Because although this tradition, more than a millennium old, completely ignored modern science, it was the only form of medicine with which parents and grandparents thought it prudent and reasonable to treat their children, since they themselves had been healed by it. Even beyond his fame, old Dr. Ye was not remotely like a simple family doctor: any consultation with him, be it for the smallest injury, was an extraordinary event.

So, if one of my twenty-seven cousins was careless enough to cough in the presence of my grandparents, he was immediately taken down to the first floor, where he was seen without delay, thanks to the privilege that Dr. Ye gave "to the Yans on the third floor." As far as I was concerned, I had at least one good reason (even if I would have struggled to think of any others) to regret living in the residence: I still retained the vivid, bitter memory of tasting Dr. Ye's herbal soup. This soup had to be eaten after first swallowing a series of decoctions in accordance with an obscure but inarguable ritual, and its taste convinced me that the happiness of living with my grandparents in Xibianmen came at this cost. The fact that the soup got rid of my fever did not make it seem less of a negative.

One day, in the hope, I suppose, of encouraging me to swallow his herb soup, old Dr. Ye took the trouble of explaining to me that this was how my sick body would regain its balance between yin and yang. And since I stared at him wide-eyed the first time that he uttered those words, he added, "You have come to see me, little Lan, because you have too much fire in your body. In the case of a small person with too much fire, the absorption of herbs that I have chosen specially for that person will bring to her body the cold that is missing from her balance. If, on the other hand, your body had been too cold, I would have chosen herbs to bring you more fire." At that, I grew bolder, "But, Dr. Ye, what is the yin? And what is the yang?" The kindly old doctor replied, "To know that, little Lan, I think you must devote nothing less than your entire life." The most important thing was to maintain a balance between yin and yang. And that was where I thought my education in the principles of traditional Chinese therapy would end . . . until a few years later, when I was living in the countryside, I thought again about those principles and became interested enough to learn the fundamentals of what, back then, were called "barefoot doctors."

But Dr. Ye's popularity among our family was also due to the credit that he allowed Nainai at the end of certain months. And perhaps because this favor had always been one-way and offered with good grace, Dr. Ye was given a particularly warm welcome one evening, much later, when he knocked at our apartment door with a request. The question of whether, in the context of the era, it was a good idea to grant that request was never posed. Just as kind Dr. Ye had always refused to calculate the interest on the credit he gave us, our family likewise refused to calculate the risks involved in granting the extravagant favor he asked of us.

The doctor wished to entrust two trunks to the safekeeping of Gaosu, my grandmother, if that did not bother her. "Naturally, I will show them to you," our eminent neighbor had said, adding that after mature reflection this appeared the best solution to him because nobody could tell what would happen to him if the Red Guards discovered those trunks, which contained furs— very beautiful furs, as it happened. Whereas for the Yan family, or more precisely for Yan Baohang, who was a "red," not to mention a close friend of Zhou Enlai, there was nothing to fear from such a discovery.

Louwen, too, lived in the residence. In the same building, in fact, on the second floor, and she went to the same boarding school. Her father was head of the documentation department in the State Council.

On weekends, Louwen would sometimes come to play in our apartment or I would go to hers. The reason I mention her is that Louwen was my friend. My best friend, during those years. But that is another story.

3

Crescent moon, cold pale gold sickle.

—Lao She, *Crescent Moon*, 1935

November 6, 1967, just after 8 p.m.

The garden of the residence is entirely swallowed by darkness. Midfall in the lunar calendar: the icy sandstorms from Mongolia are not yet here. Fewer lights on in windows than usual. Some of the neighbors even turn off their lamps, I feel sure, as we rush to the balcony to watch my grandfather. The sudden blackness reminds me of the detestable habit the grown-ups now have of whispering into one another's ears or speaking in murmurs, or going into another room and closing the door behind them when I approach; and, when I ask them about this, their detestable habit of answering me with a "don't worry," spoken in a tone of voice that only makes me worry more.

My grandmother's "don't worry" that night is even worse. The night, too, shrinks into the darkness, listening out for any sounds, listening out for a sob or a shout.

Nainai immediately sent the ayi to warn everyone she could find in Beijing. Their youngest son, my father, "very busy at the moment," cannot intervene to find out where Yeye will be kept: he is forbidden to go anywhere, forbidden to go home or to his father's apartment. But as it happens, Mama is in Beijing; she will come, my grandmother is sure. One of my cousins, too, Lingling, who is staying with my grandparents temporarily, will be back soon, particularly since her university classes have been suspended for the past few months. And so you might think that it is my mother, or one of my aunts, or my cousin Lingling whom we are looking out for as we stand on the balcony. We also keep an eye on the front door of the apartment. In truth, though, it is he and he alone, my grandfather, whom we are hoping to see return at any moment.

That cold evening, on the balcony, the Red Guards' words are still burning my forehead. Holding tight to my grandmother's chest, I feel their venom flowing through my veins, into my flesh, through my grandmother's veins; I feel that poison move toward my heart and toward her heart, too.

Yet in my mind is Yan Baohang's face, at the moment he left his office: their insults had not altered the expression on his face. None of their cruel words had made him lower his head or hunch his shoulders or grimace. From his office, where those words had been yelled, he came out, looking serious but straight-backed and calm. He did not raise his voice; he did not struggle when one of the Red Guards grabbed him, and even that Red Guard must have sensed his natural authority. My grandfather did not need to shout in order to be obeyed; he never shouted at me, and yet I always obeyed him. Not only did that Red Guard not prevent Yan Baohang from freeing himself, but he did not hold him back when, in no rush, he went up to his wife to speak to her in a gentle voice, and then to me, tenderly placing his hand on my head as he always did.

I realized that, if the Red Guards' words continued to glow and burn inside me like embers, it was because they had the power to harm me, not my grandfather. Those words submerged me in shame, as if I were the one who had been called BAD, WRONG, LIAR. I also realized that if my grandmother stayed on the balcony instead of going to bed, if she had sent the ayi across town to search for our family, friends, and allies, if her gaze continued to move from the garden to the front door and back again, if she let me stay up with her in the middle of the night, it was because the Red Guards' words had hurt her, too. It was because those words hurt my father, my mother, my aunts, my uncles, my cousins. They sullied our entire family.

At last my mother arrived. Barely had Nainai finished telling her what happened than my mother was going through her list of contacts, working out what needed to be done, with that ability she had—and which I always envied—to prioritize the most urgent tasks, to act instead of complaining. This capacity of hers meant that some people might consider her cold, but all the same she was the one who was busy exerting herself, methodically organizing the plan intended to free my grandfather from the claws that had closed around him. Almost as soon as my cousin Lingling entered the apartment, my mother was handing her a list of instructions, and then the two of them left.

The search was on. In less than an hour, dozens of people on bicycles—because nobody had private cars back then—were racing across Beijing in all directions, trying to find out WHO had taken him, WHERE they had taken him, and WHY they had taken him.

4

The straight man does not fear a crooked shadow,
and the honest man does not dread
the devil's knock at his door.

—Chinese proverb

It was the spring of 1966. Kehui, my mother's younger brother, liked to take photographs. He had asked my grandparents to pose for him in the gardens of the residence. I was there, beside him. I thought that my uncle had chosen a perfect background for his portrait: behind the old couple, the end of a cherry tree branch hung with blossoms stretched up toward the sky. It was beautiful.

I do not remember what Nainai was wearing that day because she changed her clothes every day: sometimes a single-color blouse, sometimes one with a flower pattern, or a Chinese-style tunic with pants, a matching silk scarf around her neck. As for my grandfather, I hadn't seen him for days and his image remained as it was in that photograph. Perhaps that is also because there is less variety in men's clothing. Except in very old portraits, taken when he was studying in London, Edinburgh, or Copenhagen, when he dressed in that kind of Shandong silk crepe shirt that in the late 1930s was worn like a tunic, not tucked into pants, or in a suit, or a blazer and tie, a Western-style overcoat, black silk socks, black satin slippers with thick soles of white piqué cloth . . . other than in those portraits I always saw him in *Zhōngshān zhuāng*, that jacket with four external pockets and a short flat collar, or a raised collar in the style of officers that is (wrongly) known as a Mao collar, whereas in reality all Chinese men wore such collars from the beginning of the twentieth century, Mao among them, following the fashion of Sun Yat-sen, the father of modern China, one of the founders of the Kuomintang and the first president of the Republic that permanently overturned the Qing dynasty. For the Chinese men of that era, wearing that jacket was a sign that they belonged to the new age that was beginning in China. In fact, from the moment that that jacket had been "proposed" by the Chinese leader and immediately adopted by the 1912 government, it became more than an emblem: the official costume of China, since worn by all the country's leaders, including the current president, Deng Xiaoping, who often wears it during official ceremonies as a traditional symbol of contemporary China. As for that name—*Zhōngshān zhuāng*—it is taken from the common name of the founder of the first Chinese Republic, Sun Zhongshan: Sun Yat-sen was his literary name, more familiar in the West than in China. But the most spectacular of all the innovations of that time must have been, I suppose, the gesture that symbolized the break with feudalism: most of the men in the generation before my grandfather's had stopped shaving the tops of their heads and had cut the tight braid that they used to wear down their back, and which the Manchus had demanded as a sign of allegiance for almost three centuries.

Anyway, everybody said that my grandfather—whether he wore a suit and tie or the *Zhōngshān zhuāng*—always looked very elegant. Tall. Like most of his compatriots from the northeast, he had skin as pale as the wheat fields that have given rise to Dongbei's nickname as the granary of China.

Of my grandfather, it was always said that he was physically and morally distinguished. Sober but warm. Faithful to his friends. Generous. Very sociable. In support of their admiration, some people highlighted his ability to meditate deeply and to think for himself.

"How could Yan Baohang be a bad man?" wondered Soong May-ling, the wife of Chiang Kai-shek. This was the woman who, before she agreed to marry Chiang, had demanded that he not only divorce his wife, but also give up his concubine and embrace the Protestant religion! "How could Yan Baohang be a bad man," she asked, "when he is a pious Protestant?"

Pious? I'm not so sure. My grandfather never took me to church. He never spoke to me of Jesus Christ. Protestant? Yes: he was converted in his youth, like the writer Lao She, his friend during his years as a student in Europe, who, like him, rallied to the communist regime.

Nainai liked to tell people that at the birth of Mingfu, my father, a mendicant monk came to their home to ask for alms. My grandmother had immediately told my eldest aunt, Mingshi, a child at the time, to give the monk a few coins and to let him know that this charity came from Christians, not from Buddhists or Taoists. Proof, if any were needed, that this strong woman (all the Yan women are strong) did not hide her religious convictions.

Soong May-ling had many things in common with Yan Baohang, who was only three years her senior. They both spoke English, had both studied in the West, had good social skills, and were refined in their appearance and in their thoughts.

My father remembers excitedly that Soong May-ling once gave Yan Baohang a convertible. This was when the government was headquartered in Nanjing. Yan Baohang had agreed to lead the New Life Movement initiated by Mrs. Chiang Kai-shek and her illustrious husband. It was my aunt Mingshi who drove a Chevrolet, with my father, Mingfu, then a very young child, in the back seat. In his memoirs, he recounts the pleasure his sister felt as she honked the car's horn, which had a special sound, in Zhongshan Mausoleum Scenic Area in Nanjing, and how the two of them enjoyed watching Chiang Kai-shek's guards rushing over to salute every time they heard that familiar sound.

An old family friend also liked to tell the story of how Soong May-ling once telephoned Yan Baohang after midnight: Chiang Kai-shek wished to see him without delay. Naturally Yan Baohang went straight to the palace, and when Soong May-ling herself answered the door to him, she cried out: "Ah, Paul [my grandfather's English name], you came so quickly . . . without even shaving! That's wonderful! That's . . . perfect!"

5

Disasters never come alone.

—Chinese proverb

November 17, 1967, eleven days after the arrest of Yan Baohang,
his youngest son, Mingfu, was incarcerated

First my grandfather. Then my father.

It no longer made sense to try to shelter me from the truth. I was told about the house arrest that my father had been under for the past year, allowed to leave his office only on weekends. And then I was told that he had been arrested.

My uncle Mingzhi and his wife, both of whom worked in the Ministry of Foreign Affairs, were put under house arrest. The same thing for my eldest uncle, Daxin, even though he was an army general. One of his daughters was handed a megaphone and forced to proclaim publicly that she disowned her father and would have nothing further to do with him. And as if that were not enough, my aunt Shu Ti, Daxin's wife, a high school teacher, was publicly humiliated in front of her students before having her head shaved. According to the rumors, she remained free until further orders. Humiliated but not incarcerated.

Sometime before this, I had come out of school asking to be given a Red Guard uniform. Another time, I had worn the famous scarlet armband. When our teacher started initiating us in the art of brush calligraphy, I had planned to make *dazibaos* because I saw them all over the walls of the city in those days. My mother had severely reprimanded me for this: "Do you have any idea what a *dazibao* is?" she had asked angrily. "A *dazibao*, young lady, is something that criticizes and denounces people!" She reminded me that all students should always respect their teachers. Then she condemned the ignorance of young people who claimed to know better than their elders. What she meant when she said "young people" was the Red Guards; at the time, students in colleges and even in high schools were involved in making accusations, criticisms, and denunciations. But she was also condemning my own ignorance. On the one hand, I had been kept in ignorance; on the other, I was reproached for it. I was ten years old. I was desperately confused.

My grandmother and I watched from the windows, taking care not to be seen. Everybody watched from windows. Everybody took care not to be seen. If someone knocked and you weren't sure who it was, you pretended you weren't home. Everybody stayed in their apartments and everybody pretended they were somewhere else.

The word *arrest* cropped up in every phrase. On everybody's lips was the name of Jiang Qing, Mao Zedong's fourth wife. Even though the Party's political office had made it a condition of their marriage that the ex-starlet should abstain from all political activity, Jiang Qing was now a member of the group within the Central Committee that was in charge of the Cultural Revolution. Rumors spread of muddled and unverifiable scenarios: for example, of confessions made under torture; of a former Kuomintang general who had, through these confessions, enabled the dismantling of a group of counterrevolutionaries rampant in the northeast—with this group consisting of several current and former Red Army generals, allies of General Zhang Xueliang, and several current or former ministers.

We did not seek the source nor the evidence of these allegations. We simply translated: Yan Baohang is a former Kuomintang member. From the northeast. A close friend of General Lu Zhengcao, another native of Liaoning. A former minister, appointed by the communist government led by Liu Shaoqi. So he was the culprit. The rumor did not specify if Yan Baohang was dead or alive.

Evidence was fabricated. Conspiracies were invented. Fictions were woven around the word *treason*.

A transceiver for the sending and receiving of coded messages, crudely disguised as a transistor radio, had been seized. The suspect had been denounced as a spy for Moscow. Mao Zedong's entourage was infested with traitors. The chairman, Liu Shaoqi, and his closest ally, Deng Xiaoping, were incriminated. A network like that required a Russian speaker. Not to mention a revisionist, the name Mao now gave to disgraced Soviet leaders such as Nikita Khrushchev and Alexei Kosygin. In Mao Zedong's entourage, infested with the above-named traitors, Yan Mingfu was the official Russian translator. In all the photographs where Mao Zedong, Liu Shaoqi, and Kosygin are together, Yan Mingfu is there, too. Yan Mingfu tried to hide the transceiver at his father's apartment. The two culprits are now behind bars.

All day long, family, friends, and acquaintances paraded through the apartment with new information that we hurried to report to my mother. The most recent information contradicted the previous information. The more blatant these contradictions, the truer the story seemed. Despite all the rumors and reports, the truth was that we knew nothing; we could be sure of nothing. While my mother roamed all over the city on her bicycle, my grandmother invited people into the apartment, listened to them, comforted them, walked them to the door. Each time those people left, the person I loved most in the world would hold her head in her hands, close her eyes, and—as if speaking to herself—ask, "Do they at least have warm clothes?" I asked her whom she was thinking most about at that moment. And my grandmother saw how upset and confused I was. "I am thinking first and foremost about my son," she said.

6

The past has a stronger scent than
a bouquet of blooming lilacs.

—Chinese saying

It was the time of year when cabbages were ritually delivered, because there were no greengrocers in the cold of Beijing. Families
stored up cabbages for winter, particularly families from Dongbei, where cabbage is one of the region's specialties.

I can see them now, those mountains of cabbages in the
garden of the residence, each pile corresponding to a family's
order, the cabbages with their beautiful smooth dappled heads,
the bright color clashing with the leafless trees. It was a big job,
carrying fifteen kilos of cabbages up three floors. The cabbages
would form the basis of all our food through the winter, enliv-
ened in many different ways: with salt, with lard, with meat, with

vermicelli . . . And to prepare the pickled cabbage, which we would use to stuff the most famous dumplings I know, the ayi and my grandmother had already cleared a space in the kitchen, taken a large quantity of salt, the pots, the stones, and everything else necessary for this confection, which would accompany tofu, meat, or—the most wonderful delicacy of all—the famous northern soup, with its tofu, its meat, and its vermicelli.

Nainai and the ayi both pretended they needed my help for this preparation. The pleasure I felt at playing the role of souschef was so obvious that they realized that, for me, this was more exciting than any game or toy.

If I remember correctly, we first had to carefully wash the cabbages. Next, we put them to dry all day. The next day, in each pot, we alternated a layer of cabbage with a layer of salt until the pot was full to the brim. After that, we poured hot water into them, used heavy stones to cram the mixture down, then gave the pot an airtight seal. Even the thought of finally being able to taste our creation—something that would have to wait at least two weeks—was enough to make our mouths water.

The year before, some of the piles of cabbages had been left where they were longer than usual. This year, it was worse. The piles diminished bit by bit. What was going on? Quite simply, there were not enough men in the residence to do all the heavy lifting. So where had they gone?

The nights had become strangely silent without the funny hissing of cabbages fermenting in jars. How I wished that funny, peaceful sound would return, and with it, our happy days. In my grandmother's bed, where I often lay, I would turn toward my grandfather's bed: I missed him, too. Outside, the rest of the cabbages were rotting.

Unafraid of waking my grandmother, I asked, "Nainai, does *Baohang* mean something?"

"You know the answer to that, Nan-nan," she replied. "*Bao* is the character in the given name that indicates the generation. All Yeye's brothers and cousins have that character in common: *Bao*. Because, according to tradition, there is always an ancestor, in all our families, who decides in advance the crucial character of a family for the next ten or fifteen generations, the list being transmitted from father to son because that is a man's task. So, if you meet a man or a woman whose middle character is *Bao*, whether the second character be *Wang* or *Yan* or anything else, you can be sure that the person is a sister, brother, or cousin of your grandfather. Likewise, if you were not an only daughter, you, too, would have been given a 'middle' character. Look at the names of my children: your father is Ming—Yan Mingfu—just like your three aunts, Mingshi, Mingying, and Mingguang, and your uncles, Mingxin and Mingzhi.

"As for who Hang is . . . wait, let me think. In China, the name that we give to our children is completely invented, the fruit of our imagination. We choose whatever we want, whether because we think it a beautiful character or because it expresses a wish. With you, for example, your mother chose a very beautiful character, but it was so complicated in terms of calligraphy that you could not write it. So she decided to change it and call you Lan, which means 'orchid.' So, you see, you didn't lose anything by changing.

"As for your grandfather, whose given name is Hang: that could mean a vessel at sea. It could be a conqueror's ship . . . Yes, that must have been what his mother or father were thinking when they called him Hang . . ."

And I fell asleep.

7

Kindness in words creates confidence.
Kindness in thinking creates profoundness.
Kindness in giving creates love.

—Laozi (571–471 BCE), *Tao Te Ching:*
The Book of the Way and Its Virtue

In China, women have always kept their maiden names. My grandmother, born Gaosu (Gao was her family name, Su her given name), remained Gaosu after her marriage to Yan Baohang. He was fourteen, she was sixteen.

So, in the 1930s, at the time of the anti-Japanese guerrilla war, it was not Mrs. Yan who was sent for when they wanted someone to give refuge to a soldier in the battle against Manchukuo, that puppet state that the Japanese established in northeast China. They asked for Gaosu. And Gaosu took matters in hand.

Likewise, when my grandparents lived in Chongqing, the city that became the temporary capital of the Republic of China and the Kuomintang government, and some patriots needed help, it was Gaosu who was sent for. And the respect that she commanded meant that she was addressed as Yan Da Sao: sister-in-law of Yan. During that period, nationalists and communists fought together against the Japanese. Only the expansionist pretentions of the Japanese archipelago, so dangerously close to northeast China and to Korea, had been able to seal this unnatural alliance between nationalists and communists, who fought under the same Kuomintang banner.

From this period that preceded—and heralded—the Second World War, there was among those patriots a man named Zhou Enlai who, though older than my grandfather, called him Da Ge: big brother. As for my grandmother Gaosu, Zhou Enlai would call her "our very dear great sister-in-law." So it was not a mark of recent friendship or of circumstance when, much later, Zhou Enlai, now the prime minister, paid tribute to Gaosu by mentioning the many occasions when he had entrusted his revolutionary comrades to the care of my grandmother, knowing full well that they would be healed, fed, pampered, and safe. And, recalling that she had treated them like her own children, the prime minister had called her Da Niang and Guo Mama: the great mama. He might also have said that my grandmother's name fit her like a glove. I do not mean *Gao*, her family name, but rather her given name, *Su*, which means "modesty, reserve, simplicity."

It was due to her good heart that she naturally took control of the nursery schools in Liaobei when her husband, after the

Second World War, was named governor of the province. And after the New China (in other words the proclamation of the People's Republic of China on October 1, 1949, with Mao Zedong at its head of state and Zhou Enlai as the head of the government), Gaosu followed my grandfather to the Foreign Ministry, where she worked for the department of documentation.

My grandmother gave her husband seven children, of whom six survived.

Mingfu, the youngest, is my father. He was born in 1931.

And when, in the kitchen, alone with my grandmother, I thought of my father, I broke down in sobs in front of my morning bowl of rice because, as the proverb says: "Distant water does not quench your thirst now."

So it was that my grandmother came to tell me a story very different from the ones she usually told. This one was not funny; I could see at once that it was both sweet and serious. "It was Sai Weng [Old Sai]," she said, "who lost his horse. You don't know this story? It's a thousand years old and there is not a Chinese person in the world who does not know it. It speaks to everyone, just as it speaks to me. And it will certainly speak to you, too. It was said that one day Old Sai lost one of his horses and now he had only one animal, despite having raised two at great cost.

"'Oh well,' said the old man, 'that's life.' Because Old Sai was a philosopher, as we strive to be, too. And so, one day, not only did the vanished horse return, but it brought with it a proud and beautiful wild horse. Ah, life brings us so many surprises! thought Old Sai, who immediately asked his son to tame the wild horse. But the son found this so difficult that he suffered a bad fall. This misfortune was probably always written, the father thought. And war had broken out all over the country. All the young men of Sai's son's age had been recruited. Every single one of them, except for him, because he had broken his leg."

I am not sure that I truly understood at the time the message that my grandmother was trying to transmit to me, but after so many years I feel certain at least that, amid the misfortune we were suffering back then, her story gave me strength and courage. I stopped crying into my bread and my rice broth. I looked at my grandmother's face, full of kindness, a face that was like a sun in the night through which we were traveling, a night that proved even longer and darker than I could have imagined. That morning, my grandmother did not know where her husband and her youngest son were, nor what fate awaited her other children, but she refused to despair and gave everything she could to make sure I did the same. And yet my grandmother had many more reasons for despair than I could have known. The grown-ups were still doing their best to spare me the truth; they were careful to hide many things from me, particularly their worries for my second uncle, Mingzhi, another diplomat, seven years my father's senior, who had been his best Russian teacher. They were also worried about Daxin, my first uncle—who, rumor had it, was in quarantine—and about my mother . . . My grandmother's determination to remain confident, to keep her head high, allowed me to understand the meaning of a story that my grandfather had often told me.

The setting of that story was a ceremony in commemoration of the Kuomintang and in honor of Sun Yat-sen, the man who had negotiated the surrender of the last emperor, four-year-old Puyi, before becoming the first president of the Republic of China.

"Gaosu was beside me. I was wearing a suit, and your grandmother was in a beautiful silk *qipao*. I loved seeing her in that outfit. To reach the stage, the guests had to climb many steps, and we had been advised—in order to help the ceremony run smoothly and enable the photographers to do their jobs—that we should go up the steps one at a time, and that we should not rush. I know it must have taken a long time because I clearly remember everything I said to your mother during that climb; I also have a vivid memory of the attentive way she listened to me. It was only after the ceremony, in the car that took us home, that Gaosu was finally able to take off her shoe, which had a broken heel. As you can imagine, I told her how proud I was to have a wife who knows how to keep her head held high even in the most trying circumstances."

8

Seek the tiger's friendship;
it will always end up eating you.

—Chinese saying

There are things that I can say now. Things I have been silent about for too long. Certain things cannot be said right away. To start with, you do not believe them when they happen. Then, you are ashamed to verify them. Ashamed to say them. And on top of your shame, you also feel fear. The fear of not being believed. The fear of being denounced as a pathological liar. Shame. Fear.

I have already said that I used to want to dress up as a Red Guard. At the very beginning, when the first Red Guards appeared, they were the heroes of the moment. Little soldiers of the revolution. The vanguard of the revolution. That was how they were presented. They were young students, some of them still in high school. They were the same age as my eldest cousins. They were the very image of ardent youth, and I aspired to that image without truly understanding the meaning of this revolution. Boys and girls, they all wore a very fashionable uniform. For all children, a uniform is the most enticing of outfits. This one was khaki or blue, with a red armband and a red-starred cap. I wanted to parade like them. When I say that all children wanted that, I am not trying to find excuses for my blindness; I am just telling it like it was: we all wanted to be like them.

To start with, the words with which they were associated were the same words I could hear at home: *Revolution. Motherland. People. Justice.* And then new words appeared, words I didn't know: *Denunciation. Roundup. Raid. Auto-da-fé. Suicide.* Words that were not used at home. I also heard groups of words that always went together. The words *revisionists* and *antirevolutionaries*, for example, were always preceded by the phrase *down with*.

It began before my school closed. Before my aunt by marriage, Shu Ti, had her hair shaved off by her own students. In my school—I was in third grade; I was nine years old—the principal and the vice-principal were forced to eat excrement. Or so it was said, at least. We could not believe it. We laughed. Until the day I saw my teacher kneeling in front of us, back bent and head lowered above a sign proclaiming: TRAITOR. REVISIONIST. COUNTERREVOLUTIONARY. Then she had been forced to repeat, "I am a traitor, I am a revisionist, I am a counterrevolutionary." This was known as a self-criticism session. It is hard for me to write what happened next. And yet I must. At the end, the teacher was beaten with a belt buckle. That scene traumatized me.

It would not be true to say that from that moment on I began to believe everything I was told. But whether I believed it or not, it was terribly complicated. Lies had corrupted truth to such an extent that I was no longer sure of what I was seeing with my own eyes.

I went back home, a knot in my guts, nausea rising, and I found an apartment full of frightened grown-ups, whispering to one another, closing the door in my face so they could continue their conversations. They avoided me. Their silence, they thought, formed a protective cocoon. They did not see that I was alone inside that cocoon. At nine or ten, your heart is not well defended, even less so if you see the adults around you faltering.

The garden of the State Council's residence was now empty. We saw fewer and fewer cars. At most, a few black Volga limousines with chauffeurs who, not long ago, would calmly drop off their passengers, as well as one or two Pobeda sedans. And then suddenly, the blaring noise of a GAZ covered truck, the tarpaulin opening to release a horde, troops who rushed toward a building and disappeared into the stairwell. An apartment was chosen, the door smashed down, the rooms searched, turned upside down, the inhabitants body-searched, humiliated, insulted. We saw books and stacks of newspapers go flying out of the windows, piling up in the garden below, covered with kerosene, and burned. We watched all this furtively. The door of the ransacked apartment was left wide-open, its occupants expelled.

Everybody was terrified. On their way home, people would glance at the latest *dazibaos*, out of fear that they would see their own name listed.

Sometimes, we would hear prolonged yelling. A human beast screaming. If it was night, I would bury my head in my pillow. I could hear my heart pounding. If it was daytime, I would curl up in a ball, hold my breath.

Of all the new words that I was hearing back then, the most terrifying of all was *suicide*. When I heard someone speak that word, however quietly, and gesture with their chin at such and such a building, such and such apartment, when by chance I heard "third floor" or "fourth floor," "opposite," "on the right," horror would take shape within me. I was petrified by the idea of seeing a hanged body because I could not imagine any other method of committing suicide. I fixated on that image, like something from a nightmare, which made the sweat bead on my forehead. I learned years later that two of Dr. Ye's sons committed suicide during the Cutural Revolution. And Dr. Ye died in prison, though he was not involved in politics. The day before his arrest, Dr. Ye had administered acupuncture on Jiang Quin, Mao's wife.

Another word kept coming up: *madness*. That did not scare me so much. During happier days, it had been a word used to describe all sorts of things. Sometimes the word *madness* was even a prelude to laughter, so I found it easier to face that word, to think about it. I imagined a disease, a contagious evil, a sort of plague or rabies. A disease that anybody could catch now. An evil that had befallen the city, the whole country, maybe even the whole world, and that nobody seemed able to eradicate. It might seem like a virus, but in my mind it was more like a cancer, the infected cells multiplying chaotically. Those images had been inspired by phrases overheard from conversations between adults, all centered on the word *revolution*. It was as if that word—until now associated with the victory over ignorance, over feudalism, over the superstitions and archaisms of times past—had not only lost its substance but, much worse, had its meaning distorted to the point where it had become nothing more nor less than a synonym for *destruction*. Had I known of Goya's painting then, I would have said: that is what we are experiencing, not *Saturn Devouring His Son*, but the revolution devouring all its children.

During that summer of 1966, I heard mention of a man whom I never saw, I think—though how can I be sure of that now? In fact, I learned of his existence only much later, during the celebration of my grandfather's one hundredth birthday. The man and Ning Encheng, another of his close friends, formed—along with my grandfather—an inseparable trio. They were in London and Edinburgh at the same time as my grandfather, who was studying the living conditions of the working classes, the issues of unemployment and poverty, for his PhD thesis. Ning Encheng, who would become a professor at Stanford, was also a student, while Lao She, the man I heard of in 1966 and the third pillar in this triangle of close, deep friendships, was already teaching Chinese at the School of Oriental Studies in London.

They met in the mid-1920s during a YMCA summer camp in Mukden, in the Liaoning province. The three friends shared a taste for literature, a passion for London museums, and a hostility toward the Japanese, who were occupying Manchuria at the time. All the more so since one of them was a native of that region, and another belonged to the Manchu minority whose lives, once he became an author, he would describe at the end of the imperial dynasty and then under Japanese occupation.

So everybody was talking about this third man, who was barely four years younger than my grandfather. He had been one of Mao Zedong's earliest supporters and had returned to the country when China became communist in 1949, becoming a sort of official writer, tasked with educating the masses with his plays. But now they were not praising Lao She's great talent, as they had done in the past, nor were they fondly discussing his characters, as my grandfather would often do about the patriarch Qi or Ms. Da Chi Bao from the saga *Four Generations under One Roof*, or the famous Xiangzi from *Rickshaw Boy* . . . No, they were talking about the fact that Lao She had just committed suicide. The writer's body had been found floating near the surface of Taiping Lake in the center of Beijing, the city he had loved so much and where everybody knew his saying: "When a man is at the bottom of a well, people throw stones at him."

What could have driven that progressive intellectual to such an extremity? Lao She watched as his precious books were burned. He had been brutally interrogated, humiliated, then beaten by the Red Guards. This act might have been the result of Chinese history turning to tragedy. It could have been an act of despair but also, in a way, of revolt: the final act of a man who refuses to surrender his dignity as a human being.

Reading the works of Lao She, which I did much later, allowed me to confirm that hypothesis. In *Peking Men*, I was struck by the opposition imposed by the author between "the uncertain limits of civilization and barbarism." But it was in his magnum opus, *Four Generations under One Roof*, which he began writing in Chongqing, in the middle of the Sino-Japanese War, that I noticed the name of Qu Yuan (342–290 BCE), and it was not by chance that Lao She referred to the most famous poet in Chinese antiquity: feeling powerless before the misfortunes of his country, Qu Yuan had ended his life by throwing himself in a river. In that same book, one of the characters says: "Better to die than live without principles." And, about Ruixuan—an intellectual, a man of honor, and the novel's central figure—the narrator wrote: "He had often heard his grandmother recount how in 1900, when the army of the Eight Powers had entered the city, several important figures had committed suicide with their families, sacrificing themselves for their motherland."

9

All living beings can go to heaven.
But man? That's another story.

—Attributed to Shi Nai'an
(1296–1370), *Water Margin*

Whether Lao She decided to end his life or whether he was driven to his suicide as it was rumored—he had been viciously beaten by Red Guards on the steps of the Temple of Confucius on August 23, 1966—the author's death provided a premonition of the infernal spiral into which the country was about to descend.

It was no longer simply a question of hordes of young people, students aged between nine and eighteen, who ransacked anywhere that they judged to be bourgeois, pillorying anything and anyone that they considered to belong to bourgeois culture: classical music records broken in two because they had been recorded abroad; engravings and calligraphies vandalized and torn to pieces; bookshelves overturned, book jackets destroyed, pages ripped out, all of it trampled upon and then thrown in the fire.

It was no longer simply a question of acts of violence against people in the streets who wore glasses or well-tailored clothes that made them look like civil servants, teachers, writers, artists—intellectuals, in other words, those people whose achievements made them perfidious, privileged, harmful, and before whom those hordes brandished the Little Red Book that a certain general, Lin Biao, had distributed to them out of deference to Mao Zedong. It was as if we had been returned to the time of the Japanese conquest, when the invaders burned everything connected to the doctrine of the country's leader, Sun Yat-sen: nationalism, democracy, socialism. But these vandals were Chinese, so perhaps we had gone as far back as the Qin dynasty, in the third century before Christ, when the all-powerful emperor Qin Shi Huang ordered the burning of canonical books and the burial of nearly five hundred men of letters.

It was no longer simply a question of destroying everything that spoke of knowledge or thought in the name of a sham named "the battle against the four olds": old ideas, old culture, old customs, and old habits. Soon it would be a question of contesting the expression of all authority. So, the name of the chairman, Liu Shaoqi, was pronounced. Then it was the turn of the party's general secretary, Deng Xiaoping, the most faithful of all Mao's followers. Both these men were publicly condemned, accused of deviance because they had sought to divert the country along the road to capitalism. And the greatest lie of all was that this movement, into which the nation's entire youth found itself recruited, had been named, in high places, the Cultural Revolution.

In reality, this targeting of intellectuals had begun in the 1950s, when most of China's intellectuals had been teachers, researchers, academics, and administrators. By order of the authorities, they were forced to confess their contamination by capitalist imperialism, to plead guilty of having betrayed the Chinese people, and to give thanks to Chairman Mao for setting them on the right path. This ordeal, with its incalculable psychological consequences, degraded the image of intellectuals in general. The concept of the class struggle was reactivated, and it ended in a distinction between "good" social origins (the peasantry and the working classes) and "bad" social origins (urban, bourgeois, educated).

The issue regarding men of letters is a very old one in China. The ancestral system of exams formed a class of civil servants working for the Empire, necessarily docile because they were providing the regime with its leaders and cadres of government officials. The big idea of China's Communist Party (CCP) was to make allies of the intellectuals in the battle for the New China. In fact, most of the CPC's leaders—including Mao Zedong, Liu Shaoqi, and Deng Xiaoping—contributed greatly to this revolution, by "betraying" their origins as landowners.

However, in 1949, Mao Zedong himself admitted that the work of intellectuals was indispensable to the revolution, not only those who had embraced the communist cause, but even—a theory defended by Zhou Enlai and Deng Xiaoping—those who were not affiliated to the party.

From 1956 on, intellectuals were invited to formulate, without fear or reservations, their criticisms of the process in which different elements of the Party were engaged. This initiative was called the Hundred Flowers Campaign, following a fashion for lyrical titles at the time, and it astounded many young Westerners despite the fact that they themselves were well used to the advantages of critical thinking: "Let a hundred flowers bloom and a hundred schools of thought contend!"

There was a moment of hesitation, but as nothing happened to justify this excess of prudence, in the spring of 1957 the revolution began to be questioned for the first time. After that, there came increasingly virulent criticisms, and finally full-frontal attacks on the very foundations of the doctrine. The backlash was not long in coming: the campaign against the right began, with its reprisals and its hysterical hatred directed particularly at intellectuals. "Revisionist" and "counterrevolutionary" were among the less defamatory insults. My aunt Mingshi, who was labeled a "rightist" for defending an innocent young boy, was sent to a remote part of northeast China.

The debate about good and bad social origins was cut short. Mao came down in favor of the supposed purity of intention of proletarian origins. Among the specialists who cannot be suspected of ideological bias, the American historian and sinologist John King Fairbank—after whom the Fairbank Center for Chinese Studies at Harvard is named—writes about the terrible "ten lost years" when characterizing the Cultural Revolution between 1966 and 1976. In fact, he goes further: "The phrase 'ten lost years' . . . was only a continuation of what began in 1957." Nineteen fifty-seven: the year I was born.

From about 1937 until after the end of the Second World War, there was a united front against the Japanese, with the nationalist government (Kuomintang) in Chongqing on one side, and the communists in Yan'an on the other. The different sections of the Party's Central Committee were able to raise Yan'an, the now-mythical city in the Shaanxi province, to the level of a revolutionary laboratory for progressives the world over. Not only did communists learn to fight in Yan'an, they were also supposed to think, to set the terms of how Marxism could incorporate the Chinese way of thinking. The objective was to finally unite the practical and the theoretical. Seminars took place. Thinkers competed and debated at the highest level.

Of course Yan'an attracted the young and idealistic, and had to contend with their ardor: the city became the ideal backdrop for sentimental and utopian dreams of a radiant future. And all those young people who surrounded Mao Zedong, who supported and venerated him, were none other than intellectuals, most of them university-educated. Bourgeois. Privileged, to use the terminology that would one day be turned against them. Those young people would be prey to the stupefying cruelty of the dark years that followed. Among my grandfather's children, four went to Yan'an. Mingshi, my first aunt. Mingying, my second aunt, met her husband there. My uncles Mingzhi and Mingxin (who changed his name to Daxin when he was leaving for

Yan'an) had also found belonging in the enthusiasm and militant spirit of Yan'an.

There were certain methods there that might have alerted them. Each militant who arrived in Yan'an was subject to an examination of conscience designed to identify ways of thinking that should be corrected. Anyone who claimed to be a sincere and authentic revolutionary was urged to expose his own antecedents. What followed was a group critique, with all the ferocity, one-upmanship, and bullying that groups tend to show toward an expiatory victim. The victim was then ostracized and publicly humiliated until all self-esteem was destroyed and replaced with self-hate and self-denigration. It required a rock-solid physical and mental constitution to withstand such treatment.

10

I do not know the true face of the Lu mountain
because we are lost in the heart of the place itself.

—Chinese proverb

For just less than two weeks, my father has been held in isolation in the special prison of Qincheng, in Beijing. He is thirty-six years old. He has been charged with spying for the Soviet Union. The evidence against him is a transceiver that belonged to him. He knows all about that kind of proof, completely fabricated; everybody knows about it. He pays no attention to it. He has not been told that the transceiver was seized from his father's apartment.

What worries Yan Mingfu most is not his father, because Yan Baohang—a founding member of the People's Consultative Conference in 1949 with Zhou Enlai—is an untouchable historical figure. Mingfu believes his father has nothing to fear, despite the way this new era seems to want to overturn all established values. He was arrested by mistake. He will be released. Yan Mingfu is less serene about his own fate. He knows that he is in charge of a sensitive area of Chinese foreign policy: relations with the Soviet Union. A Russian translator for the most important figures in the Political Bureau, including the Party's general secretary, the supreme leader, Mao Zedong, he is perfectly well aware of the ideological tensions between the two communist parties, currently more like rivals than brothers.

On many occasions, he has witnessed delicate situations; that is part of the job. He has also witnessed some farcical scenes. In late July 1958, Nikita Khrushchev came on a secret visit to Beijing for a series of meetings with Mao, who informed my father that one of these meetings would take place in his swimming pool. Khrushchev, though, "does not understand the nature of water," in the euphemistic words of Shi Nai'an in *Water Margin* about someone who cannot swim. Khrushchev was given a rubber ring. While one man showed off his ease in the water, the other was furious at finding himself stuck inside an inflatable doughnut. By the side of the pool, Mingfu shuttled from one to the other.

Mingfu reviews the situation. His cell, he knows, is located in the political prisoners' "neighborhood," but he does not know where exactly because he is being held in isolation. He supposes that one of the first victims of the Cultural Revolution, Peng Zhen—a member of the Central Committee and one of the founders of the Party in 1923, who has also been arrested—must be somewhere close by. But if Yan Mingfu is categorized as being in disgrace, it is not only because of the deteriorating relations between China and the Soviet Union: in Beijing, even within the corridors of power, the highest-ranking figures have been shaken by the earthquake of this so-called Cultural Revolution. He knows he is paying the price for that, too. He tries not to think too much about his mother and his daughter, who must be safe, more or less. As for his wife, she appears to him less exposed than he is because her specialization within the foreign liaison department of the Central Committee is Western Europe, a less sensitive subject. His real source of anxiety is Mingzhi, his older brother, who, like him, learned Russian from Soviet teachers sent specially to China.

Someone coughs, interrupting Mingfu's thoughts. Someone coughs and he thinks he recognizes that cough. His father coughed like that when he caught a cold. He is so moved that he thinks for a moment of asking his guards, even though he knows that he will get no answer. He wants to call out. Then he calms down. Calm is necessary when you don't know how long you will be kept in isolation. How many months. He refuses to think about that. What calms him is the simple, soothing thought of his father's commitment to the communists of the 1930s, the soothing remembrance of his close friendship with Zhou Enlai.

11

Heaven is falling and Earth is rending.

—Chinese proverb

The Red Guards did not just appear out of nowhere. The role they would play became clear at the eleventh plenary session of the eighth party congress in August 1966, in the presence of representatives of revolutionary teachers and students.

The slogans that were formulated there would be taken literally: "Let us be the student of the masses, not their teacher. Let us judge as reactionary the scientific authorities of the bourgeoisie; let us transform education, literature and art so that they match the socialist order." One must "*dare* to make a revolution." And, most important, one must "not fear disorder."

The Central Committee highlighted the particular role to be played by college and high school students. It was these young people whom Mao was addressing, first and foremost, on August 18, in a solemn speech made in Tiananmen Square before the Gate of Heavenly Peace. At this first mass meeting, which heralded the abuses, denunciations, and searches that would follow, Mao had the idea of adding a slogan of his own invention: "It is right to rebel!"

Nobody asked who was doing the rebelling because everybody instinctively understood that the leader was becoming one with his audience. That simple, abstract commandment was also a sort of authorization that deleted the half century or more separating the seventy-three-year-old leader from his Red Guard followers, the eldest of whom were twenty-five. At these words, boys and girls stood up in an instant show of support. They all raised their arms, and in those thousands of hands were clutched thousands of Little Red Books.

At the time, Mao's publications were everywhere: 150 million copies of his *Selected Works* were printed in two years; 96 million copies of his *Poems*; more than one billion copies of his Little Red Book.

What was he hoping to achieve? He wanted to use the youth of China as his spearhead in the merciless political battle against his opponents in the party. As a good strategist, he knew that in a country where old people have always been venerated, his advanced age was actually an asset.

With hindsight, we can understand more easily what Mao Zedong was thinking at the time: to use his authority to persuade these young people to act as vigilantes, without realizing that they were doing so with the ultimate goal of reestablishing Mao's power, and that this goal would come at the cost of millions of lives.

To better understand the situation, we must rewind eight years to 1958, when Mao launched the policy known as the Great Leap Forward. It was a policy based on self-sacrifice, intended to massively increase China's industrial and agricultural production, but followed by three consecutive years of natural disasters that brought the country to the verge of bankruptcy. The word *famine* is insufficient to describe that period, which is why it became known as the Great Famine. The government reluctantly admitted that fifteen million people died; the actual figure is today estimated at between forty and fifty-five million. There are no words that can add any meaning to such figures.

One must simply reread the declaration made during a working meeting of the Central Committee, four years after the Great Leap Forward, in 1962: "When Chairman Mao says that the situation is excellent, he is talking about the political situation. As concerns the economic situation, it cannot be described as excellent; in fact, it is very bad."

Mao resigned as chairman. His calculation was that it made sense to let Liu Shaoqi and Deng Xiaoping act. They could do all the work this time. Deng Xiaoping attacked the situation with a pragmatism that would go down in history and whose formula is all the more striking because it proved successful: "It doesn't matter if the mode of production is individual or collective, so long as it contributes to increasing food production.

It doesn't matter if the cat is black or white, so long as it catches the mouse."

Once the economic situation began to improve, Mao's supreme authority would perhaps be threatened. Before that happened, he had time to find some way of infiltrating the party's various organizations. What was happening in the Soviet Union convinced him to lead a fight against the revisionists in the party. Liu Shaoqi could be China's Khrushchev.

In the summer of 1966, Mao saw the enthusiasm of the Chinese youth as a springboard. After the disastrous effects of the Great Leap Forward, he refused to be fobbed off with a strictly honorific role. Mao was determined to regain absolute power. Bereft of strong support within the Party, he decided to use his direct, intimate, almost filial relationship with the country's youth. The name of the brigades who would carry out Mao's Cultural Revolution was chosen by the young people themselves: the Red Guards. What those young people did not realize was that they were committed to a deliberate program of destruction aimed at the intelligence and creativity, the cultural and artistic heritage of this ancient civilization.

I was nine that summer. I had just finished my first year of boarding school in Yuying. When the summer was over, I would start fourth grade.

The Yuying school was affiliated to Yan'an, the elite communist school. There was nothing surprising in this choice of school, given my family's CV. It was one of the few boarding schools in Beijing. My aunt Shu Ti had taught there. Yuying was intended to be a school for the children of cadres who had trained in Yan'an. There were many children of diplomats, ministers, highly placed civil servants, and other dignitaries from Beijing in the school, and I felt good there.

But early in 1967, Yuying closed its doors. Suddenly, in the middle of the school year, I found myself deprived of my classmates and, most of all, of my teacher, whom I liked a lot. Yes, I was very fond of her pretty round face and her long, jet-black braid. I liked her cheerfulness, the trust and encouragement she showed me; I liked the gentle but invigorating way she kindled a desire within me to always be better, the way she let me know that this was precisely what she was expecting of me and, ultimately, what I hoped for, for myself. That was why I took pleasure in showing her all my respect by calling her Tian Lao Shi—addressing her as Master Tian, in other words—and I sensed that she had a preference for students, like me, who applied themselves.

Yuying was judged to be an elitist, bourgeois, harmful establishment. The Cultural Revolution demanded the closure of all high schools and universities. Younger students were transferred to the primary school closest to their home; that was the rule. So I left Yuying for Yuming.

The only thing I liked about that change was that Louwen, my friend from the residence, who lived in the same building, was also transferred to Yuming. And the school was so close that we could walk there.

Children's capacity to adapt is remarkable, particularly if—as was the case for Louwen and myself—they are pampered by their families. So we settled into our new school without difficulties. I was top of the class, as usual, and I could tell that the teacher enjoyed giving me all the perks associated with that position. I am not ashamed to say that I was the "teacher's pet," as my classmates called me.

Until that day in early December 1967 when I was summoned to her office.

She was sitting behind her desk. I stood there, waiting. It was as if my teacher had suddenly become someone else. Frowning, lips pursed, she said: "Lan, first I learned that your grandfather has been arrested."

I felt cold sweat trickle down my spine. School was the only place where I could forget for a few hours all the things that had happened to us, all that I had seen, all that I knew. And now, out of nowhere, the black hole of my despair broke through the walls of my family home and spread beyond, to this place where I no longer felt safe.

"And now I hear that your father has also been arrested. Is that correct?"

I lowered my eyes. I could no longer bear to look at her.

"And as if that were not enough, Lan, I also know that your mother has been placed under house arrest. Is that right?"

"No, that's not true!"

The lie escaped my mouth in a yell. Well, I suppose it was not exactly a lie, rather a refusal to acknowledge the truth. Tears of rage poured from my eyes. The teacher's expression grew even harsher, and her voice boomed:

"It is pointless to deny it. You must think about this now.

Think about it, and immediately confess all the crimes that have been committed. Admit that your grandfather, your father, and your mother are criminals, despicable counterrevolutionaries!"

I couldn't stop crying. I couldn't speak. That word, *crime*, had changed the nature of my tears. I was no longer rebellious; I was destroyed. In a very small voice, muffled by sobs, I said that I knew nothing about it. And then the teacher left me standing there, alone, abandoned, sobbing, while she walked away without a word.

Outside in the yard, I did not dare go near my classmates. Besides, they kept away from me as if I had scabies. And for the first time, the names they called my friend Tian Louwen were directed against me, too.

I have not yet explained what the problem was with Louwen because, for me, there was no problem with Louwen. I played with Louwen, I spoke with Louwen, I messed around with Louwen just like I did with all my classmates. In fact, I had more fun with her because this cheerful, pretty girl with large dark eyes was my friend. And since Louwen acted exactly like everybody else did at our age, it was easy for me to forget that she was very small with bowlegs because she suffered from a terrible bone deformity. She had a good heart and she was a faithful friend, so I invited her to my apartment and she invited me to hers, and the two of us grew very close. When people called her "cripple," it hurt me as well as Louwen. "Cripple" or "freak" or "monster" or "ugly." I don't even want to repeat the other words they used. The only thing that could comfort us was the knowledge that we were inseparable, united in adversity.

There was a new ritual in the class now: there were forms to fill out, and for us, this became a form of torture. I say "for us," because Louwen was in the same situation. My hand trembled as I had to write that my father and grandfather had been arrested. And as if that were not enough, I had to add the reason for their arrests: "Anti-revolutionary activities."

Likewise, Louwen's hand trembled as she had to write that her father, head of the State Council's archives, was currently under investigation. Our family names, previously a source of pride, now marked us out as pariahs; writing those names suddenly became an ordeal because those names were associated with infamy. When we walked to school together in the morning, we both felt nauseated. Neither of us felt able to eat breakfast.

Encouraged by the sudden change in the teacher's attitude toward us, our classmates looked over our shoulders the first time we had to fill out those forms, then grabbed the pages from our desks and waved them around triumphantly. The teacher had given them tacit permission to be cruel. We were now no longer merely the daughters of criminals but also cripples, freaks, monsters. Of course I lost all the privileges and special tasks I had been given for being top of the class, all those tasks I had been so proud to carry out. "No, not you!" the teacher said when I offered to help. "No, not her!" my classmates shouted as they excluded me from their games.

At the end of the day, on the way back to the residence, Louwen and I walked with our heads down. To spare our families, we did not tell them what was happening at school. We did not complain. I went straight to my room and did not come out again until dinner, and even then I had to be coaxed out. When the weekend arrived, I remembered how I used to sit on the sidewalk for hours on end, waiting for my father to arrive, to see him walking quickly from the bus stop to the residence. I had begun to feel nostalgic for that period when he was under house arrest and could at least come to visit me from Saturday afternoon until Sunday morning.

I did not picture my mother suffering, at worst, the same humiliations I had suffered. I could not imagine that, as soon as she arrived at her office in the foreign liaison department of the Central Committee, the unbelievable inquisitorial machine would lurch into action. What had she done to deserve being made the office scapegoat? A father-in-law in prison. A husband in prison. She was labeled the daughter-in-law of a criminal, the wife of a criminal. Birds of a feather . . . Particularly as, on her side of the family, there was not a single worker or peasant among her ancestors; instead her father was a "capitalist," the son and grandson of bourgeois forebears; her entire family tree was infested with "bad" social origins. Under orders—but whose, and for what reason?—her boss planned public-confession sessions in her department. She refused to say, over and over again, that the proven counterrevolutionary behavior of most of her family, their betrayals, their elitism, had led them to their prison cells, and that the people's justice should be applied to them without restraint. It was not certain that she could be reeducated; that remained to be seen. Her private life was exposed, pulled apart, turned upside down, with such a constant determination to portray her as guilty that, even though she had a tough temperament, she ended up feeling a sort of self-suspicion. She began to doubt—I know that for a fact. I have felt it myself: that shaking of your being, when you end up wondering if, deep down, despite your absolute conviction, you are wrong, if perhaps it is the others who are right. Something breaks inside you then, something that cannot always be repaired afterward. But my mother said nothing about any of this when she came to the residence at the end of the week.

During December, she informed us that she was no longer allowed to leave her office. She was under house arrest in her own ministry. It was at that moment that Louwen and I began skipping school.

12

Govern by doing nothing that goes against nature.

—Laozi (571–471 BCE), *Tao Te Ching:*
The Book of the Way and Its Virtue

I remembered that tree, shaped like a bush, in the garden of the residence. A ginkgo. My favorite tree. It is not usually mentioned as being emblematic of China. The tree known in the West as the Peking willow, whose long branches droop over the edge of the imperial Beihai Lake, north of the Zhongnanhai, is more famously associated with our country. But the lesser-known ginkgo is the one that speaks to me.

It is said that the ginkgo belongs to the oldest-known family of trees. It is said that it already existed forty million years before the age of the dinosaurs. I am inspired by that ancient life span.

This tree's character, its ability to withstand everything without dying out, is remarkable.

I love its power to resist. I love how little air and earth it needs. I love the fact that it has the skill to make light of the numerous predators and parasites that threaten all other species. I also like how the ginkgo, as old Dr. Ye taught me, has been used in traditional Chinese medicine since the dawn of time.

The ginkgo is also known as the silver apricot tree and the "Tree of Forty Shields," probably because its flowers explode in dazzling yellow in the spring and, when fall comes, its leaves turn golden brown before forming a wide and precious carpet around its base.

But what I liked most when I was young was the idea that there were male and female ginkgo trees. That this magnificent tree should have grown below our apartment building seemed to me the incarnation of Yan Baohang and Gaosu's marriage. And because it was now winter, because the branches of my beloved tree were all bare, because my grandfather had still not returned and I was going to have to leave Nainai to join my mother's ministry boarding school, I suddenly thought of the beautiful flowers and leaves of my ginkgo tree and how everything that had gone from my life that winter had the exact color of my golden childhood.

13

The heart of men will no longer be what it was.

—Chinese proverb

When I was a little girl, I never had to wait for my grandfather outside the boarding school. I knew he would be there. He was always so eager and happy to take me for the weekend that I knew my cousins were right when they said I was his favorite.

Some weekends, before we reached the car where the chauffeur was waiting for us, Yeye would smile knowingly and whisper into my ear: "First we're going to pick up my pay packet." So we would head toward a neoclassical building: portico with colonnades, pediment decorated with a crest in the colors of the workers and peasants, and engraved with a date, 1949. Since my grandfather had resigned from his post in the Foreign Ministry in 1959, this was now his workplace as a member of the Standing

Committee of Chinese People's Consultative Conference and also a member of the National Committee of Culture and History Archives of the Chinese People's Consultative Conference. Apart from official sessions, the senators' club also organized mah-jongg evenings, but my grandfather preferred the dance nights. The other leaders, including Zhou Enlai and Mao Zedong, shared his love of dancing.

After the limousine had been parked at an angle, in the middle of a fleet of Hongqi—the chosen car of the regime's dignitaries—I did not sit there and wait for him because I knew that what he loved most of all was having me close to him and introducing his little Lan, his Xiao Lan, "Mingfu and Keliang's daughter." Sometimes Yeye would even sit me next to him during one of the Senate's interminable meetings. Barely would the session have begun than a man of my grandfather's age would come over to us, smiling broadly, and Yeye would quickly stand up: "Prime Minister, allow me to present my granddaughter," and Zhou Enlai would look me up and down and reply, "I see, my dear Baohang, that you have prepared a successor for your renowned Yan household. Congratulations! This child reminds me of the golden days in Chongqing, in those heroic times when the Yan home was always full of children and partisans, all seated around the famous Yan table, and when Mingfu, if I remember correctly, was hardly any taller than this young lady . . ."

"Well, quite," my grandfather replied. "Nan-nan is his daughter!"

But it was the next part that I liked best. And without paying attention to what that elegant and very affable old gentleman was saying, I wondered where my grandfather was planning to take me.

Top of my list of destinations was the Perfumed Village of Osmanthus. It was an old delicatessen from the time of the Qing dynasty, located at the end of a pedestrian street. When you walked in, you were welcomed by the delicious smells of fresh cakes, some sweet, some savory. The house specialty was the famous pig's feet, marinated and grilled, which we adored. If Nainai had come with us, we would perhaps go to the famous Dong Lai Shun. There, the old maître d' would rush up to us, excitedly saying, "Ah, Mr. Yan! There you are! There you are!" As he removed my grandfather's overcoat, he would find a way to whisper to him the names of all those who were already inside this renowned restaurant. Those dignitaries of New China, those veterans of Kuomintang and Red China, would always greet my grandparents as we made our way to the little room where our table had been set. On that table was everything we needed to taste the exquisite *huǒguǒ* of ancient tradition: the cooking pot and the boiling water where we could dip fine slices of mutton held between our chopsticks.

And if we did not go to the Perfumed Village of Osmanthus or to Dong Lai Shun or to the Cultural Palace of Minorities, where we also sometimes went, I would be able to guess where our chauffeur was taking us because, if we followed the direction of the imperial Beihai Park, I knew we were going to that part of the Forbidden City, north of the Jade Island, where the emperor liked to go with his concubines to watch the paper lanterns during the Lantern Festival.

There, Yeye would look out at the lake and the bridge and, pointing beyond the bridge, would say, "That is the headquarters of the central government of the Communist Party of China. That is where Mao Zedong lives. And the weeping willows that you can see all around, the ones that are often reproduced in ancient Chinese paintings . . . well, you should know that in the West, most of that tree's admirers are not even aware that it comes from China . . . And here is the Jingshan Park."

All Yeye's stories were, for him, ruses to educate me. So he would recount the history of a restaurant, whose specialty was the imperial cuisine of the Manchu dynasty, and whose two characters, *Fang* and *Shan*, had been traced with a calligraphy brush by his friend, the writer Lao She.

In the early days of Fangshan, Yeye told me, this place was reserved exclusively for the emperor. But in 1924, the twelfth and last emperor of the Qing dynasty—young Puyi—had to flee the Forbidden City. So it was that the palace's former cooks began to offer their expertise at preparing princely feasts. And so in 1925—as long as you'd received your pay as a state civil servant, Yeye added with a wink—the restaurant became popular.

Every year, my grandparents took me to the celebrations of the New China. On October 1, the national celebration of the communist victory, everybody got three days off work. But my personal privilege—and I had no idea how exceptional this was, nor how precarious—was to climb the steps of the official gallery, one hand in my grandfather's, the other in Nainai's, and then to look down on Tiananmen Square.

First we watched the military parade in front of the central gallery where Mao Zedong sat with all the dignitaries, the guests of honor, and the entire government. Then, in the evening, there was the big fireworks display. On October 1, 1964, I was seven years old; the grand finale had just ended and everybody was applauding when my grandfather stood up and headed over to a couple whom I didn't know. Both had a modest appearance. The woman was very simply dressed, and the man, who was very thin, wore little round glasses and a humble, grayish *Zhōngshān zhuāng*. While my grandfather greeted them with great deference, my grandmother whispered to me: "Look, Lan, it's the little emperor." It was as if, in my head, a megaphone began blaring, just like the ones that, during the parade, had broadcast slogans: "BAD. EVIL. BAD ARE THE LANDOWNERS, AND EVIL ARE THE RICH. BAD IS THE EMPEROR, AND ALL THOSE USELESS PARASITES WE OVERTURNED! . . . LONG LIVE THE REVOLUTION!" Those same words that I had heard constantly at school ever since kindergarten. And deep within me, that megaphone seemed to be lecturing me, ready to check whether I had learned my lesson correctly.

Now that we had joined them, my grandfather proudly introduced his little Nan-nan. And gesturing to the man, he did not say "the little emperor," but simply, "This is Puyi Yeye." Puyi immediately put his hand in one of his pockets and took out a handful of candy, which he handed to me with a pleasant smile. As I stared at him sullenly, Puyi asked me, "How old are you, Xiao Lan?" And even though I was familiar with the Chinese habit of offering candy as a way of being friendly, even though I appreciated the thoughtfulness of the gesture during a period when everything—including candy—was rationed, I was torn between my childish desire for that candy and what I had always been taught.

Finally I could not control myself and I shouted, "I DON'T WANT CANDY FROM THE LITTLE EMPEROR!" Puyi looked shocked. The little old lady lowered her eyes. My grandparents were deeply embarrassed. As for me, panicked by my own boldness, I turned around and ran away.

My grandmother never told me off. But this time she did, severely, because of my lack of education and respect for the little emperor. I was mortified. My grandfather, who had been a teacher in his younger years, took a different approach.

"Nan-nan, do you know why we call the man who was only one of the Emperor Daoguang's great-grandsons 'the little emperor'? Because when that little boy, at the age of two years and ten months, ascended the throne of imperial China, he cried his eyes out. He cried and shouted and struggled all the way through that ceremony. In other words, he cried for hours, in the presence of all the princes of his lineage, the Manchus. He cried while his father, Prince Zaifeng—who was not the emperor, only the regent—held the little emperor in his arms and could think of nothing that might calm him but to whisper, 'Don't worry, it will soon be over; don't worry, it's almost over,' and to repeat this throughout the ceremony. You see, Nan-nan, we now know how farsighted those words were, because, as you know, all of that is over. Less than four years later, the last emperor of China—to whom you had the exceptional honor of being introduced—abdicated. The last dynasty, the Qings, who had ruled China since 1644, bowed down before the new Republic in 1912.

"What I have just told you, Nan-nan, is not the fruit of my imagination: Puyi wrote all of that in his autobiography. It has just been published. It is called *The First Half of My Life*. Reading that book confirms, if confirmation were needed, how right the revolutionaries around Dr. Sun Yat-sen were to want the establishment of a Republic of China, and how eager they were to see China become a modern nation. To give you an example: when Puyi, as a child, was carried in a palanquin, two young eunuchs accompanied him to satisfy all his desires. Behind him, another eunuch held up a large silk canopy, and behind *him* came a herd of eunuch valets of the 'imperial presence,' some attached to the Imperial Tea Office, others to the Imperial Pharmacy, and then there were the eunuchs in charge of the commode and the chamber pot. The chancellery of the imperial court employed more than one thousand people, not counting the palace guard, the eunuchs, the lower servants, and those who—when the child behaved badly—had to suffer the punishment in his place, since the emperor was *untouchable*. Puyi writes that, when he was a very young boy, he would have the eunuchs whipped at the slightest excuse, sometimes until death. As far as his education was concerned, it was customary for his tutors to heat up the shell of a tortoise so that they could decipher the cracks as if they were auguries.

"The two of us talked a lot while he was writing his autobiography. In many respects his fate was tragic. Undoubtedly he made some grave errors of judgment—he thought that the

Japanese would give him back his throne—but, although he was condemned for war crimes, Chairman Mao believed that he should be pardoned. His autobiography is the fruit of a conversation with Zhou Enlai, who encouraged Puyi to write about his life. In the prime minister's opinion, Puyi's testimony was of great historical significance. While Puyi did untold harm to his homeland, particularly in allowing the Japanese to become rulers of the puppet state of Manchukuo, the prime minister was inclined to believe that historians would be grateful for a first-hand account, and that there was every reason to stop our cruelty toward someone who was, ultimately, a reject and a victim of the feudal age.

"In that sense, the People's Republic of China was not guilty of barbarism in the eyes of its people—like the Soviet Union in eliminating Tsar Nicholas II and his family. Because he recognized that he—as a symbol—had been constantly manipulated, Puyi was able to make amends for an existence that he had never really controlled. Furthermore, the conversations with Zhou Enlai, in which it appeared that Puyi aspired to nothing higher than living in a natural environment, led to him finding work as a gardener in the Beijing botanical gardens.

"He has always had health problems, aggravated I suppose by some of the old-fashioned customs he experienced, such as being breastfed until he was nine. He was kept in such confinement in the Forbidden City that it is not surprising he was unable to bloom physically or intellectually. What that has produced is the sort of candor that you witnessed, as well as a feeling of persecution. He is still haunted, he says, by those murderous intrigues, the atmosphere of permanent conspiracy that held sway at court, all those plots that drove his biological mother—from whom he was separated at the age of three—to kill herself. He did not choose his first wife, nor his concubines. His first and third concubines demanded divorces. The second died under shady circumstances. The imperial wife, Wanrong, became an opium addict. That's quite a lot to deal with, don't you think? Mao Zedong told him one day: you are still young, you should re-marry. Just over two years ago, he married the woman you saw beside him, Li Shuxian. She is not a princess—she's a nurse. He overcame the obsession, among his entourage, that he ought to marry a woman from the Manchu lineage, like himself.

"Today, Puyi lives in a modest square courtyard house, an overcrowded *dazayuan* that is home to dozens of families. He spends most of his time in the courtyard, surrounded by chil-dren. He plays with them as if he were the same age as them. That is what he likes most: playing with children. There is always a crowd of them around him, and he hands out candy to them. His pockets are always full of candy. One of his little playmates asked him the other day if it was true that he was 'the little em-peror,' and he replied—this is what the child told me—'I didn't have a happy childhood like you.'"

14

Let me look at plums to quench my thirst
or draw me a pancake to sate my hunger.

—Chinese proverb

"First we're going to pick up my pay packet." It was not always possible to devote ourselves to the ritual announced by my grandfather's magic phrase. Most often, at the end of the week or the night before the celebrations at the residence, Yeye's question to my grandmother was: "Do we still have some money left?" Although my grandfather was a highly placed civil servant, although he rubbed shoulders with the most famous men of his era, between the help he gave to his children and his many friends in need, money seemed to slip between his fingers like sand.

And it was not only a question of money. After the Liberation, the People's Republic of China had brought in a rationing system, distributing tickets without which—in cities, at least—no food could be obtained, or only a limited amount of it anyway. Ration tickets were distributed to families, the number of tickets depending on the number of children; they were necessary for the basic staples, such as rice, wheat flour, and oil, as well as for candy and even cotton. The purchase of a bolt of fabric or of ready-made clothing required a cotton ticket. Parents of children who were in the middle of growth spurts—particularly boys, who were always hungry—would come toward the end of the month and lament that they had spent all their cereal tickets. Life wasn't much easier in the countryside, since there was no private land and the harvests were all strictly monitored. This rationing went on even after the end of the Cultural Revolution; it was not phased out until the 1990s.

Yeye's ritual question to Nainai was never asked in a whining or anxious tone. The joy of seeing the dining table extended so that it could seat the whole family—children, spouses, grandchildren—as well as friends, and so that they could all be fed with as much warmth and generosity as possible, was more important to my grandfather than any financial worries. When it came to controlling the purse strings, Nainai was the "minister of finance," as my grandfather put it. But Nainai was too resourceful ever to answer that all the money had gone; she had all sorts of clever tricks for making ends meet.

It would have been unbearable for Nainai to puncture my grandfather's good humor with what she considered small, fleeting worries. The Yans were proud of their tradition of welcoming people into their home, and she refused to give up on that, on top of everything else. And this happy tradition of the "open table" was always associated with laughter, with lively, passionate debate, even if it could sometimes turn to arguments, as was the case with my eldest cousin, known to other family members as Da Pangzi ("Big Guy"). But that didn't matter, because my grandfather loved to discuss world affairs with him.

The packed kitchen, the overworked ayi, the bowls steaming between our hands or on the table, the extra mattresses in the bedrooms: this was the picture of home that Nainai liked best. Sometimes an unexpected visitor would knock at the door and ask if, by chance, not wishing to disturb anybody, his compatriot from the northeast, Yan Baohang, whom he had never had the opportunity to thank in person for a favor he had granted long ago, might have a spare moment . . . My grandparents loved that kind of thing. They would both open their arms wide in welcome before ushering the visitor inside.

15

I like fish, but I also like bear's feet. If I cannot have both, I will leave the fish and take the bear's feet. I love life, but I also love morality. If I cannot have both, I will renounce life and keep morality.

—Mencius (372–289 BCE), Book VI, Section 8

When all the Yans were present, there were a lot of people: Mingshi, my first aunt, had eight children. My second aunt, Mingying, had six. Mingguang, my third aunt, had seven. In the 1940s, even before the establishment of the New China, they had been sympathetic to Mao Zedong's speeches about the birth rate: his theory was that a great nation must have a large population. The more Chinese people there were, the better their chances of defeating American imperialism. This was the polar opposite of the one-child policy of the 1980s and beyond that would arise from a need to control the rapid population growth. Mao's pro-birth policies had even been backed up with practical benefits, even if they only favored cadres of a certain level. Three children gave you the right to a nanny, six to two nannies. These incentives proved highly effective.

Until the mid-1960s, the great ritual at the residence was dumplings. For people from the northeast, no celebration could be complete without dumplings, a long-standing tradition in Dongbei. It is a ritual at once highly codified and very informal. It was not enough to bring ready-made dumplings in a bowl and place it in the center of the table, with everybody seated calmly, waiting for the mistress of the house to be served before they could begin eating. No, everybody had to help make them, all of them talking loudly at the same time. This ritual required at least twenty guests, all of them ready to pitch in.

Everybody helps. Wheat flour, salt, water. First, they make the pasta receptacle: it can be made in different shapes, and there is a sort of competition for who is the most skillful creator. Sometimes, you will test the consistency of the pasta with your finger; sometimes, you will taste the stuffing by raising a finger to your mouth. These things are tolerated, even encouraged, as the water boils and the pasta rests before being dropped into it. The dumplings are lined up on the table in military order. The children try to taste the first batch in the kitchen. They are eaten partly in the kitchen and partly in the dining room, with or without a bowl, with spoons or chopsticks. You can eat from your neighbor's bowl, and I often find that other people's dumplings taste better than your own. You are allowed to feed other people, to dangle the dumplings above their nose before letting them eat, even if it means treading on each other's toes. The idea is not only to eat, but to eat while kneading, while cooking, while chatting. Adults hoist children onto their laps; children climb onto adults' laps. Everybody boasts that the dumplings they made was better than their cousin's, their brother's, their mother's, their neighbor's, sometimes better than any dumplings ever made. The dumplings serve as starter, main course, dessert. It can be eaten with sweet-and-sour sauce, or with spicy sauces. It can be eaten without hunger, hot, lukewarm, or cold. At midnight, you must throw all the dumplings in the boiling water and wish one another happy new year. Before you eat the first dumpling of the year, you must make a wish. And whoever finds the "surprise dumpling," containing a piece of candy or a coin, will have good luck all year. The later the night gets, the better the dumplings taste. There must be all kinds of dumplings and you must taste them all: with vegetables, with meat, with or without scented mushrooms, dipped in vinegar and soy sauce or not. The mistress of the house stares happily at every empty bowl. Anybody who asks for more is met with a beaming smile. The great acrobats of dumplings are the children, and I should know: we would race across the apartment to be the first to taste it and to find the "lucky dumpling." I was pretty good at that game.

Sometimes both my parents would be there. Despite being diplomats, they were not rolling in money. They were paid only a small amount of money by their ministry for their foreign missions.

But Mama always found a way to bring me something from Paris, Geneva, or Rome. I remember the first book she brought me from Paris and the delight I felt as I turned its pages. Compared to what existed in China at the time, it was all so sumptuous: the shine of the paper, its thickness, its immaculate whiteness, the beauty of its colors and their innumerable shades, even the smell that those books gave off, all of this gave me even more pleasure than I would have felt had I been able to read French.

The atmosphere of those celebrations at the residence was nourished by the countless memories shared between family, between friends, between partisans. And it was the intensity of those memories that communicated to all of us the singular joy to be found in revisiting and rekindling the past.

I was not so sure that the events they described were as cheerful, funny, and free of danger as they made them sound. What made me doubt this was my grandfather's silence. Well, he was not totally silent, but he limited himself to correcting a date or the name of a place or a person. Of course he listened, and he did so very attentively. Sometimes he would lightly nod his head in approval. But when everybody else was laughing loudly at some remembered episode, he merely smiled. And yet he was the hero, the principal character, in most of these stories. My grandfather's discretion regarding his past, his great modesty, seemed to me the condition of all true heroism.

Within these accounts, there were many things implied and unspoken. I understood that these events had taken place during the period of resistance to the Japanese occupation. The shadow of the Japanese invasion, the Japanese occupation, the Japanese abuses had grown and grown through the 1930s and 1940s, ending only with the Liberation of 1949.

For me, aged seven to nine, it was clear that there had been two kinds of partisans fighting against the Japanese on Chinese soil. On one side, the Kuomintang, the nationalist party founded by Sun Yat-sen after the overthrow of the Qing dynasty in 1912. He had come to power under the direction of General Chiang Kai-shek in 1928, and his government had been based in Nanjing. On the other side were the communists. They were not in power, far from it, but they were just as patriotic as the nationalists.

But between my grandfather and the others with whom he spoke, there was enough talk of the fate of contemporary China that I was able to grasp that the fratricidal battle between the Kuomintang and the Communist Party of China had begun very early. A ferocious, intransigent, deadly battle, despite their common enemy, the Japanese empire, which was skilled at taking advantage of these dissensions to conquer, enslave, debase, massacre.

So, inasmuch as my grandfather had occupied—and continued to occupy—important posts within Zhou Enlai's communist government, under Chairman Mao Zedong, I found it hard to understand how that connected to these words, reported to me by my father or one of his sisters: "Anyway, Papa was always under the protection of Soong May-ling." Now, who was Soong May-ling if not Mrs. Chiang Kai-shek?! And it was strange how amazed they sounded when they said that, some of them as stunned as spectators watching a man walk across hot coals without burning his feet, others awestruck not only by the supreme skill but also the courage and sangfroid of someone willing to risk not only his own life in the name of his convictions but the lives of his family, too.

16

Is it not delightful to have friends coming from afar?

—Chinese proverb

In addition to Nanjing, where the Yan family once lived, another address cropped up regularly during our family gatherings, with an emotion that was sometimes intercut with bursts of laughter: Villa 17, Chongqing Village, in Chongqing, the capital of Sichuan.

In November 1937, the Japanese were waging total war on China. In the north, all the major cities had already fallen. In the south, Nanjing, where the government was based at the time, suffered for six weeks as its people were relentlessly robbed, raped, and murdered during the infamous Nanjing Massacre of December 1937. In Beijing, the Japanese inflicted the humiliation of a "temporary government" intended to replace the Kuomintang. Which is why the Kuomintang opted for a base as far as possible from the Japanese army: Chongqing, in the inland province of Sichuan. This "mountain city," as it was known, was needed to give what remained of China a temporary capital, as well as provide the seat of Chiang Kai-shek's government. A refuge, in other words, for all the country's dignitaries. All of them were there, without exception. In Chongqing, they also had to reckon with the presence of communists. The most active communists were underground because while, on the face of it, nationalists and communists were united by their common enemy—imperialist Japan, which was trying to force China to its knees—in reality the communist partisans and Chiang Kai-shek's troops had been fighting bitterly against each other since the unified front had been destroyed. Another reason why the Japanese wished to target Chongqing.

To my child's ears, those events all seemed far in the past. The same was true for certain catchphrases, such as the famous "House of Yan" and the "Great Yan Table," not to mention the incomparable welcome one always received "at the Yans'." These expressions might have been born in the northeast, and strengthened during my grandparents' stay in Nanjing, but it was in the climate of permanent danger in Chongqing that they finally acquired their magical and essential value.

Sometimes, said my aunt Mingguang, there were as many as ten mattresses on the living room floor; turning to my father, she would say, "How many times did Gaosu come to our respective bedrooms, after midnight, and tell us we had to give up our bed for some strange visitor who'd just arrived?"

And, laughing, Mingfu, my father, would reply, "I must have been about ten when we were in Chongqing, and there were always lots of visitors, but I was not allowed to go upstairs. And upstairs there was a little room without a window where I would have loved to play! I was so frustrated because the only ones who were allowed to go up to that room were my father, accompanied by an 'uncle' with very thick black eyebrows. And what did they do up there, Yan Baohang and 'Uncle' Zhou Enlai, because that's who it was, in that little room? Well, they never told us. Not a word. We pretended that they were playing mah-jongg. But their games of mah-jongg lasted entire afternoons, and I still wasn't allowed to go in that room! But what's strange is that, as soon as they came out, Gaosu rushed into the room, emptied all the wastepaper baskets, and ran to the toilet. I always wondered what my mother could be doing in the toilet with the contents of those wastepaper baskets!"

My third aunt, Mingguang, took over the story: "Our parents' determination to let in anyone who needed help, to give them bed and board purely because they'd heard about the famous 'Yan household,' had one minor drawback: spies could come to our house, too, whenever they liked! I must have been ten or twelve, and I remember a young man who was with us in the living room, and as soon as my parents turned their back, he started bombarding me with questions: Where are your brothers? What does your father say? What does your aunt do? But the funniest thing was this young man's obsession with going upstairs: he was desperate to go up to that little room without a window. Sadly for him, his obstinacy always came up against Gaosu's. And yet, despite all my parents' precautions, years later we found information files on the whole family in the Kuomintang archives. We even found a plan of the inside of Villa 17. And it was actually quite funny to see such a meticulous rendering, so rigorously precise, of all those rooms where we lived in private." At that moment, Mingguang would pause for a few seconds . . . "Particularly if you bear in mind," she would then add, "that they never found any kind of transmitter in our house! No underground cell! Nothing that proved Yan Baohang belonged to the Communist Party!"

"But the constant coming and going of comrades in our house," my father interjected, "was bound to arouse suspicion. Remember that day when three policemen, more enterprising than the others, came inside and declared point-blank: 'We've heard that you're running a clandestine gambling den. We're going to search the house!' And at that moment Baohang played his trump card, quite literally: he took from his jacket pocket a business card bearing the name of Dai Li, chief of Chiang Kai-shek's secret police, with a few words in his handwriting addressed to Yan Baohang. The policemen left without further ado."

Sometimes, one of my aunts, one of my uncles, or some old partisan from the northeast mentioned to my grandfather how often the Yan family had just skirted disaster. The conclusion being that, despite their conviction that they were fighting on the "right side," despite the feeling of justice and, therefore, invulnerability, there had been an element of luck during all those years spent in Chongqing, those years of coexistence, daggers drawn, between the Kuomintang and the communists, when they really had no idea which side would end up victorious, when it seemed perfectly possible, until the end of the war in the Pacific, long after the war in Europe was over, that Japan might defeat China and rule over most of Asia.

I realized that my father was no longer reeling off his memories of being a little boy. More and more, it was the sophisticated gaze of the grown-up diplomat that set the scene of Chongqing, where all the most divergent interests, convictions, and strategies coexisted and intertwined. On one side, the contacts with Chiang Kai-shek had been known to everyone; on the other, the meetings with Zhou Enlai had always been kept secret. While Zhou himself had officially joined the Kuomintang government, he had asked Baohang to clandestinely join the Communist Party of China in order to help him transmit any useful information that Zhou might obtain as a member of the military committee and an advisor to the policy department in the Kuomintang.

"Courage and boldness were not enough," said my father. "It was imperative that this courage be allied to intelligence, sometimes even to a sort of duplicity, so that all relationships could be used to serve the cause and to save comrades in great danger. It needed both a capacity to accurately assess the risks we were running and, at the same time, convictions solid enough that, if one were to sacrifice oneself, it would not be for an ill-considered and suicidal act."

17

How can you catch tiger cubs without
entering the tiger's lair.

—Chinese saying

It was in this context that the Kuomintang's political police would
arrest a communist agent. Whenever Mingfu began recounting
this episode, my grandfather, I observed, always turned pale.

In those years, with an arrest of that nature, we knew that
the agent would be tortured. We also knew that this comrade
knew that Baohang was secretly a member of the Party. I had
no idea, of course—I was only eleven—but I could see that Papa
was upset. It was only much later that I found out the dilemma
that was eating away at him. If he left Chongqing immediately,
it would be tantamount to denouncing himself. But if he didn't,
he was relying on the agent not talking. How could he know? In

any case, he had to take into consideration the danger that this represented for his family.

That night, at midnight, I hear footsteps very close to the villa. And they are not the footsteps of Zhou Enlai's personal secretary, which I would recognize easily, but those of the "uncle" himself: Uncle Zhou. I get out of bed and groggily leave my room and I hear my father exclaim, "You shouldn't have come! It's too dangerous!" before hugging him tight.

In Chongqing, Zhou Enlai lived in a house very close to ours, and both houses could be reached discreetly via a small path that ran behind the buildings, and which very few people used. But Zhou was very strict about safety: we must never visit him, that was the rule. Even in an emergency, it was Uncle Zhou who would come to us. That day, Uncle Zhou told Baohang to leave the city, to lead his family to a safer place. My father refused.

When my grandfather was still among us, I remember that there was also much discussion of a village, Beipei, not far from Chongqing.

The family liked to reminisce about the beautiful natural landscape around Beipei: a rugged terrain, heavily forested, with lakes and rivers and waterfalls, with parks and gardens and natural hot springs. All of this made Beipei, at that time, a highly prized vacation resort.

My grandparents took their children there regularly. They had to take a small boat to travel from one riverbank to the other. During the crossing, to see that elegant couple looking so relaxed—Gaosu in a cloche hat, Baohang in a polo shirt under a summer jacket—and to see how nicely dressed their youngest children were, you would have said they were the very picture of a good bourgeois Chinese family.

My grandfather insisted on the importance of this appearance; according to him, their impeccable wardrobe was their most certain means of protection. Because of this, it was out of the question, as he explained to Mingshi, that she should remove her high-heeled shoes to run; such an act would rumple the smooth image intended to ease any suspicion among those people who might be observing or following them.

While the younger children ran into the garden to play hide-and-seek as soon as they arrived at the house in Beipei, Gaosu kept watch as Mingshi took out the transmitter hidden in a bucket of rice and removed the typewriter and the coded transcription "bible" from under the wardrobe's false bottom. Mingshi's mission, within the secret cell set up by Yan Baohang, which included one of Gaosu's cousins and Li Zhengwen, who was sent by Zhou Enlai to assist my grandfather's secret-agent work, and his wife, could now begin.

You needed a steady nerve for this kind of work. That day, for instance, in the middle of the transmission, Li Zhengwen detected interference on the line from a nearby station. They all knew that US-trained Kuomintang agents were patrolling outside, attempting to intercept any clandestine communications. So, while my grandfather often complained that there was "no point having information if we don't have a machine to transmit it," there were times when, for urgent security reasons, the cell was forced to hide its equipment and not go near it again for three or four days.

There was also the day when some "workers" came, while my grandparents were absent, to do some supposed repair work on the house's exterior. Barely had the Yan family arrived in Beipei than they were warned by a neighbor that some "wires" running over the roof and along the facade had been inadvertently torn off by workers. Nainai, in a panic, had asked, "Workers? What workers? What work were they doing? We didn't need any work done on the house!" They had been forced to find another house in a rush.

As for the most serious incident . . . my aunt Mingguang would wait until I had left the room to mention it. She lowered her voice, which, naturally, made me listen more carefully: a plan to murder my grandfather had been secretly hatched within the Kuomintang!

One of the agents recruited for this mission was present during a meeting attended by Dai Li, the chief of Chiang Kai-shek's secret police. He had been surprised to see Dai Li interrupt their meeting to greet Yan Baohang, warmly and at great length. The agent in question had deemed it prudent to find out more. "Yan Baohang is a close friend of Mrs. Chiang Kai-shek," he was informed. In a panic, the agent did his best to leak enough information to doom the plot to failure.

18

I am filled with infinite delight when I
awaken memories. He is filled with infinite
delight when he awakens memories.

—Chinese saying

It was 1962, and I was five years old. I was spending the vacation
with my parents in Beidaihe, on the Gulf of Bohai, in the province of Hebei. We were there at the invitation of Deng Xiaoping,
head of the Communist Party, who had been in power for thirteen years.

Beidaihe is the closest beach to Beijing, less than two hundred miles to the east, not far from the place where the Great
Wall reaches the coast. The sand on the beach is fine and golden,
formed from ocher rocks and heated by the sun. Dunes planted
with cypresses and pines, colonized by birds and the bird-

watchers who come from miles around to observe them. The place is known for that, and for having become a sort of "summer capital."

Before becoming the favorite beach resort of China's leaders, this fishing village was popular among British railway engineers in the 1890s; it was they who built the first beautiful single-story villas here. They were followed, in the 1920s, by businessmen and diplomats seeking to escape the furnace of Beijing or Tianjin, as well as aficionados—from China and abroad—of the *viennoiseries* offered by the local tearoom supplied by Kiesling and Bader.

That summer there was a subject on the agenda that directly concerned my father: the withdrawal of economic aid from the Soviet Union, with whom all relations were now broken. He had to prepare meetings, consult papers, translate speeches. Liu Shaoqi, chairman of the People's Republic of China since 1959, spent all his summers in Beidaihe. Deng Xiaoping, the Party's secretary-general, had a large villa there, hidden away behind parasol pines. Marshal Chen Yi's villa was pretty nice, too. The man who had completed the communist victory between 1948 and 1949 by leading his troops into Nanjing and Shanghai had been working in the Foreign Ministry for the past four years. My father worked with those three men in a new building that housed offices, meeting rooms, a movie theater, and a ballroom. Our leaders loved to dance, as I had always been told.

Deng Xiaoping told my father, "In Beidaihe, we'll have to work all summer. It's a big house." So it was that he invited my father to stay, along with his wife and daughter.

When my father mentioned this to my mother, she imposed

a condition: "If I'm coming, I need to have something to do. Why don't I set up a little summer English school for the children?" No sooner said than done. The class was composed of Rong, whose nickname was Maomao, the third and youngest daughter of Deng Xiaoping; Pingping, one of Liu Shaoqi's daughters; and Shan Shan, daughter of Chen Yi.

And so, every morning, Mama taught those girls English.

In 1995, Maomao published a biography of her illustrious father. Given the exceptional stature of this man of state, to whom we owe China's openness after the Cultural Revolution, she decided to retrace his political journey, which many people identify with the history of contemporary China itself. For me, Deng Xiaoping was not only a great leader who changed China's destiny, but he was also the man with whom I enjoyed several summer weeks in an atmosphere of bonhomie and familial affection.

Maomao often told me how much her father enjoyed having his children, grandchildren, nephews, and nieces around him. And the Deng household also included Xiaoping's sister, her children, and his stepmother—their father's fourth and final wife—whom they called Grandma. It is remarkable to think of this man, whose political commitment began in adolescence, actively desiring a "Chinese-style" family life, in-laws included, the utterly traditional lifestyle of "four generations under one roof," in the words of Lao She. In fact, there were five generations in Deng's case! It seems admirable to me that he continued this way of life until his death, but it is also easy to imagine what a source of comfort and support his family must have been in difficult moments.

That summer, a few of us were learning to swim. Seven or eight children would crowd around Deng Xiaoping, each with our rubber ring, waiting at the water's edge for our swimming master's instructions. Deng Xiaoping challenged us. Then it was time to go back to the villa to eat dinner in a lively atmosphere where everybody talked about his or her day while Deng Xiaoping remained silent, happy to listen to the cheerfully chatting children.

More than fifty years later, I was very moved to hear Deng Maomao recall, at the publication party for my father's biography, the strong impression that my mother had made on her: "A very beautiful woman. Tall. Slim. Impressive." All the more so, I thought, for little girls who had heard her speak in three foreign languages: English, French, and Italian.

"Of course," Maomao told me, "that was part of the reason why Keliang became our idol. But most of all, before the Cultural Revolution, the wives of the founders of the People's Republic usually dressed very simply. And what enchanted us about Wu Keliang was her 'Western-style' appearance."

And in the contemplation of that summer, captivated less by the memory of the beach resort of Beidaihe than by the thought of a time long gone, Maomao remembered a completely white suit that had dazzled not only the girls but their mothers, too, and—most of all—a pale yellow suit that had driven them wild.

Maomao did put a damper on my nostalgia, however, by reminding me of my mother's intransigence toward me. I ended up bursting out laughing at the retelling of one particular episode: one evening in Beidaihe, everybody was sitting at the dinner table except for me. And so Professor Wu Keliang, the idol of those young girls, had suddenly fallen from her pedestal after exclaiming:

"Oh! I'm sorry, I'm sorry! I completely forgot to let Lan out. I locked her in the bathroom to punish her this afternoon and . . . I just didn't think about it again!"

Maomao and her mother had told Deng Xiaoping about this, and he had laughed, "Oh, that Keliang is harder than a warlord!"

Mao Zedong, too, had a villa in Beidaihe. He went there almost every summer between 1953 and 1965. The tradition of mixing business with pleasure was so well established that a whole host of meetings, symposiums, and speeches were scheduled for July and August.

I remember one evening we all went to see a performance of Peking opera in a large theater hall assigned to the leaders. The first few rows remained empty. We understood the reason for this when Mao Zedong made his appearance. He moved forward and greeted a few people before taking his seat. Then the show could begin. But that evening, although Mao Zedong had the place of honor, in reality he had withdrawn from the presidency. This distancing could be interpreted as a wise decision, but that is not exactly the case: his resignation, in favor of Liu Shaoqi, had come after Mao had been put in the minority, three years before, in the Party's committee following the disaster of the Great Leap Forward and its millions of dead.

But while Liu Shaoqi was preparing to recommend a return to private business and Deng Xiaoping to defend food production at all costs, Mao—who refused to recognize the Great Leap Forward as a failure—opened hostilities at the end of that summer in Beidaihe, in September 1962. Not content to minimize the production crisis that was overwhelming the countryside, Mao Zedong was returning to the dogma of the class struggle.

At the tenth plenary session of the eighth Central Committee, he would begin by touching on the question of youth and the necessity of its revolutionary training in order to fertilize China's roots on the path to socialism. As for the countryside, he faulted the peasantry's incorrigible tendency to dream of owning land, which added to the inertia of the government's administrative cadres. Those two factors, he claimed, put the socialist plan in danger of being strangled at birth. Lastly, Mao talked about culture. He believed that leaving this realm to the intellectuals would inevitably lead to the restoration of a bourgeois, capitalist ideal of society.

Nobody could have guessed then where the three themes outlined in Comrade Mao's speech—Youth, Countryside, Culture—would lead us. Hindsight shines a starker light on his thoughts, which would take time to mature. In the years that followed, those three themes would melt into one apparently harmless concept, and circumstances would change. Then it would explode.

19

What he did is making his relatives heartbroken
and the haters happy.

—Chinese proverb

At the very beginning of the Cultural Revolution, my grandfather received Gao Chongmin one evening at the residence.
He, along with Wang Huayi, had been Zhang Xueliang's closest
colleague before being named vice president of the parliament
after the birth of New China.

They soon started discussing the famous journal that Wang
Huayi had long kept. Mr. Gao explained that the hundreds of
notebooks composing this journal had been entrusted to him
just before the author's death. But Mr. Gao seemed anxious, ner-
vous, in a rush. He began telling my grandfather that, very recently, in Beijing, some young and less young people, who called

themselves Red Guards and were recognizable by the armbands they wore, had piled in the streets journals, books, and other documents raided from the homes of "ideological suspects" and burned them.

The thousands of pages of Wang Huayi's manuscript journal had been given to him by the deceased's own children. Mr. Gao had read them all from beginning to end, and he could testify that it was a very important historical document. According to him, part of the interest in his document related to the way of life in China between the end of the nineteenth century and the start of the twentieth, but it was above all the political aspect of the entries from the 1930s to the Liberation of 1949 that most needed to be preserved.

Mr. Gao insisted: an attentive reading of this journal allowed him to affirm that, in light of the current political climate, these documents would be highly compromising for whomever was in possession of them. And that was why, given Yan Baohang's close friendship with the prime minister, Zhou Enlai, the descendants of Wang Huayi and Mr. Gao himself believed that the journal of their father and his friend would be safe nowhere else but in Yan Baohang's apartment.

It is only now that I am able to date these events. So many things happened so fast to me between the summer and the fall of 1967 that my emotions at that time remained frozen beyond time.

At the very beginning of the Cultural Revolution, in 1966, the eldest of my cousins, Da Pangzi, was twenty years old; Nainai and Yeye's first grandson was starting university, funded by my grandfather. In choosing to study Russian history, civilization, and language, my cousin was following a family tradition begun by two of his uncles.

At that time, my grandparents were even more concerned about my cousin since his mother—my aunt Mingshi—had been accused of "rightism" in 1957 and, consequently, exiled with her engineer husband and their eight children. Their place of exile was Anshan, a steelmaking town in the province of Liaoning. Their situation was so difficult that I remember the instructions given to all the members of the family: that they should send them some money every month, and even some secondhand clothes.

Da Pangzi came to the residence every month, and each time my grandfather was so pleased to be able to talk with him that I became aware that the "Big Guy" was now in fact one of those "great people" whose knowledge and judgment are always sought. Da Pangzi was generally considered to be my grandfather's "other favorite."

Over time, however, everybody noticed that Da Pangzi was changing. Certainly, the relationship between grandson and grandfather no longer had the serenity necessary to all good conversation. In fact, there were times when my cousin grew so irritated that he left the apartment without saying good-bye to us. My grandfather kept his temper, while Da Pangzi appeared to be trying to pick a fight. One day, having barely arrived, already furious, he started a very heated debate from which I remember only one phrase: "Well then, if that's how it is, I'm going to join the Red Guards right away!" he said threateningly to my grandfather.

It would be several months before we saw him again at the residence. Finally he came, with a mocking expression on his face and the famous red armband over his biceps, after first making sure that my grandfather was absent. That day, he insulted everybody, telling us that he had just come from Xinjiang, that his group of Red Guards had "made revolution" there, repeatedly yelling, "Pillage! Pillage! Pillage!" I can still see my cousin's face now, unrecognizable in its fury, its hysteria, shouting those three words, and I can still see the shock on my grandmother's and mother's faces.

Flanked by other Red Guards, he had come to demand that we hand over Wang Huayi's journal, though we'd had no idea how he even knew about it. When we refused to give it to him, arguing that its historical significance meant it should be entrusted to the National Archives, Da Pangzi ordered his stooges to search the apartment. They caused considerable damage and, in the end, Da Pangzi got his hands on the precious journal.

Immediately after this, Yan Baohang was arrested.

20

Poverty gives rise to a desire for change.

—Chinese proverb

Yan Baohang was born in the spring of 1895 near Fengtian, the capital city of Liaoning province. He was born into a poor household in the village of Xiaogaolifang, though it was no poorer (or richer) than any of the others in that village. One more mouth to feed, but two more arms to work. A boy, too; always better than a girl. As the fourth in a line of six boys and three girls, he had little chance of being given any of the rare privileges reserved for the eldest, particularly as he had to show his respect to his elder brothers and sisters, in accordance with the family ethical code that governed all habits in the old Empire.

His mother's family name was Dong. Sadly, the given name of the woman who was my father's paternal grandmother is no longer known. Besides, in a family of more than twenty members, it is likely that she was always addressed by her rank within the successive, always "arranged" marriages: third sister-in-law or daughter-in-law, fourth sister-in-law or daughter-in-law, etc. I don't even know if she was given the usual offering reserved for new mothers—eggs, brown sugar, and millet—when she gave birth to her fourth child, my grandfather.

My grandfather's father's name was Yan Decheng. In China, as I have mentioned, the family name always comes before the given name. The child's given name was Yuheng. Yes, that's right: Yuheng, not Baohang. I should explain that in China the given name is not necessarily permanent, the way it is in the West. There is a distinction between the childhood name, for use only within the family, and the social given name, generally settled on when the child starts school. But there are all sorts of circumstances in which a name might be changed, for example to mark the passage into adulthood or to mark a change in one's personal journey.

Having seen those little peasants' shacks, I can imagine the few windows decorated with paper or gauze. I visualize the *kang*, that large bed which takes up almost all the space and which can still be found in northern China, made of bricks warmed in the embers of the fireplace, big enough that the new mother can lie there with her other children. One of her sisters-in-law is perhaps at her bedside, having brought boiling water during the labor.

In the fields they cultivated corn and sorghum. They also raised a few pigs. Men and women both wore the short, ordinary tunic, sometimes fleece-lined, of simple people who work with their hands; they would wear it over shorts or pants. Nobody in the village wore the long robe of aristocrats or intellectuals, except for the teacher, brought there from a larger village by the least poor families to instruct their eldest sons.

When greeting one another, the usual expression was "Have you eaten?" The most common saying, "An empty belly is the most important truth." So, you can see how life was for them. Hunger and cold at least proved to them that they were alive. Which was not the case for the third boy born in the Yan family, who died at a very young age.

In 1895 the Empress Cixi had been ruling over China for thirty years, and the Qing dynasty had been in place since 1644. All over the country, people feared changes of dynasties. They feared change, period, in fact, since change always exposed poor people to violence, pillage, and rape. It was already hard enough dealing with the hazards of the weather: droughts, floods, tornadoes, locusts, bad seasons, bad harvests . . . And that was without even taking into account the risk of sickness.

So was Yan Baohang's birthday a good day or a bad day? All we know is that, on that day, there was fighting in the surrounding villages. Japanese troops attacked the Empire's soldiers. Eleven days later, on April 17, the Treaty of Shimonoseki ended the Sino-Japanese War that had begun the previous year. But at what a price! China surrendered Formosa and the ninety islands in the Pescadores archipelago. In the province of Liaoning, the peninsula of Liaoning was surrendered, including Port Arthur. China recognized Korea's "independence," now under Japanese protectorate; agreed to pay 200 million yuan of silver in war compensation to the Japanese empire; and had to open seven of its ports to Japanese merchants. This treaty, among so many other unequal treaties, is known in China as the "treaty of dishonor." At the same time, the Western powers were developing territories all over the continent. In other words, Yan Baohang was born in a country that had lost almost all control of its own destiny.

Worse, the Great Qing Empire that was selling China off so cheaply was unable to pull the country out of its semifeudal state, with its population mostly poor, illiterate peasants.

The feeling of humiliation at being colonized was a heavy burden for the Chinese elite. The poor people, however, were less affected by the death throes of the weak regime than by the famine that would hit the entire northern part of China the following year after some unusually disastrous weather.

Yan Baohang was born on April 6 under the sign of the goat. This is not necessarily a good sign. Chinese astrology states only that its dominant aspect is the yin. Of all the signs in the zodiac, the goat is the most generous. He likes to be useful; he defends the weak, the poor, the oppressed. He is empathetic and selfless.

21

The fool chatters, the monkey listens.

—Chinese saying

Until he is old enough to work in the fields, the fourth child, twelve years old now, looks after the pigs. He is in charge of the pigpen. At a time when the pig is a symbol of abundance and prosperity, the job of swineherd is an important one, though obviously his role is to feed and fatten the pigs for sale, not to eat them. And for that, the pigs must be in good health. He must watch over them to ensure they do not hurt themselves by fighting; he must keep the pigpen free of rats, keep the boar on a tight leash, and the sow, too, when she is in heat; he must keep the piglets, still suckling in the spring, sheltered from the cold, and feed them on vegetable peelings and corn husks; he must collect their manure to fertilize the vegetable garden; he must feed the weaned piglets on acorns, while also taking care of the henhouse.

The fourth child is managing pretty well. Fishing pole in hand, he walks through the dirt alleys of Xiaogaolifang. On his way to the river, he passes the little house where the teacher stands, in long robes, holding a switch. One classroom. Six students. A window without paper or gauze, through which the fourth child can hear and see the lucky children reciting the *Sanzijing*, the famous three-character primer, and among those lucky ones is Ersuo, who is the same age as the fourth child. The difference is: Ersuo's parents can afford to pay the teacher.

He has asked to be able to study, even though he is not aware of the Chinese proverb: "All professions are worthless; only study is noble." His mother does not necessarily disagree with this proverb; it is just that they do not have enough money. The little money they do have, the father has decided, will be spent on sending the second child to school. The first child will be a farmer, the third child is dead, so you, fourth child, are the swineherd.

There is nothing unfair about that, the fourth child thinks. The only injustice is to see, through the school's window, how bored Ersuo looks. How eager he is for the class to be over so he can go out and meet the fourth child. So that he and his friend can go to the river, because Ersuo finds it more enjoyable to herd pigs and go fishing in the Taizi, whereas he, the fourth child, is so desperate to learn.

That day, Master Fan is beginning the famous *Sanzijing* of the Song dynasty for the umpteenth time.

Master Fan's method is always the same: "Like someone throwing fruit to monkeys," as the saying goes, Master Fan recites the first verse in a series of four, each one composed uniquely of three characters, and he points at one of the students, who is supposed to know the next line by heart. This handbook of elementary education is so skillfully composed that, in just 356 characters, it touches upon all the essential general knowledge regarding grammar, arithmetic, historical chronology, literary classics, and Confucian morality. Any young Chinese person who learns this recital will become familiar with the common Chinese characters, how to read them and how to pronounce them. In fact, this form of teaching was common until the Cultural Revolution banned the supposedly feudal ideological foundation of education.

But let us return to Master Fan, who is reciting *ren zhi chu*: "Men at birth . . ." And with the point of his switch, he asks Ersuo for the next line. But Ersuo is daydreaming. He has not heard the master. He is miles away. He is brought back to earth by a flick of the master's switch. Through the window, the fourth child sees the livid, red, painful mark, the same mark he has seen so many times on his friend's hand after coming out of school. Pitying Ersuo, he starts hissing the correct response, hoping that his friend will hear him and that the master won't.

xing ben shan are naturally good . . .
xing xiang jin are naturally all the same.
xi xiang yuan they differ through the habits they form.

Well, either Ersuo is deaf or he is utterly absorbed by the pain. In either case, he says nothing, so Master Fan strikes him again with the switch before attempting another verse:

san guang zhe the Three Rules are ...

And the fourth child answers, a little too loudly:

jun chen yi the affection between father and son ...
fu fu shun the harmony between husband and wife.

The switch remains suspended in the air, and Master Fan turns to the window and demands, "Who are you?"

22

There are tigers and dragons among you.

—Chinese proverb

"I'm just my father's swineherd," the fourth child replies. And fearing that his intervention might worsen Ersuo's fate, he defends his friend, explaining to Master Fan that it was the fear of being struck that prevented Ersuo from responding because he knows the verses. Ersuo has recited them by heart many times when he has gone fishing with his friend in the Taizi River!

Master Fan is not taken in. He begins by ordering the fourth child into the classroom and then launches into a diatribe against Ersuo, whose father is slaving away to allow this lazy boy to learn to read and write, instead of which, by learning nothing, Ersuo demonstrates a lack of the basic respect owed to a father and a lack of the basic respect owed to a teacher. Then, turning toward the fourth child, "And you, swineherd, what do you know of the *Three-Character Classic* that your friend does not?" And the fourth child recites the forty-four rhymed verses of the first chapter on the nature of man, the necessity of education, and filial piety, concentrating on correctly pronouncing the Mandarin language despite the strong accent of the dialect that is commonly spoken in the northeast. "And do you know the rest?" the master asks, increasingly intrigued. So the fourth child reels off the sixty-six rhymed verses of the arithmetic and the object lesson.

"And what do you know of the good books?" the master asks.

"I don't know them all, just a few bits," the fourth child replies.

"Very well. Let us begin."

For those who study
there must be a beginning.
After the elementary study of characters
come those of the Four Books.

And the fourth child continues:

The teachings of Confucius
comprise twenty chapters
in which his disciples
transcribed his wise words.
The *Mencius* comprises seven books
about the Way and Virtue

and teaches the principles
of altruism and justice.
The *Doctrine of the Mean*
was written by Zisi.
The Mean is what does not deviate.
Once the Classic of Filial Piety has been learned by heart
and the Four Books understood,
we will move on to the Six Classics
that can now be started.
The *Classic of Poetry*
the *Book of Documents*
the *I Ching*
the *Book of Rites*
the *Rites of Zhou*
the *Spring and Autumn Annals*
are the Six Classics
that must be explained and studied in depth.

"But I'm not too sure after that," says the fourth child.

The master, somewhat taken aback, realizes that this boy, by listening through the window, has benefited more from his lessons than his friend has, sitting in the classroom. Now he wishes to find out if the fourth child can write. On this question, the boy admits that he has never used a quill or a brush, but that he has been able to write in the sand of the riverbank with the aid of a bamboo stick, and—using his index finger—he demonstrates the first characters of the *Hundred Family Surnames*, the most famous of the ancient texts. True, Master Fan spots a few errors, but that is not what he plans to talk about this evening when he goes to meet the fourth child's father.

That Master Fan, the only man in Xiaogaolifang to wear the long robe of the learned, should deign to visit a peasant: this alone is enough to impress Yan Decheng. But the master does not go inside. He simply wants to know what is stopping the fourth child's father from sending him to school. Yan Decheng stammers that he has no money. The master interrupts to tell him that the fourth child has a favorable disposition, and as this compliment is a rare source of pleasure in a life where opportunities for rejoicing are so few, the father exclaims: "Well, in that case, we'll see . . . perhaps I can find enough money for the fourth child." But the master replies: "Listen, the time has come for your fourth child. As far as money is concerned, there will be no need to pay anything for that son."

And so it is that for two years in Xiaogaolifang, Yan Baohang attends Master Fan's classes and does not fall below his expectations. In 1909, Yan Baohang is fourteen. Master Fan decides to tell him, "I have nothing more to teach you. For you, Xiaogaolifang is over. You must go to Haicheng now. I'm going to talk to your parents about it."

23

To know one's nature is to know Heaven.

—Mencius (372–289 BCE), Book
VII A, Sections 1 and 4

The idea that Yan Baohang should go to Haicheng, nearly a hundred miles from his home village, was not something his parents were willing to accept. The fourth child would be lost to the farm, to the plot of land and the pigs; he would be lost to them. Neither parent had ever studied, but they knew, as did all Chinese people in those days, that three things ran contrary to filial piety: The first was to encourage parents to do something bad through flattery and a shameful indulgence, exactly as Master Fan had done to them. The second was not wishing to work for money to relieve the poverty of one's aged parents, which might well happen if the fourth child went to the city to study. The third was not to marry or have children. Of those three faults, the most unforgivable was to remain without posterity, said Mencius.

So the first thing that Yan Baohang's parents did was to give their son a wife "to connect the heart." It was high time, anyway: the fourth child was fourteen years old and, as was customary, the young girl had long been chosen. The usual practice was to marry two children who knew each other well. Sometimes this agreement on a marriage was concluded between the families as soon as the mothers became pregnant: "If it's a boy, keep him for my daughter," they would say. And if that wasn't the case, then the custom was to employ a matchmaker. Needless to say, no feeling was required, merely the accomplishment of a duty.

The fourth child protested that he did not want to marry, but it made no difference. His mother ordered him to put on new clothes to welcome his spouse.

But when they returned from the parents-in-law with the girl in tow, Yan Baohang had disappeared. The wedding was about to take place, and everybody was present . . . except for the groom. At that moment, Master Fan entered. As his intention was not to stir up trouble but to calm the situation, he took care to step inside their humble abode on this feast day so that everybody could see how honored Yan Decheng was by the presence of the robe wearer. Master Fan asked to speak with the fourth child's father.

Man to man, they put their cards on the table. Yan Decheng

went first: "The time for studying is over. The fourth child must marry!" Master Fan let him speak for as long as he needed to express his opinion, and he acknowledged what he had to say. Yan Decheng felt better for having gotten it off his chest, and the master took advantage of his relief to suggest that, if the son performed the most important duty of filial piety by taking a wife, the father could then agree to let him pursue his studies. Master Fan made it clear that the fourth child had a special talent and that it would be a shame to let it go to waste.

For a long moment, Yan Decheng was speechless. Then he thought that, after all, his own wife would have some extra help with the presence of the young bride in the house, so all was not lost. And who knows, perhaps if they were lucky the fourth child might be allowed to take the imperial examinations. In the middle of this impossible daydream—because Yan Decheng was not aware that the imperial exams had been abolished three years before by order of the empress—he suddenly thought about all the guests who were waiting outside to find out if the wedding would go ahead or not. So he gave his agreement.

Gaosu was a peasant girl of sixteen. From a neighboring village, she spoke the local dialect (and her strong accent would resurface years later, even when she spoke Mandarin almost exclusively).

Born under the sign of the snake, her astral data, her planet, her element, and her color showed no incompatibility with those of her young husband. Or so the matchmaker said, at least. That same day, Yan Baohang informed Gaosu that, directly after their wedding, he would go to the city to study.

Very well, she replied.

On her side, Gaosu had a request, too: her feet had been bound; she wanted that to stop.

Very well, he replied.

And so they took an immediate liking to each other.

24

And so I could suffer even more from having wished
to avoid suffering, and when my heart would
be all suffering I would forget the suffering.

—Lao She, *Four Generations under One Roof,* 1949

A few words about bound feet.

For more than a thousand years, women in China suffered from this tradition. With the exceptions of Manchus and Mongols and, more generally, of nomads—because the women rode horses—practically all the others (particularly the Hans, who were the majority in China) were mutilated in this way.

It was at the end of the Tang dynasty, in the tenth century, that this practice was supposedly begun. The Taoist emperor Tang Aidi asked one of his young concubines to accord him this favor in order to stimulate his desire during the lotus dance.

Associated with life at court, and therefore with nobility, the custom became widespread through the following century among the higher realms of society, particularly as women were required to perform very few tasks that required complete freedom of movement. But soon, it became commonplace among all the classes, except for the very poorest, to the extent that a good marriage was inconceivable if the girl did not have shrunken feet. The practice of bound feet, having begun as a fetish, became a mark of social distinction—it was impossible to work in the field if you had small feet—as much as an aesthetic demand. The outcome was that any girl with "big feet"—i.e., normal-sized feet—would not find a husband.

The natural growth of the feet began to be inhibited from the age of five, sometimes even younger. The toes were firmly folded down, except for the big toe, toward the interior of the arch, which was severely bent, if not broken, in order to reduce its length; then the foot was held in this shape, day and night, with the aid of a very tight ligature. Finally, the foot was slipped inside a beautiful embroidered slipper with a pointed end, in smaller and smaller sizes, until the foot had obtained the "correct" size and shape to represent a lotus bud. The instep was exaggeratedly arched, and only the big toe pointed toward the end of the small thin shape, making it extremely difficult to walk. As for the pain, let's not even talk about that.

Fractures, necrosis, engorgement, edemas, and other infections inevitably accompanied the operation. Despite the absolute necessity of changing the bindings daily, of applying antiseptic solutions, of eliminating dead skin and ingrown nails, instances

of septicemia were common. The custom made it practically ta-
boo to show one's bare foot, since it was impossible to exhibit it
without the bindings and slippers.

The need for her to work in the fields spared my grandmother, at least for a while. Then she had the courage to tell her
new husband that she disapproved of this tradition, and Baohang
agreed with her that these were customs that belonged to another age and that it was better for her to be unbound.

In this regard they were ahead of their times, because while
it is true that three years after their wedding the government
outlawed foot-binding, it continued to happen secretly. It was
not until 1949 that the ban was enforced. But for Gaosu, whose
parents had hesitated between the need for her to find a husband and the need to have her working in the fields, it was already partly too late.

In her case, the cessation of the binding allowed her feet to
recover some of their natural shape, but the fractures and irre-
versible necrosis had already affected her metatarsals. My beloved grandmother showed me her feet one day, her eyes lowered
out of modesty, and what I saw appeared to have the consistency
of tofu and resembled nothing so much as overcooked dumplings. It was very strange.

25

If a man takes no thought about the future,
he will lose his present.

—Chinese proverb

There are periods in a life when time moves faster. So Yan Baohang thinks, aged fifteen, when he begins his secondary studies
in Haicheng.

In his country school he had learned the neo-Confucian
canon by heart because, since 1313, the subjects of imperial examinations were always taken from those texts.

But those examinations had been abolished. There was now
a Ministry of Education. The modern schools, partly Western-
ized, had begun to replace the traditional academies.

Not so long ago, the Empire's functionaries had spoken
only the classical language; this was the language of official

documents and history books. Now, suddenly, it was possible to express oneself in the vernacular language: the "language of rickshaw boys and soy-milk vendors," as its detractors labeled it.

Not so long ago, the Empire had seemed unshakeable, and the "tonsure decree," first enacted during the accession of the Manchus, requiring all men to wear their hair in a braid, was still in force. But now a general movement in favor of a nationalist revolution was coming into being. Among the protesters was the Society for the Renewal of China . . . not to mention the Revolutionary Society, founded in Tokyo in 1905 by a certain Sun Yat-sen.

At my grandparents' wedding, they had prayed to the god of sun for happiness and protection; they had prayed to the god of ditches and walls against sickness; they had honored the spirits of Heaven and Earth. They had not rebelled against the Confucian precept that requires the bride to leave her family for good, and they had compensated her family for the labor they had lost. On the other hand, it did not go unremarked that the groom, Yan Baohang, in agreeing to let his wife stop binding her feet, was going against tradition by allowing her to come and go freely, beyond the strict domestic space to which other women were confined. Had he not been such a good boy, Yan Baohang might have been suspected of being a believer in those new morals that, so it was said, favored the man's wife over his mother.

Yan Baohang's discovery of city life was filled with other equally exciting novelties: the desire for modernization expressed by the reformists of the Hundred Days, grouped around Kang Youwei and his "modern party," was starting to bear fruit. In place of the "three teachings" based on Confucianism, Taoism, and Buddhism, the "foreign school," in which Yan Baohang was now being taught, extolled the merits of scientific knowledge. He learned about the deficiencies in hygiene and the obstacles to the rational development of agriculture caused by the peasantry's Taoism. Consultation of the *Yellow Almanac* was criticized. Decreed by the imperial palace, this almanac listed the celebrations, prohibitions, and sacrifices required each day. The word *superstition*, rarely uttered before, was now used to describe such practices. There was much talk of progress, of reforms, of the aspiration to a modernized China. For a young man, thirsty for knowledge, eager for fulfillment, those first ten years of the twentieth century were rich with promise.

The promise was not false. In 1911, when Yan Baohang was sixteen, Kang Youwei's subversive theories were exploded by the victorious insurrection of October 10. This was the Xinhai Revolution, led by organizations that brought together intellectuals, students, and workers. Soon, a white sun against a blue background—the symbol of Dr. Sun Yat-sen—could be seen everywhere, or almost.

What were the principles behind this new emblem? First, Chinese independence and the eradication of foreign imperialism. Because, lest we forget, the Empire had, since Yan Baohang's birth in 1895, been making ruinous and humiliating reparations to Japan and to the Western powers, in addition to the regime of concessions. Second, the rebels were demanding an end to Manchu domination.

This was a huge event. The Republic swept away the Empire

that had governed this continent-sized country for more than two millennia. The "double ten" (October 10) is now celebrated as the date of the 1911 revolution. The dragon and the red sun of the Qing dynasty gave way to the flag with five horizontal bands of color symbolizing the union of the five Chinese ethnicities, putting an end to the Manchu domination. A commoner entered the Forbidden City. The government set up base in the Zhongnanhai. It abandoned the ancient system of *shichen*, which divided the day into twelve units, each lasting about two hours, although the precise length varied with the season. And, as with the French Revolution, the calendar was completely changed: the lunar calendar was abandoned on January 1, 1912, the date when Sun Yat-sen took up his new position as the president of the first Republic, and the nationalist party—the Kuomintang—founded by Sun decreed that from that moment on the years would be counted from this new era. The world had been turned upside down.

The next year, in 1913, Yan Baohang passed the exam to enter the teacher training college in Fengtian, a city even larger than Haicheng. Once again, he shone academically.

But the political situation remained fragile. China had no democratic traditions and was still dominated by rich warlords, each with his own army. Emperor Taishō of Japan saw in the weakness of Chinese institutions an opportunity to strengthen his country's economic and political stranglehold over China, which had existed since the Russo-Japanese War of 1904–05, when the Japanese victors granted themselves Liaodong (Port Arthur) and colonized Korea. In 1915, the Japanese emperor's twenty-one demands were all met without resistance, whereby he advanced another pawn as part of his plan to make China nothing more than a protectorate.

Yan Baohang was furious. The time had come for action. While he started studying for a degree that would make him a teacher, Baohang was at the heart of the growing protests. He published articles in newspapers and magazines, organized his first meetings, gave his first speeches calling for a new public awareness necessary to fight against the Japanese. He was becoming an activist, a progressive, a new kind of man known as an intellectual.

26

As the ancients said: the learned man who returns
after three days should be considered another eye.

—Lu Xun, *The True Story of Ah Q*, 1921

Very close to the college in Fengtian (today called Shenyang)
was a Protestant church. There was nothing surprising about
this, given that the headquarters of the Young Men's Christian
Association—better known as the YMCA—was not far from
there either. This evangelical organization, founded in London
in the middle of the nineteenth century, had spread all over the
world. But unlike the first Portuguese missionaries, who arrived
at the beginning of the sixteenth century, or the first Italian Je-
suits at the end of that century, the Protestant pastors prudently
avoided proselytizing, preferring to welcome everybody, boys
and girls, religious or not.

Their vast premises were open to modernity. There were thousands of reasons for Yan Baohang to go inside. Free access to the books in the library; conversations with other students in the common room; the chance to attend meetings, see shows, take part in seminars on the most diverse and controversial subjects; to join the debate himself; to ask for assistance with problems of accommodation, health care, work, or family; to enroll in evening classes, schedule meetings, drink tea while leafing through the Chinese and Anglo-Saxon newspapers . . . There were hundreds of activities on offer there, not only spiritual activities but also convivial, intellectual, artistic, social, even athletic (basketball and volleyball).

Like most Chinese people from the northeast, Yan Baohang was tall. He was easily persuaded to start playing basketball and soon proved himself one of the best players on the team.

Baohang did some digging. He found out what motivated the man who founded the YMCA: a growing awareness of the terrible working conditions of young laborers in London, their physical and moral distress, the spiritual abandonment.

Some of the meetings organized by the YMCA concerned the doctrine of social Christianity, the idea that all Protestants were expected to be personally active in helping the poorest sections of society in order to help produce greater social justice.

The values of mutual assistance promulgated by these Protestant pastors spoke all the more to Baohang, who had not forgotten the active support he received from his first schoolteacher. And soon his mind was ablaze with the idea that he must help others in the way that he himself was helped.

Like all educated Chinese people at that time, he closely followed the seismic events provoked by the fall of the Empire, and the convulsions that came in its wake. He was aware of what a rare opportunity he had: to be at the center of such a massive change in his country's history.

Questions crowded his mind: How was it that the Empire, more than two thousand years old, could have folded like a house of cards? Why had China not benefited from the same kinds of reforms that the old empire of Japan had instigated since the middle of the nineteenth century? Why were Western science and industrial modernization struggling to penetrate Chinese society? Why did this essentially agricultural country keep being struck by famine, as was the case in 1907 and 1911? How could one of the most ancient and dazzling civilizations in the world have reached such a point of disintegration that it could be pillaged by the Western powers and offer so little resistance?

In the YMCA's premises, these topics were passionately debated by young students and graduates. Some highlighted the corruption of the entire system. Others pointed out the specific misdeeds of Manchu despotism, which left the country defenseless against the aggression of Western and Japanese imperialism, leading the Empire to close its doors and withdraw into itself while the Western world went through two industrial revolutions.

But they all agreed on one point: the system of mandarins perpetuated by the Empire—otherwise known as the production by the Empire of an elite trained to reproduce the state orthodoxy in exchange for civil and military posts—was responsible for leading the country into apathy. And one day, Yan Baohang went a step further: "What is the state orthodoxy, if not the inherited teachings of Confucius and Mencius? A humanist philosophy, perhaps, but one confined within the narrow limits of traditional thought. What else can we call this perpetuation of a tradition where society and family are structured on the model of the Empire from the fifth century BCE to the beginning of the twentieth century, except feudal or semifeudal? In other words, how valid is the first line of the *Three-Character Classic* as we have learned it, 'Human nature is essentially good,' when millions of peasants, millions of poor people, millions of illiterate people are left by the wayside?"

Yan Baohang said all of this in a single breath. The others were swept along by his speech. He had a natural confidence, and it was clear that he had read many books. Perhaps he had already consulted the famous magazine *New Youth*, launched in Shanghai in 1915, where Western ideas were set forth, along with liberal and Marxist ideas. Yan Baohang would never cease to be this brilliant orator, taking care to conclude his argument with an erudite reference, if only to prove that he "knew his classics," too. So, today, he quoted the first verse of the poem "Shi Cangshu's Hall of Drunken Ink" by Su Dongpo, an author from the Song dynasty, who lived between the eleventh and twelfth centuries: "Our troubles begin when we learn to read." Naturally, as a good dialectician, he was only citing this line in order to turn it on its head: "Everything begins when we start to read!" he concluded.

The new secretary-general of the YMCA, the pastor Joseph Platt, having just learned that Yan Baohang had converted to Protestantism, heard these words and immediately became more interested in this young man.

27

Give man a fish and you feed him for a day. Teach him how to fish and you feed him for a lifetime.

—Confucius (551–479 BCE), *The Analects*

In addition to Joseph Platt, there were a large number of English expats in the hierarchy of the Shenyang YMCA. Soon, they were all agreed that it would be a good idea not to let Yan Baohang's mind go to waste, so they decided to send him to study at a good university in the United Kingdom.

But words such as *emancipation* and *liberation*, uttered at every protest meeting organized by Yan Baohang, were not merely meaningless slogans for him. Anybody who imagined that the political activism of his student years would give way to more mature reflections when he became a teacher had not really been listening.

He was teaching now. But he had not given up on the fight against the Japanese, who, since 1905, had taken over Shenyang from the Russians. Not only did his teaching post not prevent him from continuing to organize meetings and protests, but he also led his own students into the resistance. His idea was that only an educated people could free itself both from the country's feudal legacy and from the legacy of colonialism and neocolonialism. So he explained to his compatriots that the strengthening of the Japanese presence in the northeast has been facilitated by the increased power of the warlords since the fall of the Empire. On these subjects, he led think tanks and set up action committees. He also became a father for the first time: his daughter Mingshi was born in the spring of 1916, when Yan Baohang was only twenty-one.

In this context, the YMCA leader realized that Yan Baohang was not ready to continue his university career in England just yet. But beyond these objective reasons, Joseph Platt came to see that there was something else different about this project.

This something else consisted in an observation: without the fortunate generosity of a kindly teacher, Yan Baohang, the son of a poor family, would never have been able to get this far. Yan Baohang's plan, then, was to create free schools for children whose parents did not even dream that their offspring might go there. But an absence of tuition fees was not enough. They would also have to provide paper, ink, brushes, everything the students needed, and teach them the techniques that would allow them to earn a living, to give them a profession, to elevate them from quasi-serfdom, to liberate them from the alienation that was a result of their birth status. And Yan Baohang went further: the question of funding, however fundamental, would be dealt with later, but as far as the premises were concerned, he boldly asked Joseph Platt, "The hall where your evening classes take place, the one in the ancient Taoist temple . . . you would agree that it is not in use during the day? Why not install this school for poor children there? Until we have a better option. It wouldn't cause any real disruption, would it?"

And so Joseph Platt granted him the use of that hall for his crazy project of a school for local poor children. He also made it clear that Yan Baohang's plan was absolutely in agreement with the most cherished values of the YMCA.

Yan Baohang did not get much sleep that night. He was too busy thinking about the best way to promote his school in the poor neighborhoods of Shenyang. And like all young idealists, he imagined that no sooner would the posters go up on the walls than he would be overwhelmed with applicants. That was not what happened. As he came to realize, it was more complicated than that: it required a great deal of courage for anyone to make inquiries. To ask why, for instance, the school was in a Protestant church, and why these foreigners would want to educate young Chinese students if not to convert them. They also had to verify that it was *really* free, to overcome their shame at admitting they were poor and, in most cases, illiterate.

In fact, he had to seek out his first students himself in the poor neighborhoods. This took time, but after a month he had his first seven students eager to learn, each of them reminding him of the child he had been.

The school for poor children in Fengtian opened in April 1918. To start with, Yan Baohang did everything himself: the teaching, the cleaning, the organization of supplies. But how could he fund the necessary purchases? How could he earn a living? Joseph Platt thought about some foreign friends who wished to learn Chinese. So Baohang started giving private classes. He soon became indispensable to this influential community, who were aware of the importance of what he was doing and wealthy enough to help pay for it. Furthermore, Gaosu, who had stayed behind in the countryside and become a pillar of strength for her in-laws, would often send him supplies of food. So much so that, during the first spring celebrations in his new school, it was Professor Yan Baohang who gave New Year's gifts to his students: a kilo or two of rice, or flour, or soya. That may not sound like much, but for poor families such contributions were far from negligible. And it also provided the school with positive publicity.

Some of his fellow students from the teacher training college were interested in Baohang's new educational and social project; certainly it was not the salary he offered that lured them to work for him. As the school's reputation grew, however, donations allowed him to hire other teachers. By the end of the year, Yan Baohang was officially appointed the tutor for the students of the YMCA of Mukden: he was a functionary. In other words, in the China of those days, a notable man. His happiness became even greater when, in 1919, Gaosu gave him a second daughter, Mingying.

28

Every man has a moral sense that cries out
against what is intolerable.

—Mencius (372–289 BCE), Book II A, Section 6

Among the major donors to the school, Yan Baohang could count
on the support of Zhang Xueliang. The "young marshal," as he
was known, gave his friend great moral and spiritual support,
because Zhang Xueliang was a pious man. He, too, had converted. He was also able to provide considerable financial support, thanks to his father's fortune. This support was constantly
growing because, surprisingly, the two men shared a mutual
sympathy despite their disparate social origins: one the son of a
poor peasant from the northeast, the other—only four years his
senior—the son of a wealthy warlord. Because Zhang Xueliang
was none other than the son of the powerful Zhang Zuolin, who

held military control over his home region: the three provinces that comprised Manchuria and formed the whole northeast of China.

The young marshal was a native of Liaoning, just like Baohang. They were even from the same district, Haicheng. This created a bond between them at a time when the only military adversaries that the Japanese encountered in the region were the rich and powerful armies of the undisputed leader Zhang Zuolin. And even though the young marshal—who, that year, had been named his father's personal bodyguard—had benefited in his youth from a series of private tutors, he chose to complete his education at the YMCA in Fengtian.

Zhang Xueliang admired Yan Baohang. Essentially honest, he was aware that he owed his prestige as the "young Christian general" only to his birth, whereas his younger friend's reputation had been built, step by step, with this madly ambitious project of a school for poor children. And that was why he felt so much satisfaction at being able to introduce his "dear compatriot Yan Baohang" to many figures from the local high society and the foreign communities.

Then something happened to bring the two men even closer together. Transferred to Beijing as the chief tutor to the YMCA of Mukden, Baohang arrived in the city as its simmering discontent suddenly turned to a blaze of indignation. The students who protested outside the Tiananmen gates had been outraged by the Treaty of Versailles, which the Chinese had refused to sign. This was the start of the events of 1919 that would be known later as the May Fourth Movement or the New Culture Movement.

Among those rebellious students was a certain Zhou Enlai, then twenty-one years old.

Despite fighting in the Great War alongside the Allies, the Republic of China—to general stupefaction, and in contrast to what the country was entitled to expect—had not been given back, in the Treaty of Versailles, sovereignty over the peninsula of Shandong, in the north of China, then under the control of the German empire. Worse, this vast territory had in fact been handed to the Japanese, who had used the cover of their alliance with the Allies to strengthen their positions on the Chinese continent.

For the first time, it was no longer a question of a "national inferiority complex," as the writer Lao She would later call it, from which the majority of the Chinese population had, until then, seemed to suffer. Because while this unprecedented nationalist uprising was principally directed against Japan, Baohang also noticed that the behavior of the Western powers was being questioned with a new virulence. And this surge of feeling did not affect only the Western nations outside of China, but also the Europeans in the concessions and legations on Chinese territory. Those nations, claiming to defend the Chinese against the Japanese aggressor, were in fact accomplices in the pillaging of a country.

The intellectual and the warrior, Yan Baohang and Zhang Xueliang, were spectators to the emergence, apparently out of nowhere, of a patriotic conscience.

Beyond this sudden burst of patriotism, what was being expressed was a radical protest, as if the heavy lid of the imperial regime had finally been lifted, as if it had been held in place by some force of inertia despite the establishment of the Republic seven years earlier and it had taken all these years for the people in Beijing and in Shanghai to realize that they were no longer living in an era when the passage of the emperor would empty the streets, and that the streets now belonged to them.

But what stunned and intoxicated them was to hear young intellectuals of their generation, young professors whose vocal demands were the same as their own aspirations. From the Rights of Man to Lamarck's theory of inheritance, by way of the socialism of Babeuf, Saint-Simon, and Fourier: all of these ideas were in the air. But what all these young progressives—including Yan Baohang and Zhang Xueliang—demanded most loudly and clearly was an end to the dead weight of traditions, the power of the mandarins, the oppression of women, ignorance and feudalism. An end to the suffocating family hierarchy. And what did they want in its place? Progress, science, democracy, sexual equality. An end to arranged marriages, to the binding of women's feet, to concubines, to women being driven to suicide by the pressures of Confucian morality. They wanted China to change. For people to speak a modern language, not classical Chinese. They wanted China to open up. The possibility of learning about Western culture, about other cultures. That a new China should finally rise up. And that the "revolutionary spirit of May 4" should live on.

From that fateful date, the iconoclastic movement that continued until 1921 shook, for the first time, the two-thousand-year-old dogma of the "Confucian father figure." The most visible symbol of this "patricide" was the destruction of the beard on statues of the previously sacrosanct Confucius by hordes of protesters.

Ideas circulated, and so did books: from Canton, one of Baohang's colleagues brought *The Communist Manifesto* by Marx and Engels, a biography of Lenin, and *The Dream of the Red Capital* by Qu Qiubai—the title a parody of the famous *Dream of the Red Chamber*, one of the four masterpieces of classic Chinese literature—which was less an attempt to render the reality of Soviet life than to understand the spirit and the soul of this new world taking shape.

Hungry for everything "new"—the magic word—they became insatiable. Baohang got hold of every book he could find related to the social sciences. He created the first study group on socialism in northeast China, seeking to translate something that did not yet truly exist. He launched his own magazine, *Clarity*.

These events led directly to the founding of the Communist Party of China (CPC) in 1921. Chen Duxiu was among the founders. Inevitably, Yan Baohang was interested in this development. Chen Duxiu was an intellectual whose pro-Western and Francophile magazine *New Youth* had been read by Yan Baohang; its pages contained other bylines that would soon become famous. The first was that of Lu Xun, who claimed the spotlight that same year with his novella *The True Story of Ah Q*, serialized in the Beijing *Morning News*. A vitriolic satire of Chinese society and, in particular, the unfinished revolution of 1911, the story was notably written in Baihua, the vernacular language;

in other words, the language spoken by the vast majority of Chinese people, the language of modern China.

Baohang also noticed an article written by a certain Mao Zedong on morals. But it was still too early for that name to mean anything to him. Yet it was only three years later that he met his first militant communist during a painting exhibition that served as a cover for Han Leran.

The man who would later be known, not entirely accurately, as the "Chinese Picasso" impressed Baohang less with his art than with his fierce commitment to the anti-Japanese struggle. He was also the first artist to join—the year before, at the age of twenty-five—the nascent CPC. Later, Baohang would learn that he had left China for Europe in 1929. For the moment, though, Han Leran had been sent on a mission by the Shanghai communists to approach influential progressives. Yan Baohang was one of his targets. From the moment of that meeting, the members of the socialist study group formed by Yan Baohang in Shenyang would read all the Party publications. Because they wanted to be well-informed.

29

Nothing is impossible to a willing mind.

—Chinese proverb

Yan Baohang's schedule was packed: the YMCA had made him president of the summer university for Christian youth, which he had to organize. Moreover, in a new center for working-class families, he offered classes for the children and jobs for the women. He was very attached to the issue of the emancipation of women through work, particularly since a textile factory had just opened that would ensure the financial autonomy of the school for poor children. It was all coming together.

Of course, this did not leave him much time for Gaosu and their children. They had two girls and two boys now, aged nine, six, and three years old, with little Mingzhi a baby of eight months, having been born the previous November. They had all come to live with him in Shenyang.

It was in this context that the sad news arrived in the spring of 1925: Sun Yat-sen, the father of the Chinese nation, had died of cancer at fifty-nine. Knowing that his time was short, Sun Yat-sen had established more and more initiatives for the country's future. He had worked relentlessly to renegotiate treaties with the Western powers and constantly sought talks with warlords to bring peace to the provinces. This latter objective was far from easy, and it concerned the very future of China itself. The fires of civil war had to be extinguished at all costs in the provinces where the warlords, through the wealth and power of their personal armies, held a power that the central government lacked, preventing it from uniting the country.

Yan Baohang wondered about the future of the Kuomintang. What would become of the nationalist party's program as defined by Sun Yat-sen: the fight against imperialism and feudalism? The president had dictated a message to the nation on his deathbed, expressing his wish that the Kuomintang and the Communist Party should continue to work together for the good of China.

In spite of the sadness that he shared with the rest of the population, it occurred to Yan Baohang that his scheduling of summer university seminars on the student movements' relationship with socialism and lectures on Marxism-Leninism and dialectic materialism had been well-timed. This schedule was in agreement with both the president's last wishes and with the national zeitgeist.

Sun Yat-sen left behind a widow, Soong Qing-ling. Although she came from an illustrious family that was fiercely pronationalist and anti-communist, the wife of the first president of the Republic of China would be the only one of her clan to soften her positions in favor of the communists. And she would do it in such a sincere, enduring way that, much later—in 1968—she would be elected to the position of vice president of the People's Republic of China until 1972, before becoming honorary president in 1981.

Sun Yat-sen's death occurred five years after Chiang Kai-shek began a relationship with the third Soong sister—May-ling—who was twenty-three at the time, eleven years younger than Qing-ling.

Like her sisters, May-ling had received an English education in Shanghai, where she was born, then for ten years in the United States. Back in China for the past three years, she was proving herself faithful to her family's Christian convictions as one of the managers of the Young Women's Christian Association when she met Chiang Kai-shek.

Defying the last wishes of Sun Yat-sen, the highly anti-communist general continued his gradual takeover of the nationalist party until, soon, he commanded the Kuomintang's armed forces and became the party's sole leader.

By the time Chiang Kai-shek and Soong May-ling married, the general had already launched his northern attack on the warlords who still controlled most of the country. Among them was the powerful chief of the "Fengtian clique," Zhang Zuolin, who ruled Beijing. The other important Kuomintang leader, Wang Jingwei, presided over Wuhan. Chiang Kai-shek, meanwhile, was about to move his government to Nanjing.

This was the era when Chiang became alarmed by the rise in power of the communists, which worried him far more than the very real threat of the Japanese. So he launched a deadly raid against workers and communist leaders who had gathered in Shanghai. The massacre was carried out without taking into account the support that the Soviet Comintern had given both the Kuomintang and the Communist Party of China. This tragedy led to the destruction of the united front that had heretofore linked those two organizations against their common enemies—the Japanese and the warlords—with the aim of uniting the country.

But in this rift, it was Chiang Kai-shek who was in control. He ordered a purge of communists within the Kuomintang. And his determination to go it alone was reinforced by Wang Jingwei's decision to rally to the nationalists. From that point on, the irresistible rise of Chiang Kai-shek was set in motion.

The political situation in China at the time of Sun Yat-sen's death in March 1925 was not the only factor that would overturn Yan Baohang's existence.

Since his friend and ally Zhang Xueliang had offered to pay for his trip abroad, he now had no reason not to go. All that remained was for him to speak to his wife, the mother of his first four children, about his plan to study in Europe for two years.

30

Bring a little money. And also a pure heart.
Always have a pure heart with you!

—Lao She, *Four Generations under One Roof*, 1949

In the early days of the school for poor children—before that philanthropic enterprise started receiving private donations, then the respect of city councillors in Shenyang and beyond—Gaosu had to prove herself ingenious to find the money to keep her household going.

She had one, then two, then three, then four children to clothe and feed, with what little remained of Baohang's salary after most of it had been diverted to pay for the school. She never complained. There was an understanding between them that Baohang was the dreamer, the creator, the planner, while Gaosu held the purse strings.

He told her about his ideas, his vision. She listened. Without ever revealing what ploys she would use to provide for the household's needs, she took care of her side of things—and agreed to all his initiatives. This was no mean feat, since it was quite common for her to be sent a compatriot from the northeast in distress, or a family that had been through a disaster, all of them aware that Gaosu's door would always be open to them and that whatever help she could offer, she would do so graciously.

The first school for poor children had now been open for more than ten years. And in that year, 1927, a fourth school had opened while a fifth was planned. These schools were all located in different neighborhoods of Shenyang and now functioned with the support of the local teachers and board of education. This network covered almost the entirety of the city.

In the midst of all this, Baohang told Gaosu that he had to leave. For him, the moment had come. It was time—yes, it was high time—to go abroad, to observe, to compare and discuss the social situation of the working classes and their organizations in the ports, the mines, the factories, to see how the unions and the workers' hostels and the cooperatives functioned in other lands.

Because, he added, after a certain time, books were not enough to understand; even photographs were not enough, even the newspapers from those countries, which he read. Gaosu did not interrupt him. She did not protest. She did not ask in a panicked voice how many thousands of *li* from Shenyang those places were: London, Edinburgh, Copenhagen. She simply forced herself to remember these names; she handed a piece of paper to Baohang and asked him to write them down. And when Baohang had set down those characters in his careful, elegant calligraphy and heard Gaosu decipher them, he realized how far she had progressed since he had first started teaching her to read and write. There was nothing extraordinary in her illiteracy; every girl of her generation and social class was illiterate. But what was extraordinary, in her eyes, was that her husband had shown such determination to convince her that this was not an inevitability. In fact, she had gone to evening classes with little Mingshi in her arms.

Although Gaosu had no ambition to appear to be somebody she wasn't, to falsify her origins, she swelled with pride at the idea that her husband would never be ashamed of her, would never hesitate to introduce her to any of the important Chinese and foreign figures that formed his circle of acquaintances. Because Baohang had seen the considerable progress that Gaosu had made, he suggested that she make the most of his exile to learn English. After all, there was no shortage of English friends at the YMCA prepared to teach her their language. And so, during the two years that Baohang was in Europe, Gaosu asked Mingshi (then eleven years old) to look after the three youngest children while she went to take English classes. Much later, Mingshi would remember her mother's question, asked half anxiously, half mischievously: "Mingshi, do you think your father will have forgotten Chinese when he comes back?" And when Baohang got off the train that had taken him from Europe back to Shenyang, he was less surprised to see the crowd of their friends waiting to welcome him at the train station, less surprised to discover that his littlest girl was no longer a baby, than he was to hear his wife speak to him in English.

But for now, Gaosu was busy comforting her husband. He was leaving, but she was the one who had to console him. Don't worry, she told him, everything will be fine; he could go there without any anxieties; she trusted him absolutely. And to make sure that he didn't think these words contained any hint of reproach, she smiled as she recited these verses by Zhong Changtong, whose poem "Talking with Myself" she had studied at evening class:

> Raise your ambitions to the hills of the wild west,
> Let your mind wander east of the seas.
> Ride the wind as if it were your only horse,
> Sail on the seas of High Purity,
> Answer the call with elegance and good cheer!

31

Different people have different aspirations.

—Chinese proverb

The long friendship between Yan Baohang and Zhang Xueliang became more intense just before my grandfather left for Europe.

What united them was not merely the fact that the wealthy one had financed the other's stay in Edinburgh, Copenhagen, and Moscow; it was that Zhang Xueliang had behaved in such a way that his generosity could be accepted without embarrassment or constraint.

Yes, he had argued, a part of himself—the best part—would accompany Baohang and walk beside him as he grew to know the West. Their time with the Christian youth had opened a window for both of them on the possibility of other knowledge, other ideas, other ways to read the world than the traditional Chinese way, and although only one of them was actually leaving to confront the reality of these Western practices and philosophies, which they had studied before only in theory and in books, it was clear that the one who stayed behind would also benefit from this wonderful education.

This manner of presenting the situation had greatly moved my grandfather. In the days that preceded his great journey, he and Zhang Xueliang shared long conversations together, and the things his friend said to him gave Yan Baohang the feeling that their relationship was a kind of brotherhood that would last all their lives and even beyond.

During one of these conversations, Zhang Xueliang had drawn up a sort of overview of their intellectual and spiritual evolution. "We know our Auguste Comte and our Émile Durkheim, we have drunk from the well of positivist thinking, and that is why we can say, today, that it is a 'social phenomenon' and that we are able to define the concept of collective consciousness. We have also studied the doctrine of Robert Owen, and his *Book of the New Moral World* holds few secrets for us now. Our teachers have guided us through the complex thoughts of Max Weber and the relations he highlighted between the spiritual values of Protestantism and their investment in the real world, which formed one of the engines of the Industrial Revolution. We have talked of Marx and Engels and followed with fascination the events that have occurred in Russia since the October Revolution . . . It might be said that, through our generation, the aspirations of our Chinese Republic have encountered those of the Western world . . .

"But we have also," he continued, "taken care of our souls, in the phraseology of our pastors. We have studied the Bible. We have gone to church. Our schools of thought, which have made us what we are since time immemorial, have—through us—touched that other God of the world. And when I have struggled to understand certain passages in the Old or the New Testament—because it is more difficult for a warrior to meditate on such matters than for a man of peace—it was you who made them clear to me, you who showed me the truly extraordinary things in the Bible. And you have enlightened me so expertly that I sometimes think perhaps I will manage to become a good Protestant in the second half of my life! Who knows?"

At that, Zhang Xueliang burst out laughing, as if the idea that he could become a "good Protestant" was merely a wisecrack, without suspecting the prophetic nature of these words, because, ten years later, imprisoned in Taiwan on Chiang Kaishek's orders, the former warrior so pious, during the course of a captivity that lasted half a century, that he attended a religious service every day.

But this was long before such things were even imaginable, and the two friends talked freely and easily, Yan Baohang insisting on the idea that the Bible could indeed be considered an extraordinary book, just as Jesus Christ was an entirely admirable figure. At that, Zhang Xueliang grew serious again. Was Yan Baohang able to tell him not only that he understood the teachings of Christ, but also that he believed them, that he had faith?

To this, Baohang replied that the Bible demanded deeper study than he had been able to give it up to that point before he could answer that question. What seemed admirable in the wisdom of the New Testament was the figure of Christ, savior of humanity. It is true, he added, that Buddhism, too, claimed that its purpose was to save all souls. But what he most admired was the idea that Christ had accepted his own sacrifice for the salvation of humanity. That, and the fact that Christ chose to take the side of the poor, not the side of the powerful. In a way, it seemed to him that there were not so many contradictions between the knowledge they had been given to understand the world—and to transform it into a better world—and the message of hope communicated by the pastors in the name of Christ.

We can see two distinct characters taking shape in this exchange. In my grandfather, we can see the pragmatism that led him not to rule out anything, whether it be the Protestants' social doctrine or Marxist-Leninist theory. In Zhang Xueliang, we can sense a little bitterness when he confided to his friend that, in his younger years, he, too, had dreamed of being useful. But could this warlord's son embrace another life, choose another path, than that of weapons and war? "I wanted to study so I could save men, but I was trained to kill them."

32

Opium teaches only one thing: beyond
physical suffering, there is no reality.

—André Malraux, *Man's Fate,* 1933

Another of Baohang's friends traveled with him to Great Britain: Ning Encheng, whose journey had also been funded by the
young general. In London, the two friends met up with another
alumnus of their old teacher training college, Lao She, who
had been teaching Chinese there for the past three years at the
School of Oriental Studies.

Although he had not yet published anything, Lao She spent
all his spare time in libraries and bookstores, in search of new
European and American authors, although according to him
none of them could compare to his favorite writer, Charles
Dickens. In fact, the influence of this prestigious author was

still palpable on Lao She when he returned to China in the early 1930s, as his first novels were appearing. At that time, Lao She still displayed the same hostility toward Chiang Kai-shek's government. So much so that, in 1946, he decided to leave China again for the United States, before returning when communism—whose cause he had espoused in the meantime—triumphed in 1949.

While Baohang took classes in philosophy and geopolitics, in preparation for his PhD in social science in Edinburgh, the three friends met up as often as possible in London.

While he was there, Baohang investigated the workings of the cooperatives and the educational system, two subjects whose study also took him to Denmark. But his full schedule did not prevent Baohang from spending time with his friends.

Those evenings seemed endless, particularly when they had been able to procure some Hatamen, those famous extralong cigarettes that flooded China from the beginning of the century. Sadly, they could not hope to enjoy a Beijing fondue, nor even a small *baozi* filled with steamed meat or vegetables to help soothe their homesickness.

Ning Encheng arrived one day with the February 1927 edition of the *Literary Digest*, its cover showing two young Chinese women in cloche hats and spring clothing. One was wearing a short-sleeved blouse and a white skirt, the other, all smiles, a check dress with puff sleeves; the two young women were picnicking in the sun. And this illustration of a radiant, modern

China was headlined with the words "The New Life Movement for Young China."

All three of them wanted to believe in this "young," modernizing China. But in truth the news that reached them from Beijing, where Zhang Zuolin had set up his headquarters, and from Nanjing, where Chiang Kai-shek had set up his, told the story of a situation that was much more unstable and fragile than the magazine cover suggested. Because as yet, nobody could attest that the intentions of Chiang Kai-shek's nationalist troops or of Zhang Zuolin's private army were really focused on the battle against the Japanese, despite the two men's proclamations. On the contrary, there was every reason to fear that, under cover of the war against Japan, their troops were engaged in a Sino-Chinese combat with potentially suicidal consequences. The word *suicide* could also be applied to a phenomenon that Baohang had recently learned about: the return of opium addiction in China. Not that the recent rise in the drug's popularity was surprising: opium was a convenient way of enslaving people. This stratagem had not escaped the Japanese, who were supplying China's opium dens as an alternative means of waging war.

In June 1928, in a letter to Yan Baohang, Zhang Xueliang announced the death of his father. As son, he would inherit the command of the factional army that had just lost its leader in an attack by the Japanese. Zhang Xueliang was so outraged by the Soviet influence on the Communist Party of China—the support of Comintern; the Red Army stationed close to his native Manchuria—that he decided to annex the entire railway network of eastern China. The known US influence on the Kuomintang seemed to him a lesser evil. And so, in late 1928, Zhang Xueliang informed Yan Baohang that he and his troops were rallying to Chiang Kai-shek's government.

He made it clear that he believed all the patriots of the northeast, and Yan Baohang in particular, should respond to the call.

On his part, through mutual acquaintances, Chiang Kai-shek made it known to my grandfather that he felt the same way. Joseph Platt, too, urged him to cut short his stay abroad. The American-Danish pastor told him that it would be much easier for Platt to leave his post as head of the YMCA if a successor had been appointed, and that he hoped Baohang would be happy to take over from him.

All of these were good reasons to return, but there was another, too, which affected my grandfather like a poison: Zhang Xueliang, it was said, had become an opium addict. His father had been one, too, as everybody knew. But that addiction had never weakened his determination to confront the Japanese. For Zhang Xueliang, it was a different story. He did not enjoy the same reputation for ferocity as his father, and since he was already weighed down by grief at his father's death, there was no certainty that the strategy that had failed his father could succeed for his son.

So it was that, in the spring of 1929, after passing through Moscow, Baohang returned to Shenyang.

33

I am ready to die to defend the interests of the
State. I will not flee because there is danger.

—Lin Zexu, 1785 (Qing dynasty)

All of Shenyang crowded onto the train station platform to
welcome my grandfather home on that spring day in 1929 that
would remain in many minds "the year of Yan Baohang." The
new director of the YMCA, determined not to lose any time,
immediately insisted on the principle, with no exceptions, of
equality between the sexes in all areas of activity. He developed
the organization's sports teams and opened new departments in
the social sciences. But what had most animated him since his
decision to return early was the eradication of the scourge of
opium.

It was not the first time that a Chinese man had attempted

such an initiative. In China, opium addiction had a long, long history. Ever since the First Opium War, orchestrated by England between 1840 and 1842, China has been well aware of its powerlessness. The Second Opium War, in 1856—when it was not only England but also France, supported by America and Russia, that triggered hostilities—had further aggravated China's dependence on the drug: the few restrictions that had opposed this base trade up to that point were now lifted. England obtained new territories and the opening of new ports.

Since the fall of the Empire and the collapse of central power, the warlords had relied on drug trafficking to finance their military actions and the control of their territories. It was inevitable that some of them should become infamous opium addicts.

Yan Baohang knew that the Kuomintang itself must have been involved in the drug trade to finance the northern expedition launched three years earlier. After a fragile and incomplete reunification of the Chinese continent, the Nanjing government, established in 1927, inherited a country infected by this scourge, and it was well-known that the Japanese had skillfully manipulated the situation, particularly in the much-coveted northeastern region. At the end of 1928, a national conference devoted to the issue of opium had made clear the truth of this state of affairs.

So it was that Yan Baohang, with the aid of a network of northern intellectuals, artists, painters, poets, and writers, set up the Liaoning Province Anti-Opium Association to battle against narcotics. His objective: to prevent all trade in drugs, first and foremost opium and heroin, by attacking the entire process: cultivation, manufacture, consumption.

Tongues wagged. During a tennis game with Ba Lidi, the head of the post office in Liaoning province, Baohang was discreetly informed by his partner that he had just been "approached" by a Japanese businessman who slipped him an envelope stuffed with cash to ensure the reception of smuggled packages. Baohang decided to intensify seizures of illicit material, and to report in detail all instances of blackmail, extortion, racketeering, and corruption to the Chinese government.

Soon, the suspect packages were accompanied by letters addressed to Yan Baohang, their intentions unambiguous. On one of them was a drawing of a pistol and several bullets.

Almost five hundred bags of heroin and a similar amount of opium, with a value close to a million silver talents, were intercepted. But that was not all: Yan Baohang decided to destroy these illegal substances in a symbolic, and very public, ceremony. He invited the highest authorities in the province and several government representatives to burn opium; it took more than four hours to reduce this mass of narcotics to ashes. He also had the idea of inviting the British, French, American, and even the Japanese consuls to the stadium in Shenyang.

To increase the symbolism, he fixed the date of this event for ninety years exactly after a similar pyre destroyed more than one thousand tons of narcotics in order to make Queen Victoria aware that opium consumption was now illegal in China, so she would order an end to its trafficking.

Everybody remembered that date, so the symbolism was not lost. It also did not escape anybody's notice that, of all the invitees, only the Japanese consul failed to attend.

34

The clouds precede the appearance of dragons.
The wind heralds the appearance of tigers.

—Chinese saying

At that time, Japanese ambitions in China were the biggest threat to the country's security.

It was on account of this that Zhang Xueliang urgently wished to talk to Yan Baohang. Their Liaoning Association of Popular Diplomacy had been invited to join the Chinese delegation to Japan as part of the third conference of the Institute of Pacific Relations. The objective was to encourage peaceful discussion all over the Pacific zone, where geopolitical tensions ran high.

Yan Baohang had studied geopolitics in depth while he was abroad. As for Zhang Xueliang, he had a general's gift for strategy. Consequently, the two men foresaw that the Japanese would not hesitate to take advantage of this meeting in Kyoto to legitimize their expansionist policies by highlighting the benefits that northeastern China would draw from Japanese influence in the region.

In the opinion of Baohang and Xueliang, once they were at the conference, they should not issue a purely defensive riposte about the abuses that the Japanese had already committed, but should prioritize arguments that allowed them to shine a light on Japan's real objective, which was nothing less than colonizing Manchuria. And to communicate this to all the participants in the conference.

According to reliable sources, a secret document existed that had been submitted two years before, in 1927, for the approval of the 124th emperor of Japan, Hirohito. It was alleged that this document set out a plan for the conquest of Manchuria. And Mongolia. And that it did not exclude the possibility of a complete annexation of China.

But that document could only be exploited if the sources were verified and evidence established. Particularly since the author of this document was, it seemed, Tanaka Giichi, the head of the Japanese government, who was not only the country's prime minister but also in charge of its foreign and colonial affairs.

Though long regarded as a forgery, this document could be recognized as authentic following the testimony of Cai Zhikan, the man who procured it for Zhang Xueliang. He in turn entrusted it to Yan Baohang so that he could make good use of it. History remembers it as the Tanaka Memorandum.

At the time, however, in the absence of indisputable proof, it must be borne in mind that Zhang Xueliang and Yan Baohang were only formulating hypotheses. Their principle question was whether it was plausible that the leader of the Japanese government could really have written the document.

Aged sixty-three in 1927, Tanaka Giichi was, primarily, a battle-hardened soldier from a family of samurai, and general of the imperial army. A veteran of the Sino-Japanese War of 1894–95, he also fought in the Russo-Japanese War of 1904–05. Promoted to the rank of general in 1920, he was the minister of war in two successive governments, where a constant policy of military rearmament was noted. A fervent anti-liberal and anti-communist, he was the principal creator of the aggressive interventionist policy toward China, in Manchuria and Mongolia, where he himself had fought.

So yes, it was entirely plausible that Tanaka could have concocted such a plan. Now the difficulty was procuring the document. And, if possible, before the international meeting that was due to take place in Kyoto at the end of the year. Speaking of which, did we have any recent news concerning Cai Zhikan?

Cai Zhikan was the richest Chinese man in Japan, where he had lived since the age of eleven. He was a patriot, however, and also the Association of Popular Diplomacy's most frequently sought source of information.

Since Cai Zhikan was of Taiwanese origin, it was agreed that the best way to communicate with him would be to send him packages of Taiwanese delicacies. Digging deep among the intertwined strands of dried rice vermicelli, Cai Zhikan was able to extract letters from the association, sometimes providing information, sometimes seeking it, without awakening any suspicions. In return, he would send gifts of the same type: red bean paste and steamed sponge cake were especially practical for hiding messages.

In this way, they became almost certain that not only did the famous Tanaka Memorandum exist, not only did it contain all the steps intended to plan for the invasion of Manchuria, Mongolia, and then the whole of China, but they were assured that this document had been submitted to Hirohito two years before.

"Yes, but how can we be completely certain?"

"Because Cai Zhikan says he has a copy."

"Yes, but what is that copy really worth?"

"Cai Zhikan's word of honor that he copied it from the original."

"How is that possible?"

Cai Zhikan's strategy was first to exploit the virulent opposition to the political party of which Tanaka was president. It goes without saying that this approach to the most radical members of the opposition would not have been possible without the financial means of Zhang Xueliang and Cai Zhikan, without the social skills of the richest Chinese man in Japan, without a few methods for exerting pressure or the taste for very rare, expensive wines, not to mention opium, and all of this on top of the profound desire to damage the ruling party.

It is not known exactly how several corrupt politicians managed to procure for Cai Zhikan the means of entering the holy of holies, the old shogun library in Ueno, in the northeastern part of Tokyo.

The difficulty of this incursion was that it could only take place once Cai Zhikan had been introduced as a specialist in the restoration of ancient silk documents. From that point on, he was put in the presence of the "right" document fairly quickly. Then, left alone, he spent the night of June 20, 1928, making a copy of it, before being taken home in the same way.

A few weeks before the opening of the third conference of the Institute of Pacific Relations, held in Kyoto, the copy of the Tanaka Memorandum was handed over to the foreign minister by Zhang Xueliang in person. It was immediately translated into Chinese and English. As soon as Yan Baohang started reading the document, he realized that its effect would be explosive.

In this memorandum, the expansionist objective is so clearly displayed that it amounts to a step-by-step guide to conquering the world: first Manchuria, then Mongolia, then China, then Southeast Asia...

Written in 1927, it not only confirmed the warmongering policy begun even before the start of the Shōwa era, with the annexation of Korea in 1910; but it also prefigured all the events that would occur within the next five years: the invasion of Manchuria in 1931, then the northern provinces. The creation of the puppet state of Manchukuo, from 1932 until the end of the Second World War, a supposedly independent country entirely under the control of the Japanese empire, and in whose creation Puyi was manipulated.

The memorandum also predicted the invasion of China ten

years later, in 1937, the bombardment of Shanghai and Canton, and the infamous Nanjing Massacre perpetrated by the imperial Japanese army. As far as this massacre is concerned, not only did it destroy the Kuomintang, but some also claim that, without the Japanese, the Communist Party would never have succeeded in taking over China.

And it foreshadowed the occupation, between 1937 and 1942, of Burma, Thailand, Hong Kong, Singapore, Indonesia, New Guinea, French Indochina, and most of the Pacific Islands . . . all these territories were grouped together under the name "the Greater East Asia Co-Prosperity Sphere," when in reality it would serve as a source of raw materials, slave labor, and, as with Nazi Germany, "living space."

When the moment came for Yan Baohang to speak before the assembled delegations, he had already managed to have the famous document, translated into Mandarin, delivered into the hands of all his listeners. Once on stage, all he had to do was comment upon the text.

As expected, the revelation of this plan caused a general outcry. The first representative of the Japanese delegation, Yōsuke Matsuoka, threatened to leave the conference. This politician and diplomat had not yet acquired the self-assurance or indeed the notoriety he would have four years later when, in 1933, he announced that Japan was leaving the League of Nations.

The foreign minister in Fumimaro Konoe's government during the Second World War, Matsuoka was responsible for leading Japan into the Rome-Berlin-Tokyo Axis in 1940. After Germany's invasion of the Soviet Union, it was he who was asked by Hitler to support the attack with the participation of Japanese troops. Charged with war crimes in Tokyo, he died in prison before his trial could begin.

As for the Chinese patriot Cai Zhikan, he was either caught or betrayed, and was immediately incarcerated in Japan, his fortune seized. He would not be freed until after the Allies' victory. After returning, destitute, to Taiwan, he was welcomed as a hero and looked after by the Kuomintang, which was by then based solely in Taiwan.

In the days that followed this revelation in Kyoto, a price was put on Yan Baohang's head. Posters promised rewards for his arrest or for the arrest of his family. Graffiti appeared on walls threatening that he and his family would be burned alive, just as he had thrown entire shipments of opium onto the pyre.

But Yan Baohang was already safe.

35

Better die than be a salve to the subjugated country.

—Chinese adage

Then there was what became known as the Mukden Incident. Mukden was the Manchu name for Shenyang.

The Mukden Incident was intended to deceive the world, but the world saw through it. On September 18, 1931, a section of train track belonging to Japan's South Manchuria Railway was sabotaged. The Japanese authorities blamed the Chinese for the explosion, which gave them a pretext for military intervention. In reality, the Japanese, convinced that Chiang Kai-shek and his Kuomintang army were uniting the country, felt that they had to establish a foothold in China as quickly as possible or their imperialist strategy would be doomed to failure. Consequently,

Japanese troops on horseback immediately took possession of Shenyang.

The next day, a delegation of several representatives of the city, including Yan Baohang, went to the UK and US consulates. They wanted to let the world know the *real* intentions of the Japanese, because clearly this was not, as they claimed, a "strictly local event." The Mukden Incident prefigured a larger-scale action. But the city's representatives were wasting their time: there was no reaction from the British or American diplomats.

During the night, however, events accelerated: the Japanese army plastered the walls of Shenyang with wanted posters. A price was put on the heads of Yan Baohang and the other members of the delegation: a reward of 5,000 yuan was promised to anybody providing information that led to the men's arrest. They barely had time to flee to Beijing before the three northeastern provinces passed into Japanese hands.

The Western powers protested without conviction. China was an immense country, but it was considered weak. Japan was a small territory, but it was considered ultrapowerful. The Japanese were given free rein to create a new and supposedly independent state in the region: Manchukuo.

Yan Baohang had to flee in such a rush that he left Gaosu and the children behind. He only just had time to issue instructions for his family to be taken to the railway station and put on the last train to Beijing.

At the time, my grandmother was thirty-eight years old and seven months pregnant with my father, Mingfu. Her eldest child,

Mingshi, was fifteen; then there was Mingying, twelve; Daxin, the eldest boy, was nine; Mingzhi was seven; and Mingguang was four.

They were not the only ones to flee Shenyang that night. They all held hands so they wouldn't lose one another in the crowds that filled the platforms. Somebody recognized my grandmother: "Look, it's Mrs. Yan!" And another voice called out: "It's Yan Baohang's wife!"

Immediately the crowd opened up to allow my grandmother and her five children to pass through to a train car. Years later, my grandmother remembered this moment with tears in her eyes: there was something miraculous about that feeling of being carried by the crowd toward the train, even if their forced departure was a wrench.

Despite the warmth and sincerity of the many good wishes addressed to my grandparents, the reality was that their departure marked the end of an enterprise into which they had put all their energy and hope. And while that packed train rolled toward Beijing, fleeing the Japanese aggressor, the new government issued a decree closing all Yan Baohang's schools after fourteen years of good and faithful service and the education of almost a thousand students.

On his part, Yan Baohang had barely arrived in Beijing before he and a handful of exiled comrades were busy uniting various anti-Japanese circles into a single organization under the banner of the Dongbei People's Patriotic Union Against the Japanese. Having laid the foundations of the organization in Beijing, he started traveling back and forth to Shanghai to gather funds.

On September 27—less than ten days after the Japanese invasion of Shenyang—the first meeting of the organization brought together four hundred people. Zhang Xueliang authorized his officers to participate. The Patriotic Union's three central goals were to "fight against the Japanese invasion, recover the occupied territories, and protect our territorial integrity."

Power had left Beijing three years before when Chiang Kai-shek moved his government to Nanjing. And with Zhang Xueliang rallying to the nationalist government and engaging his troops in the anti-Japanese guerrilla war, Beijing had gradually become a ghost city. It was here that my father, Mingfu, was born on November 11, 1931.

36

Live in the Cao camp but with one's heart
in the Han camp.

—Chinese proverb

Chiang Kai-shek persisted in believing that the advance of Japanese troops was, all things considered, less damaging than the penetration of communist ideas in the country. For him, the priority was to guarantee and strengthen the influence of the nationalist party.

He was on his way, at this time, to becoming the strongman of China. He had managed to remove a number of adversaries from his own camp and, not content with being the head of the Kuomintang, was now the de facto leader of the central Chinese government. A desire for confrontation animated the life of the general in all domains: military, political, and romantic.

At his wedding in Shanghai, where his wife May-ling had been born twenty-five years earlier, one of his witnesses was the secretary-general of the YMCA, a close associate of Yan Baohang. So when Chiang Kai-shek, for political and strategic reasons, decided it would be a good idea to approach Zhang Xueliang, the intermediary was soon identified: Yan Baohang. My grandfather already knew an extraordinary number of people within the Kuomintang and elsewhere, and he was also a Protestant, which recommended him to May-ling, who shared his faith. There could be no doubt about it for Chiang Kai-shek: this was the kind of man he wanted on his side.

So Mrs. Chiang Kai-shek explained to Yan Baohang that she wanted him to lead her newly formed New Life Movement. Because Soong May-ling, far from confining herself to the role of Chiang Kai-shek's wife, had begun her own political career.

She already had an important role as an advisor to her husband, particularly in the realm of Sino-American relations, since she had lived in the United States for so many years. Her familiarity with Western habits and customs, her charisma, her social skills and oratory talents made her the official spokesperson for the Kuomintang, so much so that one journalist described her as the "greatest man in Asia."

So Yan Baohang had to take this invitation seriously, since he knew it came effectively from Chiang Kai-shek himself, even if he was, at the same time, a little embarrassed by it.

Because what was this New Life Movement *for*, exactly?

It was a moral initiative founded on recommendations from the most traditional form of Confucianism. Essentially, it existed to promote the values of politeness and rectitude, discipline and morality, and to recommend certain codes of dress and behavior. With no fear of appearing trivial, Chiang Kai-shek gave a few examples of its rules: do not go topless; do not spit on the ground; do not urinate in a public place; do not curse; walk straight; take a break for lunch, do not eat in the street; remove one's hat and stand up for the national anthem; respect the laws against smoking, gambling, and prostitution . . . and the Kuomintang leader insisted on the anti-capitalist nature of this movement.

Given the importance that the movement, already announced in the press, seemed to possess, given the honor of the offer made to Yan Baohang, and given the affinity that existed between Mrs. Chiang and Yan Baohang due to their years abroad, my grandfather must have expressed his reservations with a great deal of delicacy and diplomacy.

He argued that, in his opinion, the priority at that moment was the fight against the Japanese, to which he wished to devote his time. Chiang Kai-shek responded that the New Life Movement included a political and social dimension with a view to combating the Japanese, and that this movement aimed to reform China by modernizing it while retaining its traditional values in a way that would inspire the country's youth. My grandfather must have asked for some time to think the matter over before deciding.

And then he wrote to Zhang Xueliang to explain his dilemma.

Zhang Xueliang made it clear that refusing was out of the question.

His highly pragmatic argument was that there were not enough compatriots in the northeast occupying important posts in central government. Every meeting that Baohang would organize as part of his new job, every contact he would establish, would serve Dongbei's cause. He could not let such an opportunity slip through his fingers. "Anyway, if I understand correctly, it was Mrs. Chiang who made the offer. Why refuse?" he concluded.

Bearing in mind the deep friendship that had long united Zhang Xueliang and Yan Baohang, and which was not ideological in origin but patriotic, this argument was irrefutable.

My grandfather accepted the post, and the whole family moved to Nanjing. Within the Kuomintang, Yan Baohang soon became an inescapable presence in political life, attending numerous meetings, seminars, public interventions, and youth conferences. Everybody who wished to approach Soong May-ling knew that they first had to go through my grandfather, who had the first lady's complete trust.

However, this skillful sociopolitical construction harbored a secret.

The secret was that my grandfather was already a committed communist.

37

How could such a delicious bit of lamb
end up in the mouth of a dog?

—Attributed to Shi Nai'an
(1296–1370), *Water Margin*

All things considered, the 1930s appeared as murky, ideolog-
ically speaking, in Asia as they were in Europe. Not only was
Chiang Kai-shek anxious to stem the rise of communist ideas,
but he was also suspected to be on the verge of breaking off
relations with Europe and the United States in favor of a rapprochement with . . . the Japanese.

It was true that Chiang Kai-shek had good reason to fear
for his grip on power, to judge by the irresistible progress of the
Long March, a trek of more than seven thousand miles under the

direction of the Red Army. This immense procession included a vast horde of partisans, as well as a group of Communist Party leaders who were being hunted by the Kuomintang national army.

For more than a year, these marching soldiers, weakened by the civil war and the resultant famine, gradually became a legend. During the next part of the country's history, having been part of the Long March or not, having been among the survivors of a terrible massacre, and above all having been among the brave few who surrounded the young Mao Zedong, having contributed to shaping his image as a leader, having been in his proximity, having surmounted extraordinary difficulties, having witnessed the birth of a hero: all these elements would contribute to one's chances of being appointed to this or that important position after the communist victory less than fifteen years later, in 1949.

It was during the Long March between 1934 and 1935, that—according to a reliable source—Yan Baohang was informed of the increasingly sensitive rapprochement between Chiang Kai-shek and the Japanese.

In this context, my grandfather tried to show Zhang Xueliang why his reticence toward the communists had to be overcome and why it was imperative that his army cease attempting to exterminate the communists, since that combat served only to strengthen the interests of the Japanese empire.

Zhang Xueliang listened. He thought deeply about my grandfather's words, which shook him. But the general was sentimental by nature: emotions always trumped reason, for him.

1935. From left to right: Daxin, Lan's older uncle; Mingzhi, Lan's younger uncle; Yan Decheng, Lan's great-grandfather; Baohang, Lan's grandfather; Mingfu, Lan's father; Gaosu, Lan's grandmother; Mingguang, Lan's youngest aunt.

1936. From left to right: (back row, standing) Mingzhi, Lan's younger uncle; Mingshi, Lan's oldest aunt; Mingying, Lan's middle aunt; Daxin, Lan's older uncle; (front row) Gaosu, Lan's grandmother; Mingfu, Lan's father; Mingguang, Lan's youngest aunt; Baohang, Lan's grandfather.

1936. Lan's father, Mingfu, at five years old.

1966. The last photograph taken of Lan's grandparents before Baohang was jailed a few months later.

1955. Lan's parents, Mingfu and Keliang.

1947. Lan's grandfather, Baohang, and his wife, Gaosu. Baohang had just been appointed governor of Liaobei province.

1965. Eight-year-old Yan Lan with her parents.

1975. A photograph of Yan Lan reunited with her parents after her father's, Mingfu, seven-and-a-half-year-long detention.

1927. Lan's grandfather, Baohang, in London with Lao She and Ning Encheng.

1929. Baohang returns from England to a hero's welcome.

1934. Baohang with Chiang Kai-shek and his wife, Soong May-ling.

1946. More than fifty thousand people protesting against the civil war in Shanghai.

1949. Mao Zedong greets Baohang.

1957. Lan's father, Mingfu, accompanying Mao Zedong to a tribute to Lenin in Red Square, Moscow.

December 7, 1960. Mingfu with (left to right) Alexei Kosygin, Leonid Brezhnev, and Liu Shaoqi in Moscow.

1965. Mingfu speaking to Mao Zedong, with Liu Shaoqi (left) and Alexei Kosygin (right).

He was disappointed by what Yan Baohang told him about Chiang Kai-shek's ambiguous positions, and this disappointment was all the greater because he had forged an image of Chiang Kai-shek as an incorruptible patriot. It was a short leap from disappointment to anger, and he turned that anger against the head of the Kuomintang, whom he could not forgive for his dalliances with the Japanese. So it was that Zhang Xueliang secretly fomented a maneuver that he himself would call his "coup d'état."

This coup d'état perpetrated by Zhang Xueliang would go down in history as the Xi'an Incident. It took place on December 12, 1936. Taking advantage of Chiang Kai-shek's official visit to Xi'an, Zhang Xueliang kidnapped the head of the Kuomintang and took him hostage.

He laid down his conditions: he would not release his prisoner until Chiang Kai-shek committed to ending the civil war, until he renounced his battle against the communists, until he agreed to establish a united front with them against the invader.

My grandfather would later say about this affair that while Zhang Xueliang was experienced in military strategy, he was quite naive when it came to politics. The proof of this was that after several days of impasse, Zhang Xueliang did not suspect a trap when Chiang Kai-shek proposed to discuss all these questions in Nanjing, his headquarters.

The ruse was so obvious that Zhou Enlai in person advised Zhang Xueliang not to accompany Chiang Kai-shek to Nanjing. Zhang Xueliang was indignant: he believed in the Kuomintang leader's word of honor and was certain that nothing would happen to him.

As might have been expected, as soon as they were on their way to Nanjing, the nationalist leader ordered the general's arrest.

Yan Baohang rushed to the government headquarters. Soong May-ling gave him a mission: if he could persuade Zhang Xueliang to return ten fighter planes to the Nanjing government, the general would be released.

Yan Baohang asked to meet the prisoner. "Should I go back to Xi'an? Should the airplanes be returned?" To both these questions, the general responded in the affirmative. He added, "Chiang Kai-shek and I discussed it, and we came to an agreement. Once the planes have been returned, I will be freed and allowed to go back to Xi'an."

Once the operation had been completed, however, far from being released, Zhang Xueliang was sentenced to life imprisonment. Yan Baohang was shocked by this news. It was an unspeakable betrayal. Once he had calmed down, he asked to see Chiang Kai-shek as soon as possible and managed to obtain an audience with Soong May-ling. After many months, when he was finally received by the Kuomintang leader, his pleas fell on deaf ears. The only favor granted to him was a meeting with the prisoner, who—so it was said—was to be placed under house arrest for the rest of his life in Fenghua, in the province of Zhejiang, within the walls of the Xuedou Temple in the town of Xikou.

The meeting between my grandfather and Zhang Xueliang took place in February 1937. That Buddhist temple, a favorite of the Song dynasty, is sometimes called the Snow Grotto because of its remote setting at the top of Mount Xuedou. At that time of year, the snow has not yet melted. The cold is penetrating, the light at dusk dim and sinister. My grandfather told me, "As soon as I entered the temple, I felt horribly alone, horribly sad."

He was led to a small cell. Zhang Xueliang was silent and looked strangely afraid for somebody who had never feared anything. My grandfather started speaking, but Zhang Xueliang motioned him to say nothing, gesturing with his chin at the high windows as if to suggest they were being spied upon.

And my grandfather resigned himself to saying good-bye to Zhang Xueliang, not imagining for an instant that his friend would outlive him. Because Zhang Xueliang remained imprisoned for more than half a century!

Chiang Kai-shek's bitterness toward him was so deep-seated that once the Kuomintang leader had been deposed, he went to a great deal of trouble to have his prisoner taken with him to Taiwan, where the communist government had driven him into exile. And in the event that Zhang Xueliang should outlive him (which he did), Chiang Kai-shek wished to perpetuate his vengeance. Before dying in 1975, he bequeathed the care of the prisoner to his son. So Zhang Xueliang was not released until after the death of Chiang's son in 1990.

Finally, in 1991, my third aunt, Mingguang, flew to New York to visit this man, freed after more than fifty years of captivity. Later, my parents traveled to Hawaii to meet my grandfather's closest friend.

The old man's first question to his visitors was, "Tell me—and please, don't hide anything—how and in what circumstances did your father die?"

Despite the ordeal of his long incarceration, Zhang Xueliang—who died in 2001, at the venerable age of a hundred—had outlived my grandfather by more than thirty years.

38

Our people will never forget that they suffer because of
other men, and not because of their previous lives. . . .
Those who have given a consciousness of their revolt
to 300 million wretches were not shadows like men
who pass—even beaten, even tortured, even dead.

—André Malraux, *Man's Fate*, 1933

Less than a year later, on a very slight pretext, the imperial Japanese army overwhelmed the northeastern territories, crossed the Marco Polo Bridge (a.k.a. the Lugou Bridge) on July 7, 1937, and—on the instructions of the Emperor Hirohito—began the invasion of the whole of China. This was the first act of the long Sino-Japanese War that claimed, according to today's historians, more than twenty million lives. This conflict, among the bloodiest in the history of Asia, would drag the whole world along with it. It was from this chaos that China, as we know it today, would emerge, united for the first time by nationalistic fervor.

Just after this offensive, Zhou Enlai was officially put in charge of the Communist Party's negotiations with the Nanjing government in order to consolidate the front against the Japanese. He set up and led the KMT-CPC liaison office. On August 13, 1937, when the Japanese invaded Shanghai, Zhou Enlai went to see Yan Baohang.

The two men had a series of long conversations. They talked about the war, of course, but also about the future, and the communists' determination to drag China out of the old feudalism that still dogged it. They mentioned Mao Zedong's peasant origins, which put him on the same level as the majority of the population, on the same level as the country itself, which, unlike the West, had never been through an Industrial Revolution. They talked about the Kuomintang, about its relentless drift toward dictatorship, and about the corruption that had gnawed at the ruling party for nearly ten years.

And, as with more or less all the subjects they broached, Yan Baohang spoke very openly about his own belief in Christ during his younger years. Zhou Enlai replied that the church had formed a number of thinkers—Copernicus, Giordano Bruno, Galileo—who had advanced humanity. It had the same objective as they did: to help the poorest people construct a better, more egalitarian world. Those values, Zhou went on, should lead Yan Baohang to strengthen his position within the Communist Party, which could benefit from the precious network that Yan Baohang had spent so long refining within the Kuomintang.

Nobody, after all, could suspect any kind of deceit from a dignitary who had shared Chiang Kai-shek's offices since being put in charge of the New Life Movement. Who would ever mistrust this close friend of Soong May-ling, with his reputation for being affable and charming, the indispensable polyglot guest at all the regime's parties, as well as all the private parties organized by Zhou Enlai?

This discussion was well-timed: the whole of China—and, more generally, all of Southeast Asia where Japanese troops had penetrated—was now ablaze with war. This new situation demanded a new form of engagement.

It was clear that alliances were shifting, that the Kuomintang was on the verge of surrendering to the siren songs of the Germans and Japanese, who were extolling the virtues of a rapprochement with China against the Soviet Union. Yan Baohang was strongly nationalistic and eager to win the support of anybody willing to help rid his country of foreign invaders. He was also deeply touched by the Communist Party of China's determination to fight against the Japanese.

It was in this context that my grandfather secretly joined the CPC in September 1937. The operation was obviously clandestine—and dangerous, given the efficiency of the Kuomintang's secret police. Throughout the years that followed, the chief of the secret police would constantly seek to thwart my grandfather, failing only due to a lack of proof.

Zhou remained a stakeholder in the nationalist government. My grandfather continued to be employed by that government as a policy advisor and member of the military committee. On the one hand, this enabled them to obtain the release of communist political prisoners held by the Kuomintang. On the other hand, it allowed them to establish communist influence within the administration.

In 1938, government organizations were forced to retreat inland to Chongqing, in the Sichuan province. Yan Baohang became aware of the increasingly insistent attempts by German diplomats to win over the Chinese, claiming that they would soon no longer be able to count on the Allies. The military attachés who surrounded Chiang Kai-shek were unsparing in their efforts to convince him to seek terms with the Japanese. Once China and Japan were on the same side, they told him, they would be able to crush the communists—not only in the Soviet Union but within China, too. And, of course, this was exactly what Chiang Kai-shek wanted: absolute power over all of China.

It would be years before the historic importance of the intelligence work carried out by Yan Baohang was discovered. The most precious fruit of this work was harvested in 1941, at a cocktail party in Chongqing held by the nationalist government. It was one of the most lavish events ever put on for high-ranking members of the Kuomintang.

Among the operations carried out by secret agent Yan Baohang, this was perhaps the most dangerous, since it had to take place not in secrecy and darkness but out in the open, in plain view, in the white-tie dress code imposed by protocol. If anything went wrong, it would be impossible for him to claim that he wasn't there. But this type of party was only for "secure" guests whose identities and affiliations had been duly verified.

In the story as told by my grandfather, and then my father, the Chinese military attaché posted in Berlin addressed a secret telegram to Chiang Kai-shek in early May 1941, informing him that Hitler had already planned the attack on the Soviet Union to begin around June 20.

This news was met with great enthusiasm by the nationalist leaders. Once the USSR had been crushed by the Reich's troops—an outcome that seemed unquestionable in their eyes—the Japanese would find it easy to crush the Chinese communists, who would be powerless without the Russians' protection.

The party in question had been organized to celebrate this wonderful news. As soon as Yan Baohang arrived, knowing nothing of all this, he sensed the unusually festive mood. The guests were all making toasts. Some honored Chiang Kai-shek, some Soong May-ling, some the Kuomintang, some all three at the same time. Surprised, my grandfather asked Sun Ke, the son of Sun Yat-sen, what was going on. And that was how he learned the secret.

My grandfather pretended to be indifferent when Sun Ke whispered this into his ear, but he quickly sought to corroborate the information. Later that evening, he talked to the Senate president, Yu Youren, who confirmed that the information was correct and even claimed he had heard it himself from Chiang Kai-shek.

Yan Baohang feigned illness then, and left the party. It was impossible for him to go directly to Zhou Enlai's apartment: he would risk compromising them both. By chance, Li Zhengwen, who belonged to the same spy cell, was spending the night at the Yans' home. He could speak to Zhou without risk, and then Zhou would only have to relay the information to Mao Zedong in Yan'an, who would immediately transmit the news to Stalin. It was June 16, 1941.

Of course, it was no secret that Germany was planning to attack the Soviet Union, despite the famous nonaggression pact. But the date of the attack was unknown, and this question was crucial since Stalin was worried about his troops' preparedness. As soon as he came into possession of the information, the Soviet leader gave his thanks to "the Chinese comrade who was able to intercept it."

In 1962, during a meeting at the Great Hall of the People in Beijing, Zhou Enlai discussed the reciprocal support between China and the Soviet Union. "It was not only the Soviet Union that aided China, but China which gave the Soviets important information about Hitler's attack," he explained, before adding, "I do not remember exactly who it was that gave me that information." My grandfather, who was attending this meeting, was startled by this sentence. Immediately afterward, he wrote a detailed report on his intelligence activities related to this episode and sent it to Zhou Enlai. And so, twenty-one years after the events in question, Zhou Enlai found out how the information had come into his hands.

There are some historical events so remarkable that they are celebrated after the deaths of the protagonists and even after the demise of the political systems that existed at the time. In 1995, half a century after the Allied victory over Nazi Germany, Boris Yeltsin awarded three decorations in the name of the Russian people. The first medal was given "in recognition of the contribution of Yan Baohang to the victory of the Allies in the Second World War." Daxin, my first uncle, received this posthumous decoration on behalf of my grandfather, alongside his wife, Shu Ti—the aunt whose head had been shaved by her students during the Cultural Revolution. My first aunt, Mingshi, was awarded the second decoration for her assistance to my grandfather's work. She could not be there in person to receive this award for health reasons, so it was Mingfu, my father, and Wu Keliang, my mother, who received it on her behalf. The third decoration was awarded to Li Zhengwen, the agent my grandfather sent to transmit the information about Operation Barbarossa to Zhou Enlai.

Another of my grandfather's great achievements came in 1944, when he gave the Soviets crucial information about the Japanese Kwantung army, stationed in the former territory of Manchuria.

To understand the strategic importance of this contingent of a million men, armed with the best military equipment of the time, it suffices to say that this army's intention was to remain secret until its planned deployment on Chinese soil. The Japanese general staff preferred to send any other contingent into battle rather than using this reserve army. It was all the more important to spare this elite force since they were also there to protect Japan from a possible American attack.

When the Red Army decided to attack it, the Soviets possessed all the details they needed about the organization and logistics of this army that was designed to be self-sufficient. They had maps showing the positions of airports and weapons, and they knew the name of every general and every marshal. The information that Yan Baohang sent from Chongqing enabled the Soviets to dismantle the largest and most prestigious part of the Japanese army on August 9, 1945: one week before the planned date of the invasion of China. The Soviet intervention thwarted this danger and put an end to the puppet state of Manchukuo.

Lastly, my grandfather was the man who informed the communists that Japan was planning an attack on the American naval base of Pearl Harbor, in Hawaii. In November 1941, Chi Buzhou, a brilliant mathematician trained in Japan, who was working for the Kuomintang's military intelligence bureau and was one of my grandfather's contacts, decrypted information relating to this plan of attack on the biggest fleet in the Pacific. The Japanese often used misinformation, but this data coincided with a notable increase in messages between the Japanese capital and its consulate in Hawaii concerning the presence of the US Navy on the island of Oahu and the movements of the Japanese naval air force. This information was immediately reported to Yan Baohang, who transmitted it to Zhou Enlai.

The role of espionage in this affair was such that the Chinese, Soviet, and American general staffs were informed of the attack at more or less the same time. Each reacted in its own way: Stalin interpreted it as proof of the Japanese determination to start the war against the United States; Roosevelt, on the other hand, despite being informed by two separate sources— Stalin and Dai Li, the head of the Kuomintang intelligence department—did not fully credit the information.

39

When two enemies meet, their eyes shine brightly.

—Attributed to Shi Nai'an
(1296–1370), *Water Margin*

Born on November 11, 1931, my father, Mingfu, was a war child. It began one month before his birth with the invasion of Manchuria by the Japanese Kwantung army. This explains why the Chinese character of his generation—*Ming*—was affixed to *Fu*, which means "to recover the homeland." He was the child of a war that kept growing until it spread to the West and then throughout the Asia-Pacific region in 1941, and which, in China, would last fifteen years. When he was born, his eldest sister, Mingshi, was fifteen, while his other sister Mingguang was four. Mingzhi, the youngest of his brothers, was seven, and it was Mingzhi with whom my father would remain closest until Mingzhi's death, at fifty-one, a victim of the Cultural Revolution.

It is easy to imagine how strongly he must have been marked by the war as a little boy because it was he, Mingfu, who opened the door to the young and apparently blind soldier who presented himself at their apartment one day in a pitiful state. His mother, Gaosu, looked after this young soldier from the northeast, and while he was slowly recuperating she explained to Mingfu—who was eight at the time—that the soldier was one of the unfortunate victims of the biological weapons used by the Japanese.

Mingfu had good reasons to remember that young peasant-soldier who had lost all his family and would never recover his sight, since Gaosu decided to teach him to cook. Later, Mingfu would admit that he wished the soldier's initiation into the art of cooking had not lasted so long, because his mother's kindness toward the man meant their family had to eat a lot of dumplings that were unsalted or too salted, overcooked or undercooked.

Mingfu also remembers that, during his childhood, a painting given to them by a famous artist suddenly disappeared. Likewise, Gaosu would sell her rings and her watch so she could buy penicillin—incredibly expensive at the time—for the Wang family, whose one-month-old daughter had caught pneumonia.

The war was over in Europe, but the civil war in China was still raging. When Yan Baohang was named governor of Liaobei in August 1946, the Kuomintang decided to arrest his family. To escape them, Gaosu fled Chongqing with Mingfu and

Mingguang and two of Mingying's little daughters. There followed a four-month journey by boat, train, and wagon, with the family disguised as wealthy Kuomintang members, before they reached Harbin in Manchuria. In 1947, Mingfu began his higher education at the Harbin Institute of Foreign Languages. This was Gaosu's opportunity to visit her other son, Mingzhi, who was twenty-three years old and teaching Russian at the same school.

Two years after the end of the war in Europe, China regarded the USSR as a great nation that had sacrificed twenty million of its people to defeat Nazi Germany, one of the Axis powers, along with Japan, which had inflicted so much suffering on the Chinese people. As for the many Chinese who were already believers in communist ideals, they regarded the USSR as their ideological big brother. Consequently, Russian was by far the most popular of all foreign languages in China at that time.

After graduating in 1949, at nineteen years old, Mingfu spent eight years working for the National Federation of Unions, where he accompanied Soviet experts who were in China to train people in the organization of unions. Mingfu was with these people from morning until evening, often drinking vodka with them. Almost without realizing it, he made enormous progress in his understanding of Russian.

Meanwhile, Mao Zedong was in a train on the way to Moscow, accompanied by a delegation of four people. This was two months after the proclamation of the New China in October 1949. The journey to Moscow, which took ten days back then, was scheduled to include a first meeting with Joseph Stalin. It would be the only meeting between the two men.

Those ten days spent traveling across the Russian plains were still not enough to digest the affront China had suffered, among others: in 1945, the Soviets—guilty, like the Americans, of gambling on a nationalist victory—had cynically agreed to a treaty of "alliance and friendship" with Chiang Kai-shek: a dagger in the back for the Chinese communists.

We know what happened next: after forcing Chiang Kai-shek and his last remaining followers to leave for Taiwan, Mao proclaimed the dawning of the People's Republic of China, to the surprise of the Soviets and the rest of the world.

That first (and last) contact with Stalin was disastrous, despite the fact that Mao was the guest of honor for the Russian leader's seventieth birthday, and that his name was chanted by the crowds alongside that of Stalin. While the ceremony appeared warm and welcoming, however, Mao's expression remained grave. He made it clear to the Soviet Union's representative in China (who was tasked with passing the message on to Stalin) that he had not come all the way to Moscow just to celebrate the Russian leader's birthday; he would also like to "work a little bit!"

It took two months of heated negotiations for the tensions between the two leaders to be soothed. The cause of this rapprochement was, essentially, the signature of a treaty of assistance that provided for the largest transfer of technology ever realized: Soviet experts and engineers were handed the task of establishing the foundations of China's development in which the priority—in a country that was 90 percent rural—would be given to industry.

40

Know the masculine in yourself,
but embrace the feminine.

—Laozi (571–471 BCE), *Tao Te Ching:
The Book of the Way and Its Virtue*

The whole Yan family had just celebrated Mingzhi's planned departure for the Soviet Union. It was a notable promotion, since my uncle would work for the Chinese embassy team in Moscow before returning to Beijing to join the Foreign Ministry. It was amid this family jubilation that we heard the news: Joseph Stalin was dead. All eyes turned to Moscow. Everybody pored over the smallest signs, attempting to work out who would emerge on top from the battle for the Kremlin. As is always the case, the outsiders were barely even mentioned. And, to believe the *New York*

Times, Nikita Khrushchev stood no chance against rivals such as Malenkov and Beria.

What the *Times* did not know was that, as soon as Stalin died, Khrushchev took good care to send his closest ally, Anastas Mikoyan, to Beijing. Mikoyan had already been to China once before, in secret, just prior to the proclamation of the People's Republic.

Khrushchev's skill in currying Mao's favor bore fruit. China gave its full support to this outsider. In return, Khrushchev traveled to Beijing in 1954 to express his gratitude, which took a very concrete and considerable form: more than one hundred programs of technical assistance, including some that concerned armament. Not to mention the complete modernization of the Qincheng special prison in Beijing, a detail that strikes me. All of this was accompanied by an invitation to the Moscow Conference that was due to take place in November 1957.

In 1956, my father was asked to join the central government; the best interpreters of that time were all working for the National Federation of Unions. His job was to train the members of a team and to lead the staff chosen, Mr. Zhu and Mr. Zhao, in January 1957.

In the photograph that immortalized Mingzhi's departure for Moscow, two new faces can be seen: Cao You, whom Mingshi had met at the Beaux-Arts, where she had enrolled after her passage through Yan'an, and whom she married. The other face was the delicately featured Wu Keliang, my mother, who was twenty-two at the time but appeared closer to sixteen. The smile on her face might have shown shyness, were it not belied by the strikingly frank look in her eyes.

My future parents had met the previous year. She was studying French at Peking University when they met for the first time, in May 1952. About thirty foreign delegations had been invited by the National Federation of Unions for International Workers' Day on May 1. As there were not enough interpreters, the best of New China's students were summoned. So it was that Wu Keliang was asked to welcome the Algerian delegation. Mingfu, for his part, was with the Russians. During an interminable official speech, the young woman forgot part of what had been said, and Mingfu came to her aid. She was impressed by his talent.

They would meet again in similar circumstances. After that first meeting, having broken the ice, they would greet each other and smile when their paths crossed—until, one day, they were brought together again by a new mission in Hangzhou. It was during this trip that Miss Keliang, who was feeling unwell, noticed that she was the focus of this boy's delicate attentions. In fact, there could be no doubt about it: he was courting her. This boy was freely courting a young girl who had not introduced him to her family, about whom he knew nothing, in an era when arranged marriages were still the norm among "suitable" families, despite the government's extolment of female emancipation.

It was common knowledge that this Yan Mingfu was from a revolutionary family. That he was close to the ruling regime. That he was politically committed. "Very red," as they said in those days. He was completely different from the young suitor who had already been officially presented to Keliang: belonging to an upper-class family in Hangzhou, that young man had been educated in the United States before joining the Kuomintang's air force as a pilot; he had then studied engineering in America and was now teaching at Tianjin University, no less.

This carefully planned marriage was ideal from the perspective of Keliang's parents. And it has to be said that her family were, to put it mildly, not exactly favorable to revolutionaries.

But what did Wu Keliang herself think?

In all honesty, she found the man from Hangzhou, who had given her a very pretty pearl necklace, just a little dull, a little too conventional, insufficiently curious about the progressive ideas that were spreading through China at the time and which fascinated her.

Keliang had met some young people who moved in revolutionary circles, organized meetings, gave classes to working-class children, and devoted themselves to the creation of a better, fairer, more progressive society. She had come to share their enthusiasm. The pretty pearl necklace could not compete. So Keliang made a radical decision: not only would she marry Yan Mingfu, but she would do it without warning her parents.

The cruelest aspect of this for them was not that she had chosen passion over duty, but that, in choosing Mingfu, she had opted to marry the revolutionary cause. A cause that, they knew, would condemn them to disappear, at least in the heart of their daughter. And, along with them, all that they represented.

41

When I was young, I too had many dreams.

—Lu Xun, *Call to Arms*, 1922

My mother was born in Shenyang in 1931, the same year as my father, to a typically bourgeois Shanghai family. On the rare occasions when, as a child, I met this side of the family, I remember only that they spoke a language, the Shanghai dialect, that I did not understand, and that nobody on my father's side of the family understood.

My maternal grandfather, Wu Zongjie, had been academically brilliant, joining the prestigious Tsinghua University, which mostly trained engineers. Thanks to the "Boxer Indemnity," an American educational grant, he was able to complete his studies in the United States, spending four years at the Massachusetts Institute of Technology (MIT), where he graduated with a degree in textile engineering. After falling in love with a Korean princess, he decided to extend his stay there and began a three-year course at the equally prestigious Juilliard School for music in New York. He remained in New York until 1929.

Wu Zongjie was passionate about music, and his instrument was the violin. My mother, the eldest of his daughters, told me how he would ask her to accompany him on the piano, and that his playing was so beautiful that people would stop in the street to listen. His wife and his four children—two girls and two boys—constituted his favorite audience when he played the ancient, two-stringed instrument known as the *erhu*, which had been invented in China more than a thousand years before.

Despite all the time he had spent in the West, my grandfather still considered himself the direct descendant of a literary Chinese tradition that went back several millennia. This tradition was as much about playing go as about calligraphy and painting. In fact, his academic career, which had steered a course between music and science, was very much within the Confucian recommendations that a young man's knowledge should include arts such as music, archery, chariot riding, arithmetic, poetry, painting, and calligraphy, and techniques such as medicine, astronomy, geomancy, and divination.

My mother remembers how he used to organize little choir evenings, as in a German musical family, inviting his children's classmates to his house to sing. Once a month, he would bring together a group of friends to sing Kunqu, that very ancient form of Chinese opera whose literary themes are inspired by Chinese history and mythology.

The presentations between my maternal grandparents had followed the rules of the age and the social milieu. The respective families had put them in touch with each other when my grandfather returned from the United States. As their union was uncontested, they married the following year, in 1930.

My grandmother Zhou Lixing was from Jiading, a neighborhood of Shanghai. She belonged to a very old family whose roots went back to the Song dynasty. Among their ancestors, they were proud to count the eleventh-century neo-Confucian philosopher and cosmologist Zhou Dunyi. He was the author of a long book about the lotus, and my mother used to recite this passage to me, a passage I learned by heart and that is still quoted even today to illustrate nobility of character: "Despite the silt from which it grows, the lotus flower remains pure. And despite the clear water that falls upon it, it is never vain . . ." One day, Mama read in a magazine that Zhou Dunyi was also an ancestor of Zhou Enlai and the writer Lu Xun, which meant they were our distant relations.

My maternal grandmother had received a very liberal upbringing. In Beijing, she had been the student of the painter Xu Beihong. Born in 1895, this artist—better known in France as Jupéon—is considered one of the great twentieth-century Chinese artists, as well-known in China as Zao Wou-ki. A renowned portraitist who was also famous for his paintings of horses, he had given classes in Tokyo and Paris in the 1920s.

If my mother is to be believed, my grandmother gave up on the majority of her domestic duties once she was married and spent most of her time playing mah-jongg. As the eldest child, Mama, at the age of fifteen, was given responsibility for the three others. She became very protective of them, perfectly willing to fight like a boy to defend her little sister and two little brothers.

As she was graduating high school around the time of the New China, my mother remembers the taking of Tianjin by the People's Liberation Army in 1949. Despite her social origins, she had been fully supportive of this ideal of a new society, and her greatest aspiration was to escape from her family background and live far from these people who were suddenly perceived as being horribly bourgeois. She was not the only one. She and a group of equally committed friends decided to take their exams so they could continue their education in Beijing.

Her younger sister, who was very close to Keliang, followed the same path. She, too, joined Tsinghua, but opted to study engineering. She would finish top of her entire year when she completed her degree toward the end of the 1950s. This was a time when the party was encouraging young intellectuals to contribute to the development of the New China by moving to poor and backward regions.

She left for Lanzhou, nestled in the narrow strip of land in Gansu, a province trapped between the Mongolian plateau and the foothills of Tibet, a very poor region that suffered frequent earthquakes. In Lanzhou, the Central Committee had decided to set up the first industrial center in the northwest: a vast complex bringing together petrochemistry, metallurgy, plastics, machine-tool production, and, from the 1960s on, the enrichment of uranium for both civil and military requirements.

For Keliang, her little sister's departure was poignant, particularly as she is not sure that her sister realized at the time, swept along by the government propaganda, that she would spend the rest of her life in that godforsaken place. Without any hope of return.

42

Curse the pagoda tree by showing the mulberry tree.
Curse the dog by showing the pig.

—Chinese saying

Almost as soon as she had finished her degree in interpretation and translation, Wu Keliang was informed that her excellent results had instantly opened the doors to the Central Committee. More specifically, she was assigned to the foreign liaison department, which reported directly to the party, not the Foreign Ministry. But given her bourgeois origins, this "privilege" involved a sacrifice: joining the administration of the Central Committee meant drawing a line over her past, breaking—physically and emotionally—with her family.

This department was in charge of relations with opposition parties in other countries, particularly communist parties: not an easy task in the Cold War era that had followed the Yalta Conference.

Keliang's responsibilities were toward the French and Italian representatives. My mother had never learned Italian, but she had studied Latin. All she had to do was procure a few books by searching through the shelves of Liulichang, the street of antiquarians in Beijing. In fact, she managed to find an old and very thick Italian-Latin-Chinese dictionary written by a missionary. She decided to make this book her primary teacher. Because, when learning a language, Mama had a method. This was how she explained it to me: "It's very simple, Lan. Listen carefully: every day, you must learn twenty new words by heart. To remember them, you must repeat them at least a hundred times each. After that, believe me, you won't be able to forget them."

She went on to explain to me her theory behind this method: "Imagine that the words are bricks, Lan. Before you start thinking about building anything, you are going to need a lot of bricks. Next comes the grammar, otherwise known as the technology. You should learn grammar exactly as you learn any other technique..."

The only ingredient in this homemade recipe that Mama did not mention was perseverance. That was because she had so much of it that she never even suspected that not everybody else was the same. Luck played a part, too: while accomplishing her tasks as an interpreter, she met an Italian expert whom she had to accompany on his projects in China. His wife was a teacher, and she offered her services to my mother for the next two years. My mother always claimed that her mastery of the language of

Dante was far from perfect, but nonetheless she somehow succeeded in becoming the first interpreter of Italian for Mao Zedong in the New China.

In 1955, Keliang and Mingfu decided to marry. They had already set the date and prepared all the necessary documents when they were told about a working trip that Keliang could not get out of: an international meeting in Moscow, and then in Vienna, to which the Association of Chinese Lawyers was invited. Each lawyer had to be accompanied by two interpreters, one for Russian, the other for French.

Once she returned, Mingfu had to travel to Yugoslavia . . .

One Saturday in June, while Keliang was in her office studying the paperwork that had piled up during the week, the telephone rang. It was Mingfu: he had just come back to Beijing; he was calling from the airport; one of his colleagues was willing to lend him his small apartment and, if she agreed, they could get married that very night.

The wedding was improvised in no time at all. Keliang prepared the room where their guests would come and the bedroom where they would spend their wedding night, while Mingfu called his parents and friends and bought a few snacks to serve as the buffet. The lack of solemnity was in keeping with the values of the time for a young revolutionary couple who wished to exclude all traces of bourgeois behavior from their lives. The aim, as they had learned in Yan'an, was to remain simple and modest in all circumstances.

That evening, Keliang wrote a letter to her parents in Tianjin, informing them of her marriage. Her mother sent her 100 yuan by return of post, and in that way they gave her their blessing. But Keliang could not accept that money, even though she knew it was well-intentioned, without betraying her personal politics. Nor could she return the money to her parents with an explanation that their social origin—bourgeois culture plus capital, a "bad" origin—condemned them in the eyes of the Communist Party, which required that their daughter exclude them from her life. In the end, she sent back the money with a letter explaining that she did not "dare" spend it—and did not need it, in any case—and hoped that her parents would be able to read the truth between the lines.

Sadly, while the situation was difficult for Keliang to explain, it was even harder for her mother to understand. She became angry at this refusal and for a long time she blamed Keliang for her behavior.

In the early 1950s, the New China had begun to lay down very strict guidelines concerning these issues of social belonging, but they went against an age-old feudal tradition transmitted by Confucianism and passed on from generation to generation. This tradition stipulated that one could not change one's social standing, which was determined at birth, without some form of betrayal. This was as true for the emperor as it was for the peasant. In wishing to make a clean break from the idea of social heritage, the New China had in fact made it even more rigid: irrespective of his commitments, his way of life, his political convictions, a great-grandson of a bourgeois family was doomed to remain bourgeois into perpetuity. The same was true for a great-grandson of peasants: whether he was reactionary or revolutionary, he would remain a peasant.

Added to this was an equally rigid inversion of the hierarchical order: the "good" origin now was what had previously been the lowest rung on the social ladder. The one thing that remained unchanged was the notion that one could not change without some form of betrayal. From 1958 on, the different social classes were divided in black-and-white terms—or, rather, black and red. "Red" was the good category, filled by workers, poor peasants, martyrs of the revolution, revolutionary soldiers. "Black" was the bad category, the enemy: landowners, rich farmers, counter-revolutionaries, criminals, rightists.

Hence the necessity to break all connection with one's family if one came from the "black" category. Beside the questioning and persecution inflicted by one's comrades, one also had to take into account the torture one would inflict on oneself because of this permanent suspicion of contamination and betrayal.

At work, my mother was quickly made to feel the blame and shame of her origins. She was quickly made aware that, despite her progressive convictions, it would be almost impossible for her to redeem herself. This suspicion toward "black origins" would continue to worsen until it found its apotheosis in the Great Proletarian Cultural Revolution.

In 1966, a book was published by a twenty-four-year-old student named Yu Luoke that claimed to discuss this "theory of lineage," as well as the unique "cult" of the "workers-peasants-soldiers" class. His essay was hugely successful, its message spreading like wildfire. In *On Family Origin*, Yu Luoke demonstrated in substance the injustice and arbitrary nature of this theory, going so far as to affirm that its only aim was to legitimize the new privileges. Accused of rightism and attempting to organize a political movement, Yu Luoke was arrested and then executed by the army in 1970. He was twenty-seven years old.

As soon as Mama joined the foreign liaison department, she was isolated for six months, installed in a ministry residence so that her family origins could be examined in depth.

Some of her fellow former students, with grades far less exalted than her own, were given the most important and prestigious foreign missions while she remained at her desk translating documents about France and Vietnam. The reason being that my mother could not claim a single ancestor or family member who had been a peasant, worker, or simple soldier.

Within the ministry, there were regular sessions of criticism and self-criticism. At the first of these meetings, Mama said that she felt it was unfair that she was systematically given minor tasks when her university results were among the best. She thought it questionable to prioritize social origins over professional skills. Such a declaration immediately gave rise to criticism. That first session was followed by many others. In the end, they became a regular feature of life at the ministry.

For those young people starting their careers just after the Liberation, it soon became clear that if they wished to advance they would have to cut off all family ties, particularly if their family included landowners, capitalists, the bourgeoisie, or members of the Kuomintang. Anybody who did not do this was doomed, at the very least, to career stagnation and constant vexations. So my mother cut off her family. Who can really blame her?

When the ministry assigned her abroad for the first time, she was sent to the department that provided the necessary clothing for delegations. In Vienna, where she was going, it was winter. But she could not find a single coat in that department. Never mind, she thought, I have plenty of coats at my parents' home. All she had to do was write to her parents and ask them to send some. She was careful, in her letter, not to reveal the nature of her mission nor where she was going. Like all her coworkers, she had already internalized the tacit cult of secrecy, the rule of confidentiality. Even her own boss had not revealed the destination of her trip when he first told her about it.

Once the episode of the coat became public, however, the next criticism session exploded. My mother was excoriated partly for the coats—seen as an exterior sign of wealth—and partly for her reluctance to break completely with the habits of her bourgeois family.

That was why I saw so little of my maternal grandparents during my childhood. I remember only one time when we all went to visit them in Tianjin: my mother, my father, and me. We spent very little time there, only a few hours, yet it was enough for me to realize that the beautiful house they inhabited was in accordance with my grandfather's status. Although his textile factory no longer belonged to him after the 1949 nationalization program, the authorities that had taken it from him had also asked him to continue running it as the chief engineer, since he had such a thorough theoretical and practical knowledge of his own means of production.

The last time we heard from them was in the middle of the Cultural Revolution. As "capitalists," they were targets of the Red Guards' most virulent attacks. My maternal grandparents' decline had begun. Their beautiful house in Tianjin had been pillaged. My grandfather's beloved violin—a seventeenth-century Italian model, which some even claimed was a Stradivarius—had been stolen. All that was left behind was a large, stripped bed. Then my grandfather was ordered by the Red Guards to sweep his street. Once he had done this, he was given a banner that he had to hold up in front of him, reading:

I AM BAD. I AM WRONG. I AM A CAPITALIST.

43

Lure the snake from its hole to kill it.

—Mao Zedong, during the
Hundred Flowers Campaign

At twenty-six, my father was a translator and interpreter and head of the team attached to the central government. In July 1957, the Soviet ambassador in Beijing informed him that serious events had occurred in Moscow and he urgently needed to meet a Chinese leader.

Neither Mao Zedong nor Zhou Enlai was in Beijing at that time. So it was Liu Shaoqi and Peng Dehuai—one of the most prominent leaders of the People's Liberation Army—who were first informed of the crisis that the Soviet ruler had just come through: a conspiracy aimed at deposing Khrushchev had been foiled, its ringleaders neutralized, and their anti-Party group dismantled.

Until this point, any changes in the composition of the USSR's leadership had always been publicly supported by all the other communist parties so that their approval could be transmitted by the various press organs of the Moscow party. Now, for the first time, Liu Shaoqi did not utter a word. He did not approve, he did not disapprove, he simply remained silent. As for Peng Dehuai, he expressed only puzzlement.

The Soviet ambassador left the Zhongnanhai without obtaining a declaration of support: a first in the annals of Sino-Soviet relations! As soon as he was informed of this, Khrushchev sent his personal emissary to Beijing.

So it was that in early July 1957, my father was given the task of welcoming the deputy premier, Anastas Mikoyan, and accompanying him to Hangzhou, where he would meet with Mao and a number of other Chinese leaders.

This time, the Chinese did not have to insist on Soviet aid for their development of nuclear technology: it was Khrushchev himself, delighted by the strengthening of relations between the two countries, who brought the matter up and set the terms. He also invited Mao Zedong to attend the Conference of Communist Parties in Moscow the following November, and said that he would be proud to personally welcome the Chinese leader.

All in all, Mao Zedong left China only twice. And each time, it was for Moscow.

Khrushchev was well aware of how Stalin's coldness, distance, and self-importance had wounded Mao—and, through him, the entire Chinese people—during his first trip to the USSR in December 1949. He knew that Stalin had crudely boasted of the Bolsheviks' superiority over the Chinese communists. Khrushchev was also aware of the personal political prestige he could draw from a thaw in Sino-Soviet relations. My father would be a firsthand witness to this evolution, noting how one of the Soviet leader's most important assets was his seemingly frank, direct, plainspoken manner.

For all this, Mao was not fooled. Very quickly he and Khrushchev moved on from expressions of brotherly love to a relationship that Mao would later characterize as "that between a cat and a mouse."

During Mao's second stay in Moscow, in October and November 1957, my father went with him. This was not his first trip to the Soviet capital.

On the plane, he told me, Soong Qing-ling sat in the seat opposite Mao's. Her presence was justified by the fact that, having lived in Moscow in the 1930s—just after she had broken with the Kuomintang—she was the perfect candidate to chair the Association for Sino-Soviet Friendship.

During that flight from Beijing to Moscow, the chairman pointed out Mingfu to Soong Qing-ling and asked her if she had any idea whose son this young man was. Soong Qing-ling replied that of course she knew Yan Baohang very well and she was delighted to learn that the son of "such a good person" would accompany their delegation to Moscow. As for Mingfu, he thought to himself proudly that the "young man" in question was not only married but already a father, his first daughter having been born in January of that year. As you have no doubt guessed, I was that ten-month-old little girl.

That global conference, featuring the sixty-eight delegations of the international communist movement, was supposed to conclude with a common declaration. The text of this declaration would not be easy to write, given the crises in international communism since Stalin's death in 1953.

At the origin of the tension among the world's communists was, of course, the famous "Khrushchev report," which, in February 1956, denounced Stalin's crimes, causing great consternation among militants. To begin with, Mao did not condemn the report. His primary concern was to find out whether, given the circumstances, the Soviet Union was still disposed to maintain its pro-China economic policy. On that point, Khrushchev not only reassured him, but also went further. But there was no shortage of events likely to trouble communists in those years, and Mao was undoubtedly worried.

A few months after the Khrushchev report came the Poznan Uprising in the spring of 1956. This workers' rebellion forced the Soviets to accept the arrival of Wladyslaw Gomulka, supposedly a reformist, as the head of the country.

At the end of the year, there was the Hungarian Revolution: the population of Budapest, and then the entire country, rose up against a government whose submission to Moscow's diktats they were no longer prepared to accept. The scale of this rebellion, and particularly its bloody repression, caused great unease among communists, making them question their convictions.

My father always believed that the context of extreme ideological tension within international communism in those years was what provided the ingredients for the bomb that would explode ten years later under the name of the Cultural Revolution.

In the spring of 1957, Mingfu accompanied Kliment Voroshilov, chairman of the Presidium of the Supreme Soviet, who had traveled to Beijing to prepare the Moscow Conference. Throughout Voroshilov's visit, events in Budapest haunted every conversation. All the more so since Mao had, that February, launched a new initiative designed to liberalize the country: the Hundred Flowers Campaign. This was nothing less than an attempt to grant the Chinese population, and intellectuals in particular, the authorization to criticize the party. This campaign worried Voroshilov, who told Mao directly that, in a socialist country, one could not allow this type of criticism because it questioned the very nature of the ideology. The Chinese were, he added, encouraging discontent among their people. My father barely had time to translate this before the Soviet leader hammered home his point: "This is exactly the kind of incitement to bourgeois thinking that we have seen in Hungary!"

Mao replied calmly. His Soviet comrades should not be concerned, he said: China is not Hungary. The high esteem in which the Chinese people held their chairman and their Party were in no way comparable to what we had seen in Hungary. We need not fear the kind of excesses that took place there. And the proof of this was that, as soon as Voroshilov left to visit Vietnam and Indonesia, the central Chinese government launched a new directive designed to encourage the "rectification movement" intended to benefit the Party by again inviting intellectuals to make public their criticisms and to "speak openly."

Only a few weeks later, however, Mao changed his position. On May 15, 1957, a new article appeared for internal Party use, eloquently entitled "Things Are Changing." Mao was issuing a warning to those he called "rightists." This was the first time the word had been used.

But who were these people now suddenly described as "rightists"? They were anti-Party elements, Mao said. Impostors who pretended to support the Party, who feigned adherence to the communist ideal, and who had to be removed. Little by little, the Hundred Flowers Campaign underwent a volteface: the project to improve the Party through free expression of criticism closed upon the newly empowered critics like a trap. All those who had believed in it, who had played along, were now caught in its jaws.

In fact, from the beginning of summer 1957, after the antirightist accusations had grown in intensity, the Hundred Flowers Campaign suddenly came to an end. The central government explained that the rectification movement authorized by the Party to improve its performance had been exploited as a means of attempting a coup d'état. That expression—*coup d'état*—resounded like a cannon shot. A number of these intellectual rebels, these infamous counterrevolutionaries, were arrested.

My father's analysis of this diabolical U-turn was that the Soviet Union undeniably played a part in the process. He believed it inevitable that the ideological paroxysms of China's big brother should have repercussions within the country. Contrary to what he had told Voroshilov, Mao had worried about the possibility of the events in Hungary being reproduced in China. The transformation of the Hundred Flowers Campaign into an anti-rightist cabal can be interpreted as Mao's indirect response to the questions posed by Voroshilov.

Following the Hundred Flowers Campaign, more than three million people were condemned as "rightists." Most were deported so that they could be reeducated. Among them was my aunt Mingshi. Why?

In 1957, Mingshi was forty-one years old and one of the pillars of the editorial board of the magazine *China Women*. She had occupied that post since 1951. Mingshi, remember, had been the first of the Yan clan to join the communist ranks at Yan'an, at the invitation of "Uncle" Zhou Enlai, after her commitment in the anti-Japanese struggle had been noted. Mingshi joined the party at twenty-two. Later, using her experience as a revolutionary militant, she provided her father, Baohang, with precious help and supported him in his clandestine intelligence work on behalf of the Party. Her service record, however, was not taken into account when the anti-rightist campaign infiltrated the supposedly enlightened editorial board of *China Women*.

The first accusation of "rightist behavior" came during an editorial meeting. To general stupefaction, she openly stood up for a member of her department who had been wrongly accused. And she called on the spirit of Yan'an, the Party's rear base, where it was considered a point of honor that justice be done. Immediately, she was accused of rightism and her ostracization began.

It did not end there. When she was informed by an official directive that every company in the country had to condemn a minimum quota of 5 percent of its workforce for rightism, she protested against this arbitrary measure with such forcefulness that she was instantly expelled from the Party and ordered to leave Beijing to be reeducated in the countryside, where she was sent along with her husband and their eight children for more than twenty years.

There, in the middle of nowhere—Anshan, in Liaoning province—Mingshi had to work as a laborer in a steel factory, where her husband was employed as an engineer. From that moment on, the family's financial situation became extremely difficult.

44

As they say, I who have eyes,
I could not recognize Mount Tai.

—Chinese proverb

The logistics of Mao's second trip to Moscow were very different from the first. He was accompanied by a very large staff: Mao's bodyguard (who seemed smaller than Mao because Mao was a giant), Mao's secretary, Mao's chef, Mao's nurse, Mao's personal doctor...

It would be an understatement to say that, this time, the Soviets rolled out the red carpet for him. In fact, they constantly appeared desperate to show him the greatest deference imaginable: the podiums, the expressions of respect, the banners and streamers, the jubilant crowds ... It was, to use my father's expression, a real "honeymoon summit."

After the parade in Red Square in the presence of the entire Supreme Soviet, after the pilgrimage to Lenin's mausoleum, Mao did not have far to travel to his quarters: they were inside the Kremlin itself, in the fourth-floor bedroom that had once belonged to Catherine the Great, overlooking the Moskva.

Mao did not like the room: it was too large. Let's swap, he told my father: you go up to the tsarina's room and I'll take your room on the second floor. But for security reasons, this exchange proved impossible. They had to negotiate inch by inch: Mao found the mattress too soft, so they brought him a sort of wooden *kang*. And, of course, only the linen brought from Beijing could be used: sheets, blankets, pajamas, and most important, the rock-hard pillows and cushions. It is said that Nikita Khrushchev took one look at Mao's newly prepared bed and said it looked like it belonged to a soldier who had just returned from the jungle.

He also had to be able to choose at any moment from a hundred or more books arranged within arm's reach.

As far as eating was concerned, it was Mao's own chefs, all of them from Hunan, who prepared his meals, each one spiced just the way he liked it. On evenings when the Soviet hosts had hired a chef of their own, Mao insisted that the meals be served in the Chinese style: all the dishes brought to the table at the same time. This change of protocol was then applied to the many other banquets that followed.

And then there was the delicate issue of the toilets. The Western-style bowl was not to his taste; he demanded a "Turkish toilet." So the floor was raised, several steps constructed, and a grab bar installed.

Nikita Khrushchev was keen to dine with Mao Zedong every day. He accompanied him to every ceremony and was careful to remain always one step behind so as not to overshadow his presence. Similarly, when Mao left the Terem Palace for a preparatory conference meeting, Khrushchev was there waiting for him, pacing up and down without a word of complaint. For the first time, my father said, Mao felt as if he were being treated as an equal.

During a tête-à-tête lunch, my father was able to witness an informal exchange between the two men. Mao seemed to approve of Khrushchev's victory over his opponents while also posing the question of his own succession. A formidable strategist, Mao began by saying that he was preparing to quit the presidency. In reality, only his death, almost twenty years later, would bring an end to his reign. "Have you designated your successor?" Khrushchev asked. Mao mentioned Liu Shaoqi, Deng Xiaoping, Zhou Enlai. It may be noted that while all three of these men would later suffer the wrath of the Cultural Revolution, Liu Shaoqi's fate was the cruelest, dying as he did in very harsh conditions.

Yet at the time, Mao explained that of those three, Liu Shaoqi was the most suitable successor because he was a man of principle. Then he added that Liu Shaoqi's only weakness was not being flexible enough, and in retrospect it is impossible not to reflect on this remark. To honor his lunch companion, Mao reminded

Khrushchev that Liu Shaoqi had studied in Moscow, at the Communist University of the Toilers of the East. Deng Xiaoping was presented as an accomplished politician, principled but capable of flexibility. Lastly, Mao was full of praise for Zhou Enlai: he is better than me at managing the most delicate international conflicts, Mao admitted. Highly intelligent and always quick to criticize himself ... The only problem is that he is on the old side.

At that time, it is true, Zhou Enlai was fifty-nine years old. Mao, on the other hand, was only sixty-four.

45

There are natural calamities and man-made disasters.

—Chinese proverb

In Beijing, a new theme found its way into all the slogans: the revolutionary project required industrial development on the same scale as, if not even bigger than, the country's agricultural development. To back up this statement, the propaganda claimed that no account would be taken of previous public development goals because the figures were all wrong. Those studies, described as "supposedly scientific," all neglected the sole fundamental factor to be considered in the future: the people's willingness to work.

In April 1958, Mao declared: China will not need fifteen years to catch up with the British; ten will be enough. And in twenty years, we will have caught up with the Americans.

And so began the policy known as the Great Leap Forward.

It was in this context that the Soviet ambassador in Beijing asked to speak to my father. Mingfu wondered what the correct translation of Great Leap Forward would be in Russian. In matters of economic development, it was imperative to be extremely accurate. But the translation that was currently circulating ran the risk of creating a huge misunderstanding. The Soviet authorities suspected the translation must be wrong because the eccentric idea of a Great Leap Forward did not seem something that could be applied to a planned economy, which—to their eyes—implied a steady, gradual development.

As an idiomatic expression, my father explained, this notion has no equivalent in Russian. In order to gain a clearer sense of the true meaning, you must think about the way a rabbit moves by successive leaps. For the rabbit's leaps through space, we can read the economy's leaps through time. In this way, we obtain the idea of periods crossed by successive bounds.

"But why did the Chinese want to become rabbits?" Khrushchev is said to have asked when he was informed of this explanation.

In concrete terms, this was the era when small foundries were improvised in the most improbable places: the courtyard of an apartment building, a school, a village street where all the inhabitants gave their meager tribute: a saucepan here, a wok there. Tiny steelworks were set up at the top of every hill in order to contribute to the country's production figures. China needs steel, they were told. China needs machines and equipment. A furnace was built in the residence of the Czechoslovakian ambassador. Even in the courtyard of the honorary president of China, Mrs. Soong Qing-ling, there could be found a small forge. In fact, my father remembers a little blast furnace being installed inside the Zhongnanhai, the seat of the central government. A stone's throw from Mao's quarters, there were parades of old silverware, mess tins, cooking pots, and rusty scraps of corrugated iron. Everywhere was the sound of banging, clattering, the air thick with smoke and the smell of melting metal.

One day, Mao stood at his doorstep in an unusual outfit: a hat on his head, a long shirt under a gray coat that also revealed a pair of pajama pants and a single shoe on one foot, the other one bare. He looked as if he had just gotten out of bed. But what, he asked, was that racket?

My father replied that they were making steel. So Mao moved closer to get a better view. Then he went to fetch a camera, took a photograph, and asked if everything was going well. Yes, everything was going well. Although, in their heart of hearts, some probably wondered what the point of all this was. Then again, perhaps they didn't dare wonder anything. Who would risk even thinking that all of this was madness when the idea came from the man who had led the Long March, the Liberation, the man behind the agricultural reforms? And that man was so venerated that, rather than calling him by his name, the Chinese people—hundreds of millions of peasants—preferred to proclaim him, with the greatest affection and respect, as their Red Sun, their Great Savior.

It is hard to know if the Great Leap Forward was more or less absurd than the Four Pests Campaign, otherwise known as the Kill Sparrows Campaign, which was implemented around the same time.

The pests in question were rats, flies, and mosquitoes, to which Mao decided to add the tree sparrow since it stole grain. Yes, the sparrow was guilty of depriving the Chinese peasantry of the fruit of their hard-earned labor!

This campaign, noisily and expensively launched, recommended the destruction of nests, eggs, and birds in general. It was so slavishly followed that soon, although it was true that the sparrows were no longer stealing grain from the mouths of peasants, the harvests were struck down by a horde of parasites, notably crickets, which were able to proliferate due to the disequilibrium created in the food chain.

The agricultural part of the Great Leap Forward was implemented after the peasantry had already submitted to forced collectivization. Now they had to produce at the rate demanded as part of "people's communes." Everything became collective. The traditional model of the family was jettisoned in favor of the community. The local authorities, cowed by the general atmosphere of terror, did not dare admit their inability to meet the impossible targets, so they provided production figures that were systematically falsified.

In July 1958, when Mao welcomed Khrushchev at the airport in Beijing, the Chinese chairman immediately exclaimed that the Great Leap Forward had already borne fruit, and that the harvests were considerable. Statistics were advanced in evidence, all of them false. Apparently, the Soviet leader was not entirely fooled because, when Mao claimed that the country's food reserves were so vast that they no longer knew what to do with them, Khrushchev replied, deadpan: "Well, if you don't know what to do with them, give them to us!"

The Great Leap Forward created great tension between the two men. And the tension only increased during Khrushchev's visit. My father witnessed a confrontation on the subject of military cooperation: the Soviet leader wanted China's help in forming a joint naval force and a joint long-wave radio system. Mao categorically refused both requests. He accused Khrushchev of attempting to encroach on China's territorial sovereignty by demanding access to the ports of Dalian and Lüshunkou, and of wishing to exercise military control.

Between 1959 and 1962, the implementation of the Great Leap Forward provoked a famine that would lead to the deaths of more than thirty million Chinese people. It was in this context that the Soviet Union announced it would not keep its promise to provide China with the technology necessary for the development of nuclear weapons. This reversal not only signaled an implicit condemnation of what the Soviets believed to be an economic aberration—since it was "non-Marxist" in character—but was also a confirmation of Khrushchev's desire to reduce the threat of a nuclear arms race and the possibility of a nuclear war. This was the message emphasized, in September 1959, during the first official visit by a Soviet head of state to the United States. Khrushchev and Eisenhower spoke a great deal of "peaceful coexistence." It is not difficult to imagine how irritated Mao must have been by this new direction in American-Soviet diplomacy.

At the same time, in September 1959, Mao received a Yugo-slavian delegation. My father was struck by Mao's repeated apologies to the delegation's representatives. Yugoslavia had not been thanked as much as it should have been for being among the first countries to officially recognize the New China in 1949. And to justify this absence of expressed gratitude, Mao explained that "our Soviet friends" did not like the idea that Mao's China could have a direct, personal relationship with Tito's Yugoslavia.

The conversation moved on to Stalin. Mao quoted *Dialectical and Historical Materialism* and observed that although this book had been approved by the Soviet Communist Party's Central Committee, the fact remained that its author—who was none other than Joseph Stalin—showed himself to be horribly idealistic. He concluded: "In any case, I don't like his books. I never did. And that's without even mentioning what he wrote about the Chinese revolution . . ."

As relations between China and the USSR began to fray, Mao often said that the Soviets had never truly considered the Chinese to be real communists. The three key men of that time, Mao added—Beria, Molotov, and Stalin himself—declared in 1949 that the Communist Party of China was in fact merely a nationalist party.

So it was that, by 1959, all the elements of a rupture between the two nations were in place. The following year, the USSR withdrew all its advisors, engineers, and technicians from Chinese territory. The honeymoon was over.

46

Heaven does not strike down those who eat.

—Chinese saying

My mother, who had wanted a daughter, was thrilled by my birth. But the world into which I was born, in January 1957 in Beijing, was far from offering the promise of a radiant future.

Three consecutive years of natural catastrophes—from 1958 to 1961—further aggravated the disastrous effects of the Great Leap Forward. Between 1960 and 1963, I stayed at the nursery school of the ministry where Mama worked. I belonged to the ranks of the privileged children, in that we were given food to eat every day, but even there the rations were extremely meager. As for the adults, all touched to some degree by the famine that raged through the countryside, all they ever talked about were the swollen bellies and edemas characteristic of food deficiencies.

For those adults, the deprivations were even harder to bear since they came on the heels of an uninterrupted succession of ordeals: the long war against the Japanese, the civil war, and the Second World War and its aftereffects in the Pacific. On top of all this, ever since the proclamation of the New China in 1949, there had been the impression of revolution after revolution, new slogan after new slogan.

Since the Hundred Flowers Campaign, Mao had been suspicious of intellectuals. And he would remain so for the rest of his life. Each new direction, such as the anti-rightist hunt, was designed solely to eradicate any opposition that might threaten his own power. Time and again, new class enemies were identified and new wars declared. From the end of the 1950s until the Cultural Revolution, it was as if nothing was done except seeking out, denouncing, unmasking, and punishing potential enemies. New "pests" were added to the list already containing landowners and wealthy farmers: capitalists, rightists, revisionists, intellectuals . . . The intellectuals, the party's most recently identified enemy, were now threatened with expulsion to reeducation camps, where they would work on farms, in mines, or in factories, as had happened to my aunt Mingshi.

At the same time, Mao was building a court around him that reproduced almost perfectly the cult of personality that had defined the emperors of China—a cult in keeping with the modus operandi of the feudal society that the revolution had promised to eradicate.

One member of the Political Bureau, a Shanghai native, claimed that belief in Mao Zedong must proceed from blind and absolute obedience, just as it would for a religion. Kang Sheng, the most intimate of all Mao's inner circle, particularly when it came to the party's internal battles, was the inspiration behind the reeducation camps and all of the regime's purges. In 1958, he declared that Mao's philosophy constituted the peak of Marxism-Leninism.

The same was true for the military leader Lin Biao. Promoted to the rank of marshal in the People's Liberation Army in 1955, he constantly promoted "Mao's philosophy" and was one of the most fervent supporters of the cult.

In company such as that, who would dare admit to having any reservations?

Having given birth to the desired daughter, my mother saw no reason to have any more children. She loved her job, which made huge demands on her time, and now she could devote herself entirely to her career, soothed by the knowledge that I was in safe hands as a boarder at the kindergarten reserved for staff in departments connected to the Central Committee.

On weekends I stayed with my paternal grandparents. There was nothing unusual about this. In China, it is traditional for grandparents to look after their grandchildren. Even now, it is regarded as a natural duty, and nobody questions it.

My mother was eighteen when the New China was proclaimed. She belonged to that generation of intellectuals swept up by talk of women's emancipation—a message passionately supported by the communists and Mao Zedong in particular. This state of mind, something very new in China, had been interiorized in my family to such a degree that it never crossed my mind that my mother would not work. All my aunts worked. Mingguang might have had seven children, but that did not prevent her from holding down a position of great responsibility at a state-owned company in Shanghai.

In the 1950s and 1960s, the idea that women were just as able as men to accomplish any task was illustrated on posters that showed female metalworkers, female truck drivers, female airplane pilots. In terms of dexterity, expertise, and even physical strength, nothing seemed to separate men from women anymore. Most of the seductive aspects of femininity were neatly erased. In their identical gray uniforms, with their indistinguishable figures, the two genders seemed to form a single unisex humanity. A brightly colored skirt or, worse, one with a flowered pattern, would have been regarded as evidence of a bourgeois mentality.

Despite everything, Mao's declaration—"Women hold up half the sky!"—sounded like a form of liberation. My mother made that beautiful precept her own. It was applied without reservation to my education.

For her, as for her daughter, the principle of sexual equality extolled by the New China, as well as the plan to rid society of its ancestral alienation of women, was an integral part of her adherence to communist values. I was never told I couldn't do something because I was a girl. It is hard to overstate how important such principles are in forging self-confidence. For girls of my generation in China, anything seemed possible.

47

One day of cold does not make three feet of ice.

—Chinese proverb

Just after midnight on October 14, 1964, the Soviet ambassador told my father to transmit an urgent message to Mao Zedong. Nikita Khrushchev was announcing his "voluntary" retirement "for health reasons," not only as president but also as secretary-general of the Communist Party, a decision approved in unison by the Presidium and the Central Committee of the Party.

In the presence of my father, the emergency cabinet formed around Mao, Liu Shaoqi, and Zhu De, then the Party's vice-chairman. They agreed that although the situation in Moscow still seemed unclear, Khrushchev's resignation was nevertheless good news for the Communist Party of China.

While a congratulatory telegram was immediately sent to

his successor as head of the party, Leonid Brezhnev, Mao declared that this change should encourage the Chinese to support the Party's new leaders, notably Alexei Kosygin, the new premier, and Anastas Mikoyan, who had been elected president of the Presidium of the Supreme Soviet, which essentially made him head of state. To that end, it was decided that the prime minister, Zhou Enlai, should use the next official celebrations of the October Revolution to visit Moscow. For this crucial diplomatic mission, Zhou chose to be accompanied by the prestigious general He Long because he needed someone "who did not always seek a fight." Naturally, my father went with them.

As soon as they arrived, in early November 1964, the members of the delegation noted that, despite the seriousness of their recent disagreements, the Soviets seemed very pleased to see their Chinese counterparts again. A grand reception at the Kremlin was planned for November 17, and nobody imagined, at that moment, that it would be the occasion of an incident that would for a long time ruin all hope of any reconciliation between China and the USSR.

At the start of the evening, my father told me, in compliance with Zhou Enlai's instructions, He Long joined the Soviet generals at their table. General Rodion Malinovsky approached this veteran of the Long March whom Mao had entrusted with the organization of the Red Army and said to him in a loud, clear voice that the Chinese should follow the example of the Soviets, who had managed to "eliminate" Khrushchev, by doing the same to Mao. Once Mao had been "eliminated," Malinovsky went on, the USSR and China could renew their old friendship.

Now, Malinovsky was not some minor Soviet general. As minister of defense, he was effectively the man behind Khrushchev's dismissal, in retaliation for the Cuban Missile Crisis. Khrushchev's provocative strategy, which had almost brought the world's two superpowers into a nuclear war, followed by his humiliating climbdown, was the main reason for the Communist Party of the Soviet Union's internal coup d'état.

Malinovsky's words were not translated by Mingfu but by one of the three other translators in the team led by my father, although that doesn't alter the fact that he heard every one of them. He also heard He Long's angry protestations, while some other Soviet generals intervened, assuring him that they did not agree with what Malinovsky had said. A Soviet marshal spoke up then: "Each vegetable is cooked according to its season." There followed a great commotion, and Zhou Enlai asked the translators to explain what had just happened. Once he learned the truth, Zhou Enlai went to find Leonid Brezhnev and Anastas Mikoyan.

The president of the Supreme Soviet assured Zhou Enlai that the Central Committee's position on this matter was completely at odds with Malinovsky's. The opinion was that of the general alone, he added, because the Soviets believed that Mao Zedong was a great leader. Despite this clarification, Zhou showed his displeasure by conspicuously leaving the reception, along with all the members of the Chinese delegation.

Zhou did not sleep a wink that night, he told my father the next morning before a debriefing that would provide the wording for a telegram that was sent to Beijing.

Kosygin and Brezhnev went to Zhou Enlai's Moscow

residence later that morning. Neither man had witnessed the exchange, but they told Zhou Enlai that their investigations led them to believe that Malinovsky was drunk at the time of the incident. Once again, they reassured the Chinese prime minister that what was said did not in any way reflect the Soviet position, and that despite their disagreements on questions of China's internal policies, nothing had changed in the bilateral relations between the two countries: the Soviet position remained exactly as it had under Nikita Khrushchev.

When the delegation returned, Mao went to the airport to greet them in person. He was accompanied by a hundred or so leaders, in a display of the Communist Party of China's unbreakable solidarity. And after Zhou gave him a detailed report on the incident, Mao exclaimed that, despite appearances, nothing had changed in Moscow and that "without Khrushchev, the Soviets are still doing a Khrushchev!" Relations between the two countries grew cold, and when Leonid Brezhnev invited Mao to the twenty-third congress of the Communist Party of the Soviet Union two years later, Mao declined the invitation.

We had reached the point of no return, my father told me. For us Chinese, the Soviets were mere revisionists. As for the Soviets, they saw us as dogmatic. Each party, in Moscow and in Beijing, claimed to be the true depository of Marxism-Leninism and the one true leader of international communism. No alliance was possible in such conditions.

Arguably the most important effect of the Malinovsky affair was not the long-term damage it caused to Sino-Soviet relations, but the personal shock it gave to Mao Zedong. It increased his mistrust of his closest supporters, stirring up his obsession with plots and betrayals. And when, in the newspapers of that time, Mao exhorted the people to ask themselves if, close by, perhaps under their own roof, a "Chinese Khrushchev" was hiding, when he exhorted people to spy on one another, to be vigilant, it is likely that he had in mind the coup d'état that the Supreme Soviet had used to "eliminate" his counterpart. It was enough to make him completely paranoid.

In the domain of military strategy, Lin Biao's reputation for intelligence and skill was fully established after his triumphs in the war against Japan as well as in the civil war. But the head of the People's Liberation Army, who had been minister of defense since 1959, only reached the envied status of being an influential figure on Mao Zedong from the moment when he began to personally promote "Maoism" with quasi-idolatrous zeal. When *Quotations from Chairman Mao Zedong* started to be more widely read, around 1964, Lin Biao's name became systematically haloed with a new prestige as "Chairman Mao's intimate comrade-in-arms."

The Little Red Book, which would go on to be the second most widely read book in the world after the Bible, had a modest initial print run. At first composed of thirty chapters of quotations compiled and arranged by Lin Biao from Mao's speeches and essays for the edification of the army, the book was soon reprinted for the edification of all. In 1965, and then the following year, the number of chapters rose to thirty-three. The third mass print run, in 1966, was accompanied by an exhortation: as a sign of loyalty to the party and, above all, to its leader, every citizen should own a copy. Translations in every language were published. Lin Biao handwrote a two-page preface and an epigraph, which were photocopied and printed in new editions of the book, encouraging veneration. He would remain a Mao favorite until the moment of his spectacular and mysterious fall from grace in 1971. After that, the pages disappeared. As did their author.

In the meantime, study of the Little Red Book became compulsory, from primary schools to universities. But it was also studied in offices and factories, in cities and in the countryside, in farms and in army barracks.

While the Little Red Book became obligatory reading in my mother's office, however, the use of Italian was banned. Italian newspapers no longer arrived, and books in Italian, even dictionaries, were confiscated. It was not Italian as such that was forbidden; this was a special measure, designed to vex her in particular. For my mother, this was the start of a period of about ten years when she would stop practicing that beautiful language. In the end, she would almost forget how to speak it.

On top of the regular indoctrination sessions, there now came the announcement of a new movement, led by the army. It was Marshal Lin Biao who had brought it to the attention of the population, with two articles, published in April and May of 1966 in the *PLA Daily*. The first was entitled "Let us raise high the magnificent red standard of Mao Zedong's philosophy, let us actively participate in the great socialist Cultural Revolution." The second: "And let us not forget the class struggle."

48

The wind knows the strength of the grass, and
a true friend is known in day of adversity.

—Chinese proverb

I remember that period before the catastrophe, when my grandmother was working as a volunteer for the Residents' Committee of the State Council's residence. To fund this committee's
projects, she would sell ice cream on sunny days outside the
residence's main entrance. Nainai allowed me the extraordinary
privilege of contributing to this project in my own way: by tasting every flavor of ice cream she served.

"What do you want to do, Lan, when you're grown up?"

"Sell ice cream," I always replied. To me, that job seemed by
far the most wonderful in the world.

During the summer holidays I was sent to stay with my third

aunt, Mingguang. She, her husband, and their seven children lived in a very large apartment in Shanghai in a residence for senior dignitaries. The apartment had seven or eight rooms and was so vast that, the first time I went there, I kept getting lost. My aunt pointed out the bedrooms for her daughters and the ones for her sons. In the evenings, the ghost stories that the girls told became so terrifying that after a while our male cousin Suzhe could no longer bear to hear them and he would come to seek refuge with the girls.

Mingguang's husband was the director of an industrial group that provided electricity for the east and center of China: five provinces around Shanghai.

My uncle had been one of the first revolutionaries. He was one of the most important figures in the New China, with the rank of minister in Shanghai, and it was this that enabled his family to have such a magnificent apartment.

Keliang and Mingguang would often write to each other. Though careful not to let slip any compromising details, my mother had told her about the deteriorating situation in Beijing, and particularly within her ministry. For her part, my aunt told her sister-in-law about the difficulties she and her friends were experiencing, and the growing number of cadres who had been forced to join reeducation camps without any idea how long their punishment would last nor where it would end.

One day Mingguang informed Keliang that her husband had been sent to a reeducation camp "in the countryside." Everybody was in the same boat—anxiety, fear, and uncertainty were omnipresent—and nobody seemed to be able to escape this hurricane that swept up everything in its path. For some, the interrogations, the harassment, and the bullying became so bad that suicide appeared the only exit. In China, the "code of honor" demanding the taking of one's own life did not exist, but one's dignity could be fatally harmed. Better to die than be so deeply humiliated.

While my uncle remained in his labor camp, my aunt had been given authorization to stay in the city to look after the children, and their beautiful apartment had not been taken from them. So Mingguang revived the famous tradition of the "Yan welcome," inviting all the children in the family to stay with her during the summer. And as all the furniture except for the beds had been sold or confiscated, we would spend our days running like crazy through those huge, empty rooms. Our cheerfulness was not dimmed by the fact that there was not much to eat. Mingguang had to occasionally knock on her neighbors' doors to ask if they could lend her some money or food, but staying here still reminded me of home.

49

Imprint on his bones and engrave on his heart.

—Chinese proverb

My grandfather is taken away while I watch helplessly. I am ten years old.

I think again about that date, which, for me, marks the beginning of a long series of catastrophes. I see again my grandfather's tall figure, forcefully grabbed and shoved. An oft-quoted Chinese phrase comes to mind: "When the big tree falls, the monkeys scatter." There could be no more vivid image of what I felt at that moment: the frenzied flight of all that had, until then, lived in shelter and peace beneath the branches of the most majestic tree in the forest. The moment when the totem was hacked down with an ax.

That image, very popular in China, of the great tree felled, is taken from a novel among the most famous in the country's literary history: *Dream of the Red Chamber*, in which the author, Cao Xueqin, who lived in the eighteenth century, chronicles the ascension within the aristocracy of a family that is honored and happy under the reign of the Emperor Kangxi until that family—which was, in fact, the author's own family—falls into disgrace.

Ironically, Mao held this novel in very high esteem. Inspired by him, Marxist critics presented the book not as a love story or a morality tale but as the perfect illustration of the mechanism of man's exploitation of man, "an encyclopedia of the feudal world in decline."

Until the moment when my grandfather was arrested, I had always envisioned my family as that proverbial great tree: thick trunk, high canopy, strong branches, wide protective foliage. Now that this safe, solid shelter had been destroyed, we could do nothing but flee in a panic, each toward our unknown destiny. It was impossible for me to understand how a family until then considered honorable and prosperous could suddenly lurch into such a nightmare.

November in Beijing is quite similar to November in Europe. Winter has not quite arrived yet, but the leaves have fallen, the days growing shorter. There is still the occasional sunny day. But darkened by the climate of terror back then, November became a month of unspeakable anguish. That was the month when my heart shrank.

All year long, I dreaded dusk; I feared night and its despair; I was afraid of the dark and its loneliness. My grandfather's arrest took place at sunset. It was the same time of day when I attended, with my class, the humiliation sessions in a village on the outskirts of Beijing.

For a long time, I could not escape the shadow of those times. For a long time, at the approach of dusk, I would feel a sense of despair and loneliness. Not until the birth of my son did that twilight hour lose its power to embitter my life.

50

The individual who is condemned is guilty because he is condemned, not condemned because he is guilty.

—Lu Xun (1881–1936)

Grandfather? Senior civil servant. Suspect. Arrested.

Father? Senior civil servant. Suspect. Arrested.

Having to write that tore the skin from my fingers. As if I were being forced to betray them. As if I were made part of their punishment as bad people despite being better placed than anyone to know that they were good people.

The teacher waited for me to confess before the whole class the nature of the crimes committed by my grandfather and father. She would wait, she said, as long as it took for me to admit their crimes publicly.

There was the humiliation of seeing my own family—the

most private thing in the world—brought so low. There was my own shame, because I did not want to be known as the daughter and granddaughter of anti-revolutionaries—a defamatory word.

I would always be associated with that "black" category: my family was black, or even ultra-black, since the slur was spread through several generations. Doubly black because, while my paternal grandparents were not of bourgeois origin, my mother's ancestors worsened our position, their blackness staining our entire family in spite of the distance that my mother had put between us and them.

In the end, that family stain felt like a tattoo on my skin, a sign on my chest, an indelible inscription on my forehead.

I remember that our class was taken to a suburb of Beijing for a week to help with the harvest. At the end of each day, exhausted, we would find ourselves at a sort of evening gathering in the village. As night fell, we would watch violent scenes between the villagers and the former landowners. The accused were forced to kneel, hands tied behind their backs. And I couldn't watch because those men kneeling as the vicious peasants abused them were my grandfather, my father.

I was lost. What was the first precept in the *Three-Character Classic* that all Chinese children learned by heart and recited tonelessly in class? "Men at birth are naturally good."

From the moment that my father was arrested, my mother came under even greater pressure. As she claimed not to know the reasons why her husband had been detained, the others replied that, in that case, she had no choice but to divorce him. The idea being that, if you yourself are not incriminated, divorce was a way of making it publicly known that you wish to distance yourself from the crimes committed by your spouse, who can then no longer contaminate you. Understood in this way, divorce was a kind of protection. It authorized you and your children to remain in the city; it spared you from being sent to "the countryside."

It was demanded in particular as a way of breaking the most intimate connections between people, a way of smashing that special bond between two souls—husband and wife, father and son, brother and sister—that, most of the time, held firm even amid divergences of opinion. Divorce was not the only thing demanded in order to cause this rupture: there were public renunciations, too, often conducted in a traumatic manner.

My mother knew this. She knew that, beyond the forced divorce, there were other circumstances that led to the separation of couples. And yet she did not give in. She would not divorce my father. Her conviction was clear: her husband was innocent, and the truth would come out sooner or later. She stood up fiercely to her interrogators.

51

The greatest pain in life is the separation
of one's own flesh and blood.

—Chinese adage

Less than a month after the arrests of my grandfather and father,
my mother was placed under house arrest in her ministry.

Having seen her exert herself since the arrest of her father-
in-law, supporting Nainai at the same time as she sought information from everybody who could provide it; having seen her
hold firm, forbid herself the luxury of complaining, I had comforted myself with the idea that, as long as she was there, her
strength of character would save us all. And now this pillar, too,
had been taken from us. Stunned by this news, my first thought
was that now, in December 1967, I was ten years old and I no
longer had any parents.

However, even in a situation that forced her to organize her withdrawal from family life as quickly as possible, my mother demonstrated a dauntless sangfroid. For example, when she discovered that I had not been going to school for several months, knowing that she would soon not be able to look after me, instead of becoming angry and punishing me, my mother simply said: "I can guess what has happened, and I understand." Then she added: "There is a boarding school at the ministry now. It was designed especially for children whose parents are in more or less our situation. The simplest thing would be to enroll you there. Your new school is called Yang Fan Tian, and it's very close to the ministry, which is where you will be living." I could tell that my mother sensed my apprehension, because she immediately added: "You have nothing to fear now, Lan: the children in that school are all like you, their parents are all in the same boat. You'll see: things will be very different there . . . There is no other solution, Lan, because now that Gaosu is alone, without Yeye, until who knows when, she won't be able to look after you."

And so, in the little free time granted her by the ministry's jailers, my mother had devoted herself to organizing my new life in such a way that I would suffer as little as possible from these upheavals. In those circumstances, how could I ask her when she would return?

The only opportunities we had to see each other again were during the searches carried out in the square courtyard where my parents usually stayed. In that little courtyard, located in a *hutong* called Weijia, I had a tiny bedroom of about sixty square feet that I could use on the rare occasions when I was allowed to stay with my mother. When I met her, she would always be flanked by at least two people from her ministry whose job was to monitor her closely. She forced herself to smile at me, but I could tell that she was very tense and depressed. The first time I saw her, I threw my arms around her neck and we were brutally separated and ordered to be silent.

Other than those searches, I no longer saw my mother—or, more generally, anyone from my family—for months on end.

In the ministry building where the dormitory had been set up, there were three girls in each bedroom and six girls in each two-bedroom apartment. Ministry employees were given the task of ensuring that we went directly back to our rooms from the nearby school. What Mama had told me was true: nobody there ever mentioned their family situation. And this return to psychological comfort, after so much misery and anxiety, gradually helped me regain a little self-confidence. I started playing again, like any ten-year-old girl, and I made new friends. In fact, those friendships were all the more intense because our need for affection could no longer be expressed in a family setting. Even today, I remain good friends with some of those girls.

With hindsight, I realize that all the children in that boarding school were clearly trying to forget what they had seen. That thought alone is enough to chill me.

The need to forget was so urgent for me that I never wrote to Nainai or Mama. I never gave them my news, even though that was not only allowed but encouraged. Deep down, I saw this new situation as a blessing in disguise.

Every month, I had to go to the door of the ministry to

receive the money that would enable me to buy my canteen vouchers.

Following instructions, I had to ask for Uncle Zhao (out of respect and affection, Chinese children would call any kind adult from their parents' generation "uncle" or "aunt"; it did not necessarily imply a family connection). Uncle Zhao gave me 25 yuan, and with the money in my pocket, I would leave without having seen my mother.

It was only much later that I found out how things had been for her. "Mrs. Wu," they would say to her, "your daughter is here. Hand over the money." Is that what they call sadism? Forbidding an anti-revolutionary mother from seeing her daughter, if only for a few seconds, enough time to ask her how she is? My mother would hand the money to Uncle Zhao. I have never seen Mama cry, but she admitted to me much later that the only times it ever happened were when I was standing at the ministry entrance and they refused to let her see me. She would hide in the toilet so that nobody could see her tears.

It seems to me now, when I cry in my turn, that I am crying for all the women, all the mothers, all the grandmothers of that era.

The 25 yuan were supposed to cover all my expenses for the month. Does anybody understand such a concept at ten years old? I organized things so badly that I had invariably "eaten everything" long before the end of the month. I would stuff myself at the beginning of each month: I remember once eating in a single day about ten *baozi* (little bread dumplings, steamed and stuffed) and eight or nine large pancakes. This extreme diet—

going from gorging one day to fasting the next—ended up upsetting my stomach. Even in pain, though, I preferred the torment of hunger to the thought of going back to see my grandmother. Because I now associated the residence where she lived with far greater misery than an empty belly.

One day, a woman of my mother's age approached me at the entrance to the boarding school and asked me very kindly why I did not write to my mother. She took the time to explain to me very sweetly that Keliang was terribly worried not to have any news of her little Lan. And as if I had no concept of the situation in which we found ourselves, I remember telling her that there was no reason to worry, that everything was fine, and that, quite simply, *I had nothing to say*. My mother had used all her ingenuity to find a way to contact me through this woman so she could communicate to me her anxiety at my silence, and my only response was to tell her I did not write because I had nothing to say!

I can still see the shocked expression on that woman's face as she carefully explained to me that she would reassure my mother at once, but that I absolutely had to write to her, if only to soothe her pain. When I think about it now, I can see that there was no ingratitude or cruelty in my attitude. That apparent indifference was the only means I had found to make the suffering stop: to forget, to deny, to sweep the past away. I took refuge in the imaginary world of childhood. It was my only consolation and shelter from the horror of reality.

52

Only worthless people consider suicide.

—Lao She, *Four Generations under One Roof*, 1949

Barely had the Cultural Revolution been proclaimed than Deng Xiaoping was stripped of his duties and publicly disgraced as "agent of capitalism number two," the number one being the chairman, Liu Shaoqi.

Two years later, in May 1968, China was still in the grip of this violent storm. Deng Pufang was twenty-four years old; he was the eldest son of Deng Xiaoping and was studying nuclear physics at Peking University.

One day, Pufang was taken hostage by one of the Red Guard factions that were rampant in the university. He was tortured until he threw himself out of a fourth-floor window. It was officially declared an accident.

At the hospital to which he was transported, no doctor wanted to risk his own life by attempting to save the eldest son of the "agent of capitalism number two." A long and bitter negotiation followed between the Deng family and the staff of another hospital, depriving him of medical care for several days. In the end, Deng Pufang would survive. He would remain paraplegic and spend the rest of his life in a wheelchair.

As for his parents, Deng Xiaoping and Zhuo Lin, after being held under house arrest in Beijing, they were sent to work in a tractor-repair factory in the Jiangxi province.

The era was insane enough that it was possible for Deng Xiaoping, the best of men, to be blamed for his son's "selfishness" in throwing himself out of a window. In spite of that, Deng Xiaoping did finally write to Mao, asking that his son be sent to stay with him so he could look after him. His wish was granted. As for Pufang, once the Cultural Revolution was over, he would abandon his scientific career and devote himself entirely to the cause of the disabled.

During that same month—May 1968—my third aunt, Mingguang, had a dream. Yan Baohang appeared to her, wearing a long gray coat. He was alone and lying on a stretcher in a hospital waiting room.

Her dream seemed so real that she woke suddenly in tears, as if she had been allowed to see in a few seconds the truth of what had happened, and which we would only find out about in 1977.

Yan Baohang had been in detention for seven months, his

whereabouts unknown to his family. He was registered as prisoner no. 67100 in the special prison of Qincheng—the same place where his son Mingfu was detained eleven days after his father, registered as prisoner no. 67124. At the age of seventy-three, Yan Baohang received a violent blow during an interrogation. He fell to the ground and did not get up. He was taken to the hospital, where he died on May 22, 1968.

His family was not informed of the circumstances of his death. Not then, nor later. What we learned in the end was the result of stubborn research.

But we never found out what happened to my grandfather's body.

53

One's love, like a lotus root,
linked by fibers though divided.

—Chinese proverb

It was in the spring of 1968 that I saw my mother again.

We saw each other for the first time since she had been deprived of her liberty seven months earlier.

For an eleven-year-old, seven months is a long, long time. Conversely, the time she was allowed to spend with me that day went by at the speed of light. In the confusion and the stress of this reunion, I thought I understood that she had to leave. She was going to be "reeducated," but she was vague about how long she would be gone. "A few months," she said, then added: "But during those few months, Lan, you understand, I won't be able to come home . . ." I did not say anything, but what I was thinking was: you haven't been able to come home for months anyway! The only certainty was her destination: Zhaoyuan, in the northern province of Heilongjiang, near the Russian border, almost a thousand miles from Beijing, with temperatures that fell as low as -40°F.

Our time together was short. And so, in her dignified way, she told me: "During this . . . absence, please take good care of your grandmother, Lan. Also . . . take good care of yourself . . . Speaking of which, I have made the necessary arrangements with Mr. Zhao. You will go to the ministry every month as usual, and he will give you the money . . ."

Filled with an intense but still contained emotion, my mother asked me to accompany her to "her ministry," because the time she had been given with me was about to expire.

And I said no, I couldn't.

What I read in her eyes at first was incredulity. I noticed a slight irritation. Then she composed herself and gently argued: "It's not very far, Lan, and we can speak together a little longer if you come with me . . ."

This time, I did not answer that I couldn't go with her; I said that I didn't want to, and I gave her my reasons: "I'm supposed to go on a bike ride to the swimming pool in the Taoranting Park this afternoon with my classmates, so you see . . ."

And that was how I triggered the most tragic and thoughtless dispute of my entire life.

My mother did not understand my attitude. She begged me to be reasonable. But I stubbornly repeated that I did not want to go with her because *I didn't have time*. Finally she exploded with rage. And that was how we separated. She, devastated, left for the Heilongjiang camp, while I ran cheerfully off to meet my friends.

Not until I was in the water, amid shouts and splashes, did the truth hit me. A knot formed in my throat. Anguish overcame me. I had just understood: my mother, with whom I had just argued so pointlessly and cruelly . . . it was possible I might never see her again.

54

My house is in peril.
Beaten by the wind and the rain.
All I can do now is cry for help.

> —Wu Wang, *Book of Odes* (eleventh to sixth
> century BCE, ancient royal dynasties)

At that time, of course, I could not possibly have understood that the peremptory refusal I gave my mother was, in reality, addressed to everything I was living through. It was a refusal of the successive catastrophes that had struck me, each one taking the form of a departure: the departure of my grandfather, of my father, and now of my mother. Not to mention the departures of my aunt Mingshi, my uncles Daxin and Mingzhi, and all their families.

Yet my distress was so great that it lifted the resolve I had

imposed on myself never to go back to my grandmother's residence, as a way of distancing myself from the sufferings I had
endured in that place. I had to surrender to the obvious truth:
as much as I hated the residence, it was the only place where I
would find the one person in the world who was capable of comforting me.

Gaosu, as before, opened her arms to me. She did not reproach me for not having written to her, for never having gone
to see her. She was gentle and understanding. "You must never
lose faith," she said, to console me.

I noticed that she looked very tired. No, *tired* was not the
word: she had aged. The ayi wasn't there. I asked her how she was.

No matter how tired and aged and anxious she was by the
absence of news regarding her husband and favorite son, my
grandmother still believed that one could not tell everything to
an eleven-year-old child who had been through the things I had
been through.

So Gaosu did not tell me how, after so many years of good
and loyal service, the ayi had disappeared. She did not say that,
manipulated by one of her sons, she had walked off with all the
most precious objects in the apartment. She did not dwell on
what she felt about the most recent events of the Cultural Revolution, except to say that most people seemed to feel they had
been freed of all morality. Nor did she mention the money problems she'd been suffering since the departures of Baohang and
Mingfu. My aunt Mingguang sent her a little from Shanghai,
even if she did not have much money herself. My mother, too,

brought her whatever she could. Now even those little helping hands had been taken away.

Instead, Gaosu said only that Mingguang was insisting that she join her in Shanghai. However, she said, somebody has to be here on the day when they decide to free Baohang and Mingfu. Because she was convinced that the Party would understand the truth in the end. There was no other possibility. We must not lose faith.

55

The present can hardly stand comparison with the past.

—Chinese saying

At the end of winter 1969, in the harsh, icy province of Heilong-jiang, a series of military maneuvers inflamed both sides of the Sino-Soviet border.

Not far from there, in Zhaoyuan, the "bad elements" of the foreign liaison department had been cooped up for almost nine months.

Fearful of seeing their "reeducation program" threatened by the nearby conflict on Zhenbao Island or, worse, a contamination orchestrated by the "revisionist" Soviets—the organization of a plot aimed at luring the prisoners across the border—the Chinese authorities decided to rapidly repatriate more than a thousand cadres and intellectuals to the center of the country.

The families were informed by mail that a train carrying these "suspects" would pass through Beijing, where it would stop for about two hours in Xizhimen station, in the north of the city. It was strictly forbidden for the "suspect passengers" to go into the city. But families were authorized to visit them.

I will remember for the rest of my life the sight of the train entering the station, that day in March 1969. The platform swarming with crowds. The feverish impatience of the waiting families. And, when the passengers began to get off the train, the shouts, the frantic eyes searching, then finding, the people falling into one another's arms, the tears, the laughter, the endless embraces.

As desperately as everybody else, I tried to find Mama amid the crowd. I stared at each car until finally we met some of her colleagues, who pointed out to us the car where Wu Keliang is. We headed that way, pushing our way through the massed bodies. At last I saw her, preparing to leave the car.

She had changed so much, I hardly recognized her. I became frightened and I could see that my grandmother, too, was shocked by that vision: hair chopped off, eyes darkly ringed, skin dry and craggy from working in the sun and wind, face wrinkled beyond her years, body bundled up in a shapeless black coat, the hem gaping under an old peasant's cloak. My fear was mixed with revulsion: How could I accept that my mother had suddenly become another person? I also thought about the fact that I had hardly written to her during those nine long months, and I burst into tears.

For my mother, too, I had changed. "I hardly recognized Nan-nan," she told my grandmother, "she's grown so much!" I had turned twelve two and a half months before.

56

Now, everything is fine: the daughter-in-law
with the ungrateful expression has finally
been presented to her parents-in-law.

—Lao She, *Four Generations under One Roof,* 1949

The ideological one-upmanship was so frantic in those years that some of the hotheads who had screamed louder than anybody ultimately found themselves "out-lefted" by people even more hysterical than they, and suffered the same fate as their victims.

This was what happened to my cousin Da Pangzi, whose stooges had ended up deciding he was not as "red" as he had claimed. After all, didn't he belong to an "anti-revolutionary" family, almost all of whom were behind bars?

He was arrested and placed in detention for two years before being sent to a village in the depths of Liaoning province.

Apparently he had almost no hope for the future. But he had not yet reached the bottom.

One day, the man in charge of his village told him that he was of marriageable age and that he should give the matter serious consideration because there was no chance he would ever leave that place. He then pointed to a girl, on the other side of a soy field, and asked: "Will she do?"

Da Pangzi saw a fairly pretty peasant girl, wearing a traditional headscarf; he muttered something, and the man took this for the answer he was looking for: "All right, well, now you've made your choice, we need to fix a date!"

At country weddings, the old ritual still prevailed: the spouses would discover each other in the intimacy of the bedroom, not before.

The whole thing turned out to be a con: the girl was not the one he had been shown. His bride was horribly ugly. Seeing her, Da Pangzi had to choose between the horror of marrying this charmless woman or the dishonor of refusing to marry her.

57

If you wish to condemn somebody,
you will always find a crime.

—Chinese proverb

Sometime after our brief meeting on the station platform in Beijing, Mama wrote to me that any parents who wished it were
authorized to bring their children close to their "cadres school"
in Shenqiu, in Henan province.

I was part of a convoy of about a hundred children who went
there, most of them my friends. The boarding school was in up-
roar. We were separated into age groupings. We were given instructions for packing our bags. Although I had no idea of what
awaited me, my heart skipped a beat at the idea of this trip.

Before my departure, I had to overcome, one more time, my
aversion to the State Council residence: it was unthinkable that

I could leave without saying good-bye to my grandmother. And this reminded me of the money hidden in my fleece-lined jacket.

One evening, after the arrest of my father in November 1967 but before Mama was placed under house arrest, she carefully unstitched the lining of my fleece-lined jacket, slipped 100 yuan into the V-shaped neckline, then sewed it up again, explaining to me that I should use the money only in case of an emergency and "great need."

At twelve years old, I had no idea of how much 100 yuan was worth. I didn't know that my mother's monthly wage was less than 40 yuan!

So this was how I reasoned: given the imminence of my departure, this final visit to my grandmother undoubtedly met the category of an emergency. Besides, wasn't I in "great need" of giving her some presents to show her how much I loved her? Without a second thought, I rushed to Wangfujing Street, where some of the finest delicatessens were located. I stocked up on the best tea I could find—yellow tea, white tea, green tea, and black tea—all of it insanely expensive. And then, since cigarettes were Nainai's favorite vice, I bought several cartons of Dazhonghua luxury cigarettes.

Nainai opened the door and we fell into each other's arms. I had missed her so much. We cried a lot that night. We cried because I had to leave. And we cried because Nainai, too, was preparing to leave Beijing. "There will be nobody here to welcome them," she said, "if they come home while I'm gone."

The night before I left to join my mother in Henan, I realized that in leaving Gaosu, I was leaving not only my grandmother but also the woman who had brought me up. In that late summer of 1969, I was saying farewell to the generosity and tenderness she had sprinkled over all of my childhood. And when I found myself alone on the street outside the residence that night, for the last time before my departure, my eyes were as swollen as two peaches from all the tears I had cried.

That summer, my grandmother had been diagnosed with lung cancer. Mingguang wanted to have her examined by a famous specialist, Dr. Wu, who was head of the oncology department in the Xie He hospital, the best in Beijing.

My aunt's network of friends enabled her to write directly to this eminent doctor. This was obviously a stroke of good luck on our part. Like everybody else, though, Dr. Wu knew that we were a "problematic" family and he had to calculate the risk he would be running merely by agreeing to a consultation.

Courageously, he told Mingguang that she should bring her mother to his office in the hospital. *Courage* is not too strong a word for such an act at a time when no operation could be performed without the surgeon first quoting Chairman Mao.

In his small office, with no assistant or nurse in attendance, the doctor very carefully and very respectfully examined my grandmother. After that, he accompanied her to the radiology unit and himself took the X-rays of her lungs.

Back in the little office, he outlined the clinical picture, confirming the previous diagnosis. In terms of treatment, he recommended radiotherapy, which he said could be carried out in the best conditions in Shanghai. He also took the time to explain to my grandmother that the length of the treatment meant that she should agree to leave Beijing so she wasn't left alone. Finally, at the end of this long consultation, conducted with such gentleness and consideration, the doctor handed his prescriptions to my grandmother and offered her some cookies and chocolate that he had brought back, he said, from a recent trip to Europe. Both women were very moved by this gesture.

However, his kindness did not end there. In Shanghai, once my aunt had gathered enough money to pay for the radiotherapy, none of the hospitals in the city would agree to compromise themselves by admitting a patient who belonged to a family stigmatized by the authorities. So Mingguang had no choice but to call on Dr. Wu once again, since only his intercession would enable my grandmother's admission.

Because of the aggressive treatment, Gaosu sometimes showed signs of confusion. Once she asked Mingguang to fetch the meat so they could prepare dumplings. "And hurry," she said, "because Mingfu and Baohang will be home any minute!"

58

Wealth cannot corrupt him, poverty cannot make
him swerve from principle, threats cannot bend him.

—Mencius (372–289 BCE), Book III, Section 6

As soon as he arrived in Qincheng, my father was placed in isolation. Who occupied the cells on either side of his? He didn't
know. Anytime the prisoners attempted to communicate with
one another, the guards would burst in and brutally punish
them.

From his registration number—no. 67124—he assumed that
he must be the 124th prisoner in that corridor in the year 1967.
But nothing was certain.

The cell was brightly lit day and night, and whenever Mingfu
turned over on his straw mattress, making his face invisible
through the eyehole despite the intensity of the light, the guard

would come in and shake him awake. Mingfu deduced that this measure was intended to prevent suicides.

What most upset him was hearing the screams, the blows. Sometimes the blows would rain down until the screams fell silent. The silence afterward was worse than the screaming. There was also the cold and the hunger.

He could handle the damp, insidious cold, because Mingfu was young and in good health: nothing prevented him from keeping warm by exercising, even in that confined space. But the hunger tormented him so cruelly that, by nighttime, he found it hard to sleep.

And so, during those first nights, he would go over in his mind the possible reasons for his arrest. Each time, he remembered that, just before the Red Guards came for him, Keliang had told him that the searches carried out in their square courtyard were all ordered by Mr. Zhu.

What did that mean? That Mr. Zhu, one of the translators in the team he led, was an informer. This revelation plunged my father into despair, not because he had anything to reproach himself for—he was convinced that he would be released as soon as the whole case was brought to light—but because of the devouring ambition that had made Mr. Zhu believe that, by conniving with this or that faction of Red Guards that was considered more revolutionary than the others, he would earn a promotion. Which was not impossible in the current climate. And that was what made Mingfu despair.

So when an "investigation team" came to Qincheng to interrogate him, he was pleased: not only because he could finally have some contact with the outside world, but above all because he would be able to explain the truth of the situation.

He was quickly disillusioned. First, this group of five investigators was not even in charge of his case. The investigators were here to talk about Liu Shaoqi and Deng Xiaoping, so Mingfu's responses could in no way help him to exonerate himself. Worse, their questions about those two eminent men were not designed to discredit the accusations but to support them: they wanted Mingfu to testify for the prosecution. As far as his own case was concerned, that would be dealt with by a different group of investigators.

He was given no opportunity to explain anything to this first group. He was ordered to answer yes or no: Had he translated for "those traitors to the motherland, Liu Shaoqi and Deng Xiaoping"? Mingfu protested against this question, which presumed the men's guilt. But the investigators were not here to talk about the rights and wrongs of their investigation. They simply demanded an answer to their questions.

The same question kept recurring: "Who was responsible for the Russian translations carried out on behalf of Liu Shaoqi and Deng Xiaoping?" As soon as Mingfu acknowledged that he was, the investigator went on: "So you admit, Yan Mingfu, having served the traitors Liu Shaoqi and Deng Xiaoping, who conspired with the Soviet Union against the interests of the motherland? Why are you surprised to be in prison, along with your accomplices?" My father could feel the vise tightening around him.

After several hours of interrogation, during which my father did his best not to let himself be overwhelmed, the investigators tried another tack: they opted for the carrot instead of the stick. Mingfu was young. Hence his lack of experience regarding human nature. The investigators could be lenient toward him if he could manage to remember certain details, for example any "eloquent" looks between the traitors and the Soviets, any knowing glances that might substantiate the plot hatched by those counterrevolutionaries Liu Shaoqi and Deng Xiaoping, in cahoots with the Soviet Union, as a way of taking control of the Party.

It was made clear to Mingfu that he might be immediately released in return for "simply racking your brains until you remember something." My father admitted that the possibility of freedom was a tantalizing temptation after all he had been through since being incarcerated—and he hadn't even been beaten or tortured yet. But he could not bear false testimony in order to gain his release. This was what he told the investigators, over and over again.

The interrogation went on. The investigators were hoping to wear him down. Although Mingfu repeatedly affirmed that nothing he had ever translated for Liu Shaoqi, Deng Xiaoping, or any other leaders had concerned a plot or an attempted coup d'état, he did dig into his prodigious memory to recap the subjects, circumstances, protagonists, places, and dates when he had been called upon to translate for them. But never, he emphasized, had there been any suspect glances between the Chinese and the Soviets.

He was wasting his breath: the question about "knowing looks" became obsessive. And each time they posed it, there was an added degree of threat behind their words: if proof of this "collusion" was discovered, Mingfu's sentence would be doubled.

The umpteenth mention of the "transceiver found in Yan Baohang's apartment, which Yan Baohang himself admitted he was keeping for his son" was finally enough to erode my father's composure. Yielding to anger, Mingfu replied that the Soviet embassy would be only too happy to confirm to the investigators that this "clandestine communication device" was in fact an ordinary radio.

His insolence was noted, along with other disagreeable aspects of Mingfu's personality, such as his arrogance and his manner of responding to their questions with questions of his own, all of which could only harm him in the delicate situation in which he found himself.

Finally, the investigation group in charge of Lu Dingyi's case arrived. My father felt no relief: he had just learned that the various investigations might take several years.

The new group was composed of three investigators. During each interrogation, their leader would sip from a cup of his personal tea, between volleys of questions.

From the start, the man with the cup steered the interrogation toward the exchanges between the Soviet ambassador and Lu Dingyi, as translated by Yan Mingfu.

Yan Mingfu was well aware of the career of Lu Dingyi. A leader of the Communist Party of China, he had famously joined the party at nineteen and, despite having trained as an engineer, had demonstrated a long-term interest in questions of culture, the press, and propaganda. Mingfu had met him in 1957. He was a member of one of the delegations that accompanied Mao Zedong to Moscow. Mingfu remembered that Lu Dingyi had been present with Liu Shaoqi and Deng Xiaoping during their trips to the Soviet Union. He also remembered that, after being entrusted with the culture portfolio in Zhou Enlai's 1965 government, the minister Lu Dingyi had been accused, in the spring of 1966, of promoting policies that did not conform to the ideals of the Great Proletarian Cultural Revolution: a "reactionary" line that soon led to his forced resignation.

My father knew all of this, and he confirmed this to the shifty-eyed tea drinker. At the same time, he reiterated what he had already told them: he had never translated for Lu Dingyi.

The man with the cup did not blink: "Do you deny that you, Yan Mingfu, translated words defaming Mao Zedong, words spoken by Lu Dingyi to the Soviet authorities?" My father repeated what he had already said: he had never translated for Lu Dingyi. Absurdly, the man with the cup replied: "Well, it's very simple: unless you confess, Lu Dingyi will be executed!" Mingfu furiously demanded to know if the man was trying to force him to bear false witness, but the interrogation was brought to a sudden end for the day. This was a technique designed to push prisoners over the edge.

The tea drinker's strategy evolved. If my father did not confess that he had translated the anti-Mao words spoken by the traitor minister Lu Dingyi, then he, Yan Mingfu, would be summarily executed. My father's attitude, too, evolved in response to these threats. He responded that at least if he was executed, he wouldn't be able to bear false witness! Such was the price he was ready to pay for a clear conscience.

My father saved himself by not giving up. He continued to analyze the process he was being put through, in which the removal of freedom was intended to turn that freedom into a bargaining chip.

Calumny in exchange for liberty. Become an informer if you wish to become a free man again. It must have been hard to resist the temptation to enter this infernal circle once he had realized that he was its victim. It had required another informer, after all—Mr. Zhu—to bring Yan Mingfu into this interrogation process in the first place.

Despite the lure of freedom to any wrongly imprisoned man, my father revolted against the injustice of this system.

A man's courage can be measured against the number of years he spends behind bars, separated from his family. But what yardstick could be used to measure courage against a regime like that? At what point does such courage become heroism?

I don't know.

All I can say is that, in my father's generation, many people had to ask themselves those questions. Because many people, during that moment in Chinese history, were caught in a vise, with no idea how long their ordeal would go on, nor even if they would survive it.

59

Near a big tree, there is never any lack of fuel.

—Chinese proverb

Winter 1969: I joined Mama in Henan province, where I would
spend the next five years.

It was in that place, between the ages of twelve and seventeen, that I was able to realize just how privileged I had been
before.

In the early days, I categorically refused to wear the fleece-
lined clothes that were the uniform of people in that region, giving them all the same bulging outline. "Don't be ridiculous," my
mother told me. "There are enough problems here already without building our own. Like doing everything you can to make
yourself fall ill."

This was our first fight. It did not last long. I had been raised by my grandmother, so to me, my mother seemed a sort of friend whom I didn't know very well. With time, we learned to support each other. And I can testify that what my mother had to endure in that camp was far worse than she wanted to admit in a small book she wrote for her family, whose title, *My Life in Suffering and Joy*, was taken from a Chinese saying that recalls Apollinaire's line: "Joy came always after pain."

As for myself, honesty compels me to admit that I was not really all that unhappy.

The labor camp reserved exclusively for "problematic cadres" such as my mother was organized on military lines. Each person belonged to a rank, a company, a garrison. Mama "worked" at the brickworks in the village.

Each garrison was located in or near a different village. In the dormitories filled with collective beds, men and women were separated, even married couples. Children were allowed to stay with the women only one night each week, when the occupants of those shared beds had no option but to squeeze closer together to make space.

Mama's dormitory had two rows of collective beds. Seven women in each row. The dormitory was located at the entrance of the village, not far from an orchard of apple and pear trees. It was home to the third company, which included my mother and many of her colleagues from the foreign liaison department.

In the shared bed, Mama occupied a place between two other women. One of them, I called "Aunt Xu He." I gave her that affectionate name because she was older than my mother. I could tell that their friendship had grown stronger through their shared experience of being scapegoated, suffering more than the others from the viciousness of the criticism sessions and monitored more closely, too, even inside the dormitory. I would sleep between the two of them.

Aunt Xu He was the wife of Wu Xiuquan, the deputy foreign minister until 1955, in charge of international issues on the Central Committee. A veteran of the Long March, he had accompanied Zhou Enlai to Moscow in 1950 to finalize the treaty of friendship and mutual assistance between the USSR and China. He was part of the delegation sent to Moscow for Stalin's funeral. He was also the first Chinese ambassador in Belgrade, from 1955 to 1958, where my mother first met him. It was through Aunt Xu He that I came to realize my family was not the only one persecuted. There were many victims, and they were not criminals but senior civil servants, ministers, important people. This changed my way of seeing things: I felt slightly less ashamed.

Unlike my mother, who did not know where her husband was, or even if he was still alive, Aunt Xu He knew that her husband was in prison somewhere.

After a day of forced labor from which they came back exhausted—my mother's back was extremely painful—they were then the targets of denunciations for "counterrevolutionary crimes" and complicity. Subjected to long self-criticism sessions, they had to denounce their husbands in order to help them "choose their side."

I once managed to sneak into one of those sessions. That was how I understood that my mother and Aunt Xu He were the main target of criticism in the company.

Head lowered, my mother listened. Then, when she was questioned, she replied that she had nothing to say. This was not what was expected of her. Like all the others, she was supposed to criticize her husband even more fiercely than the others had done. The objective was to set up a sort of denunciation competition, the winners of which would be able to prove that they had made "ideological progress." I need hardly say how much I hated those women who, during the day, pretended to be my mother's friends and then, in the evening, harried her like hyenas.

I lived with other children, not far from the small town of Shenqiu, in an old, vast private property whose many buildings had been requisitioned to create a boarding school. The children slept, separated by sex and age, ten to each dormitory.

The living conditions were rudimentary: there was no water, no electricity. The organization was military: we woke to the sound of a gong or a whistle and exercised before fetching the water for washing and cooking, passing the buckets along in a long line from the well.

We were organized into brigades, each with a specific task. But it wasn't so bad because it was the same for everybody. Not only that, but the buildings that housed our dormitories were so vast and full of nooks and crannies that they were perfect for playing hide-and-seek. We were spared the opprobrium that was directed at our parents in the camp.

During the week, we walked in line to school. The children of my age went to the number one middle school in Shenqiu, where the children from the town and the surrounding villages also went. Some of the disgraced cadres who had good degrees from the region's universities were allowed to become teachers at the middle school.

Compared to Beijing, Shenqiu struck me with its calmness and order, the way the students followed the rules of politeness and showed respect to their teachers, which I had not imagined was still possible. For us children, it was as if the storm of the Cultural Revolution had not reached this part of the country-side, as if the Confucian values of respect for one's elders had never been questioned.

The children of the local peasants watched us from a distance for a while before daring to approach us and, in some cases, to touch us. Each group regarded the other as extraterrestrials, until that first impression faded. In reality, the local students turned out to be very good academically. Disciplined, focused, and studious, they knew that going to the best middle school in the town was, for them, a big opportunity, and they had no intention of letting it slip.

This return to the peacefulness of academic study, in classes where nobody cared about our families or our social origins, only about abilities, helped me regain my self-confidence, and I soon returned to my habitual position at the top of the class. Nainai's fable, the Adventures of Old Sai, came to my mind, along with the moral it had taught me: sometimes a curse is a blessing in disguise. What did it matter if we had to study by the light of oil lamps in the evening? It was quite funny, in fact, seeing our noses stained black because we had moved too close to the wick.

How lucky I felt to have old friends with me, and to be able to make new ones! There was a small group of girls a little older than me, with whom I got along splendidly.

First, there was Xiao Ke, or Little Ke (*Xiao* is an affectionate diminutive). A plump little girl with a strong character. I felt very close to her because her life story was so similar to mine: her mother worked in the same ministry as my mother, and she, like me, had no idea where her father was. In fact, her story was worse than mine: her father had been accused of being a rightist in 1957 and her parents had been forced to divorce. Her mother had remarried, and then her second husband—Xiao Ke's stepfather, a renowned intellectual—had been thrown in prison.

Our small group of inseparable friends also included Yang and Shan Shan. I sometimes caught the train to Shanghai with them during the holidays, when I was on my way to see my aunt Mingguang and they were traveling back to their hometown. Of the four of us, Yang was the most gifted in poetry and literature. She was capable of reciting poems not only from the Tang dynasty, but also by Balzac, Hugo, Tolstoy . . . She had a particular predilection for Dumas and Stendhal, and we would often ask her to tell us the stories of *The Count of Monte Cristo* or *The Red and the Black*. Shan Shan, the prettiest of us all, possessed a calligraphy as beautiful as she was; it was so remarkable that her homework was sometimes pinned to the classroom walls. And while their mothers worked in the fields and mine worked at the brickworks, I have to confess that we girls were protected from the horrors that were inflicted on our parents. We sensed, obscurely, that it was our youth that protected us, and we guarded that youth jealously, aware that it was the only thing that guaranteed us a sort of innocence. The misery that prowled around us forged friendships that nothing would ever break.

On Saturdays, we were allowed to visit our parents. The distance from the center of Shenqiu to Mama's dormitory was about six miles, and several of us would walk it together or, when we were lucky, ride on a cart or in the bed of a truck, singing at the tops of our voices all the way.

For Mama, there was no weekend, at least not to start with. She was the only woman to work at the brickworks, and she was forced to work like a man: barefoot, her pant legs rolled up. She and about twenty men stood in a circle, stamping and kneading a mixture of earth, finely chopped hay, and water, which was then poured into wooden molds in the shapes of bricks and cooked in the kilns for several nights.

This work required strength and physical resilience. Most people said it was much harder than working in the fields. It is difficult to imagine anything harder.

In the evenings when I was with her, even though she was worn out, her body aching, she never cursed anybody or anything. She told me how relieved she felt to have me with her, even if it hurt her to know that I had to share her sad fate. Then she composed herself and forced herself to smile and joke: "Think how lucky you are, Lan! If you weren't my only child, you'd have to share all this with your brothers and sisters, and then it wouldn't be nearly as much fun!"

It seemed to me that the fatigue and physical pain were easier for her to bear than the psychological harassment that she suffered on a daily basis. I admired her moral strength and the tenacity needed to never admit she was beaten, despite the ordeal of those cruel criticism sessions. She never hid from me how harsh and unpleasant the others were to her, but each time I saw her after one of those sessions, she told me: "We must never lose faith in the Party." When I dared ask her about my father, she promised me that, one day, justice would be done, and that "the Party will put things right." And I believed her.

The only harsh aspect of our lives that spared nobody was food, because all of us, adults and children, ate the same meals. Throughout the first year of my stay, the food was terrible: it tasted awful and had almost no nutritional value. Since there was no wheat or rice, sweet potatoes were the main ingredient of our meals because they grew in even the least fertile soil. Cut in slices and then dried, the sweet potatoes were ground into a black flour that was used to make small loaves of sticky bread, very acidic-tasting and hard to digest, even when steamed. Eating this on a regular basis gave us chronic digestive problems and stomach pains, which I had already suffered during my last year in Beijing. It was only after three years that the cadres in the villages were told to dig a vegetable garden and run a pig farm, with the food produced being given mostly to the children.

In the spring of the following year, my mother was allowed, at the end of the week, to take me for a ride on the back of her bicycle. She used this time, which seemed to belong just to us, to initiate me into the beauty of poems from the Tang dynasty, which she loved more than any others, particularly those by Li Houzhu, the deposed emperor, imprisoned at the start of the Song dynasty, who wrote about captivity and the sadness of separation:

> You say your name: your face comes to my mind.
> Since our separation, the world has changed;
> Words freeze, the evening bell rings out.
> Tomorrow, we will take the road to Hunan;
> How many autumn mountains must we cross?

Sometimes, she would tell me about her travels in Europe, about Paris, about Balzac and Zola, about Hugo and Maupassant, whose stories I had already started reading in Beijing, thanks to her. Other times, she would recount episodes from the famous *Water Margin*, a collection of tales from the Ming dynasty, in the sixteenth century, which is one of the four classic Chinese novels, along with *Journey to the West*, *Dream of the Red Chamber*, and *Romance of the Three Kingdoms*, entire portions of which she would recite, with such a feel for storytelling and suspense that I half expected to see tigers and bandits surge out of the landscape through which we traveled.

Those texts were never taught at school. They were forbidden books. Just like the works of Li Yu, some of whose poems she could recite by heart, to my astonishment:

> Cut but not broken
> Mastered but still chaotic
> Such is the sorrow of separation
> It is also a very strange taste at the apex of the heart.

So it was not only her physical and moral courage, her rectitude, that I admired; it was also her willingness to fill the shortcomings in our education during that time and her desire to share with me the sophistication and richness of the culture that fully inhabited her.

During the 1970s, she found out that her father had died. He was seventy years old. Ten months later, when another letter announced the death of her mother, we were given special authorization to travel to Tianjin, the city to which she had not returned since finishing school. And I sensed that the rupture that had been imposed between her and her family now filled her with such a feeling of waste that I didn't even dare bring the subject up. It was not so much during the funeral, with my maternal family, that I noticed how moved my mother was, as during a long private talk when she told me about how her generation had suffered the arbitrary hazards of history. I remember how, in that moment, she prophesied a future of prosperity in China, a happy future for her descendants, freed from the weight she had felt at not being in control of her destiny. The feeling of being shackled was so strong in her that she was, she told me, almost jealous of me.

Our bodies weakened by the food we ate and the water we drank (water that was often unclean or stagnant, where mosquitoes and bacilli thrived), we were prone to dysentery, malaria, and other chronic infections, often fatal.

One evening, I was laid low by a spectacular outbreak of fever caused by dysentery. They rushed me to the hospital, where the doctors decided to warn my mother because my comatose state made them fear I would be dead before daybreak. There was nothing very extraordinary about this: child mortality in the countryside was still very high back then. My mother stayed by my bedside all night long. After three days on a drip, I was slowly recovering, but they kept me under observation. Mama, who rode her bike to the hospital to come and see me every day, began to look hopeful again, despite the fatigue and anxiety engraved on her face.

But soon, the bicycle she had borrowed was stolen. She told me then: "They say bad things come in threes, so if for any reason I'm ever prevented from coming to watch over you, you should find a way to get back to Beijing and go to your father's office in Zhongnanhai. They'll look after you there." I had an acute awareness then of her distress and perhaps even her certainty that she would spend the rest of her life in that camp. All the same, what she had just told me, despite the fact that she hadn't heard anything about my father's fate since his arrest, proved that she retained an unshakeable faith in the future. I looked at her and forced myself to find the strength to reassure her: "Don't worry, Mama, nothing bad will happen to you. Everything will be fine, you'll see . . ."

60

He is in deep anxiety and a day seems like a year.

—Chinese proverb

In May 1968, more than six months after his arrest, Mingfu was still held in isolation.

He was not allowed any communication with the outside world, and in Qincheng he had no right to any contact with the other prisoners. All he heard from them was the distant sound of talking, screaming, weeping.

Mingfu had no way of shaving or cutting his hair or his nails. He had enough water only for a cursory wash and use of the toilet. Mingfu came to realize that the lack of hygiene was just as trying as the complete isolation, the cold, the hunger, the stark light that shone on him day and night.

He ended up following the guards' unwritten rules: keeping

his face turned to the door when he slept and never lying on the floor. This last rule he learned to his cost: one day, when he was focused on the relaxation that was a necessary precursor to the practice of *tai-chi-chuan*, he was kicked brutally out of his reverie. He never made the same mistake again.

His daily meal consisted of rice soup with a few vegetables floating in it, with a small piece of corn bread. This meager ration, rather than soothing his hunger, only served to cruelly whet his appetite.

But one thing that the prisoners in Qincheng could not be deprived of was the pleasure of hearing the Beijing monks sing. That sound was what Mingfu clung to every morning to keep his head above the dark water. Because there is no better expression of vital energy and joy than those cascading songs. In his memoirs, my father explains how listening attentively, for seven and a half years, enabled him to distinguish the melodies, their frequency and their keys.

Mingfu worried about the effects of his isolation. His interrogators never gave him any indication of how long it would last. In that place, everything was arbitrary. So, to keep himself sane, he practiced a sort of mental gymnastics. He sang. In a very low voice, so nobody would bother him. His aim was to prevent his memory and reasoning from rusting over, and to avoid boredom.

He sang anything he could think of: the couplets of "Songhua River" (although that patriotic song from the 1930s was strictly forbidden), nursery rhymes from his childhood, and Soviet revolutionary songs learned during his university years.

He was allowed one newspaper (the *People's Daily*) and one book (*Quotations from Chairman Mao*, of course), and he used these texts to help him with a series of exercises designed to maintain his cerebral activity. He forced himself to learn passages by heart. Then he translated them into Russian to refresh his vocabulary. Sometimes it would take him hours, even days, to remember a particular adverb or noun, but he never gave up. He talked to himself in Chinese and in Russian. Sometimes he would stop in the middle of his exercises at the memory of all those people for whom he had acted as interpreter and translator; all those high-ranking leaders . . . what had become of them? So many seemed to have vanished from public life.

One exception was Marshal Lin Biao. To judge from the articles in the *People's Daily*, which always described him as "Chairman Mao's intimate comrade-in-arms," Lin Biao had not yet fallen from his pedestal. Another exception was apparently Jiang Qing, Mao Zedong's last wife, to judge from the loudspeakers and the guards' radios that, at all hours, broadcast the only eight revolutionary operas authorized by the Cultural Revolution. The other exception, obviously, was Mao himself, whose name was always uttered with absolute veneration.

Before the end of spring 1968, Mingfu was given forty minutes outside every day, in an open-air courtyard. Despite the barbed wire, the watchtowers, the armed guards, my father found joy in those precious minutes spent in the spring sunshine, breathing the smell of the nearby countryside. He even took pleasure in the sight of weeds growing through crevices between the stones. He hoped to be freed before the return of winter. He had no idea that he was still in the first year of an incarceration that would last more than seven years.

Later, when he was free, he would learn that at the end of that winter of 1968, the high number of deaths among the most vulnerable prisoners had provoked the intervention of Zhou Enlai. It was due to this intervention that my father was allowed a weekly shower, clippers to cut his beard and hair, bigger food rations, and a piece of meat once a week.

With an average of three readers per copy, the *People's Daily* was the most eagerly awaited cellmate of all. It was the prisoners' sole connection with the outside world, their only source of information, even if that information was sometimes relayed only as an absence of information. The most remarkable example of this was the complete disappearance, after the summer of 1971, of Lin Biao's name. Without any explanation, the name of "Chairman Mao's intimate comrade-in-arms" simply vanished from the news.

The reason was only revealed a year later, in September 1972, when the *People's Daily* stated that Lin Biao had been the ringleader of a plot aimed at assassinating Chairman Mao between September 8 and 10, 1971, in cahoots with his son, Lin Liguo. His daughter Lin Liheng denounced the two traitors. After being unmasked, the ex-marshal decided to flee to the USSR with his family, his accomplices, his allies. His airplane ran out of gas and crashed on September 13, 1971, on a desert plateau in Mongolia. There were no survivors. In the weeks that followed, the army was purged of all its high-ranking officers.

In the summer of 1973, Mao was concerned about the fate of

the Party cadres still in prison, at least those whose investigations had not proved their guilt. Zhou Enlai was quick to express this "concern" to the Political Bureau of the Central Committee, accompanied by a request to have this point deliberated. But there was a sizeable obstacle to this resolution, in the person of Jiang Qing, Mao's wife, who was now a crucial member of the Gang of Four—with Zhang Chunqiao (permanent member of the Political Bureau), Yao Wenyuan (member of the Political Bureau), and Wang Hongwen (vice-chairman of the Party)—and who attempted to scuttle the decision by not turning up to the discussions or by opposing the release of a single prisoner, all of whom, she reminded her husband, had been arrested with his agreement.

Mao returned to this issue in 1974. He received the same urgent support from Zhou, and the same stubborn resistance from Jiang Qing.

In March 1975, Mao threatened to incarcerate anybody who opposed the release of prisoners incriminated without proof. It was from this date that the investigation groups rushed to conclude their investigations and a large number of political prisoners lined up in the hope of finally being released.

61

Know glory in yourself
Accept disgrace.

—Laozi (571–471 BCE), *Tao Te Ching:*
The Book of the Way and Its Virtue

When I recall the landscape of Henan that I knew between twelve and seventeen, when I see again the laboriously cultivated fields, the villages surrounded by deep countryside, I find it hard to believe that this province has become the most polluted in China.

This thought brings back to me a harrowing episode, which could not happen now due to the radical changes in transport networks and population density.

One Sunday evening, I had to go back to the boarding

school. It was dark and raining. Mama decided to go with me so I wouldn't be alone on the empty, muddy road.

I remember that, together, we walked the twenty *li* (six miles) that separated us during the week. After dropping me at the school, my mother had to make the return journey alone. Watching her disappear into the deep black night, under a curtain of rain, I felt terribly anxious. She was the only member of my family who still lived close to me.

In Shenqiu, the consequences of our poor diet—albeit less poor than the adults' diet—also caused us skin problems. In my dormitory, there were very few girls whose faces and bodies were not covered with spots.

The female doctor in the rural cooperative system, put in place in 1968 as part of the Cultural Revolution, attributed these skin disorders to an allergic reaction caused by our bodies' habituation to city life. This woman was what was known as a "barefoot doctor"—in other words, a sort of nurses' aide, very useful in the countryside, where there were practically no doctors.

Following a speech by Mao in 1965 that questioned the country's medical system, a six-month program of medical and paramedical training was implemented, designed to support traditional doctors in rural areas. This program was aimed in particular at young people of peasant stock, and that was how this young woman from Shenqiu began to teach us a few principles of traditional medicine, including acupuncture, which interested me greatly.

She taught us the points on the body that we could touch to

reorganize the energy flows. In the evenings, in our dormitory, I would practice on my friends, testing those points on Xiao Ke, Yang, and Shan Shan, who all agreed that I had a gift for this type of healing.

I memorized the main acupuncture points and experimented with the use of needles on my own body. I learned the principles of harmony and equilibrium between yin and yang, which are the basis of the traditional conception of Chinese medicine, and the use of plants in healing—a highly practical skill in the countryside, where there was hardly any medicine at all.

I also learned a great deal from Tian Lao Shi. According to custom, the term *Lao Shi* appended to the family name denotes a master. So, Master Tian was my math teacher at the number one middle school in Shenqiu.

A woman as thin as a straight line, Master Tian made me gloriously happy when I received maximum marks and filled me with despair when she gave me only nineteen out of twenty. When, sad-faced, I would report these "bad marks" to my mother, she would gently scold for me being so silly and advise me to go and have fun with my friends. But I was completely obsessed with my school results.

The teachers at my school were the best in the region. All the villagers and local peasants wanted to send their children to the number one middle school in Shenqiu. And this healthy competition between the children spurred me so strongly that Master Tian would order me, in her severe voice with its Henan accent, to lower my hand and let my classmates speak for a change.

In the spring of 1971, my mother received the authorization for me to go to Shanghai over the summer to visit my grandmother. I had been invited by Mingguang. Despite all the changes in their lives, my third aunt and my mother still wrote to each other regularly. I was extremely happy at this news.

I will always remember that Saturday in July, the day before my departure. I was alone in Mama's dormitory when a letter arrived from Shanghai. It was from my third aunt. Excitedly, I tore it open. But when I read what the letter said, I collapsed in sobs. My grandmother was dead. She had died on July 13. In the whole of my life, I had never felt such pain. Losing the person I loved more dearly than any other . . . it felt like the sky had fallen in on me.

The next day, on the train, I felt as if I were on my way to bury my whole childhood. In Henan, I had grown to know and love Mama, but I was still more viscerally attached to my grandmother.

Thankfully, in Shanghai, I learned that my grandmother had not been alone toward the end. Two of her daughters had been with her: Mingguang, who had welcomed her into her vast apartment, and Mingshi, her eldest daughter. Because, while Mingshi had been sent to a labor camp in Anshan, where she had suffered terrible emotional and physical violence, Mingguang had managed to obtain authorization for her sister to come and visit their mother during her last days.

Just before she died, Gaosu had dictated a letter to Zhou Enlai. First, she wanted Zhou to know that Baohang, her husband, and Mingfu, her son, were both innocent.

Second, Gaosu asked the prime minister if he would cover

the costs of her medical and funeral bills. She dared to ask this because she remembered the aid that she and Baohang had given to so many compatriots who were fighting against the Japanese, as well as so many communist comrades pursued by the Kuomintang during the civil war.

She had died the next day, after passionately telling her daughters to keep faith in the Party. "Despite this drift into persecution," she added, after admitting to her daughters that she couldn't stop thinking about her "dear Xiaofu"—the affectionate diminutive she had always used when talking about my father.

But how could her daughters manage to get that letter to Zhou Enlai in such troubled times? The two sisters decided to pass it on to their sister-in-law Shu Ti. Because, while Shu Ti no longer worked as a teacher, having been sent to the coal mines in Mentougou, at least that district was close to Beijing. Shu Ti opted for the simplest, most ordinary approach. After writing this address on the envelope—"For the attention of the prime minister, Mr. Zhou Enlai, State Council"—she stuck a stamp on it, then slid it into the mailbox closest to the Zhongnanhai.

Soon afterward—to her great surprise, since she didn't expect Zhou Enlai to be in a position to help anybody in times such as those—Shu Ti was informed that, on the prime minister's instructions, all of her mother-in-law's medical and funeral bills would be reimbursed in commemoration of the many sacrifices Gaosu had made for the revolution.

In July 1971, my stay in Shanghai was almost over when Mingguang and Mingshi were informed of this development. They were very moved, particularly since the Cultural Revolution had overturned so many seemingly solid lives. And Zhou Enlai, it was whispered, was gravely ill.

Nobody was talking about the arrival in Beijing, that same month, of Henry Kissinger, President Nixon's national security advisor. His task was to lay the groundwork for Nixon's official visit to Beijing, a first for an American head of state. The visit was planned for February 1972.

Kissinger's visit was kept strictly confidential in China because it meant no explanation need be given as to why an invitation had been offered to the United States, still stigmatized in Chinese propaganda as the country's number one enemy. "Down with American imperialism!" was one of many anti-US slogans on display by the road that ran from the airport to Kissinger's residence.

The Americans, meanwhile, were hoping to influence domestic public opinion about the Vietnam War.

During the first months of 1972, the political pressure seemed to gradually lighten, both in our province and elsewhere.

Nobody knew the reasons for this new, softer approach. We were not yet aware that it was connected to the death of Lin Biao, on September 13, 1971.

The first effect of this new approach was that Mama was moved from the brickworks to the kitchen. I was slightly stunned to see how this "promotion" gave courage and hope to my sophisticated, polyglot mother, even though we still didn't know if my father was alive. I admired how her strength of character, her physical and emotional resistance, enabled her to come through so many tests and humiliations without losing any of her dignity.

One day, before I went back to my boarding school, she handed me a jar to embellish my sparse daily diet: a meat pâté that she had made herself. The smile that lit up her forty-year-old face seemed to return to her all of her former beauty. I still remember the delicious taste of that pâté, which I shared with my friends. It was all gone within two days.

62

When the Way reigns under Heaven, it is
not for ministers to decide policy and simple
subjects should not even discuss it.

—Confucius (551–479 BCE), *Analects*, XVI, 2

Although Deng Xiaoping had been stripped of all his responsibilities in 1968, then exiled to deepest Jiangxi with his wife, Lin Biao's death enabled him to gradually return to his duties.

It is true that the sinister Gang of Four, promoted at the Party's tenth congress in 1973, still controlled the levers of power. Nevertheless, in February of that year, Deng Xiaoping was recalled to Beijing.

Mao always treated Deng Xiaoping and Liu Shaoqi differently. His attitude toward Liu changed gradually during the 1960s, when their opinions began to diverge on issues such as the country's economic recovery and China's progress along the path to socialism. The Cultural Revolution was a rejection of Liu Shaoqi, who had originally been named by Mao as his successor before being denounced as an avatar of Khrushchev and a capitalist in communist's clothes. All the more so as the country's strong economic results during the 1960s gave Mao the feeling that Liu had become a threat to his power. So Mao was determined to bring his adversary down, or at least ensure that he would never recover his former status.

With Deng Xiaoping it was different, because Mao had always admired his talent, even if Deng had upset him by following Liu's recommendations on agricultural reform and economic development.

At the start of the Cultural Revolution, Mao named Lin Biao as his potential successor. Mao asked Lin Biao to maintain good relations with Deng, because Mao wanted to continue using his talents. But Deng and Lin Biao clashed, leading to Deng's quasi-disappearance during Lin Biao's ascension. Despite that, Mao did not expel Deng Xiaoping from the Party. The two men maintained contact, whether directly or through Wang Dongxing, the secretary-general of the Central Committee bureau, and without using Lin Biao or Jiang Qing (who saw Deng as a threat) as intermediaries. And when Mao appointed Lin Biao as his successor, he did so without total conviction. Deng, exiled to a tractor factory, wrote regularly to Wang Dongxing, who passed his letters on to Mao.

On August 3, 1972, Deng, having heard about Lin Biao's disappearance, wrote to Mao to assure him of his support. At the same time, he wrote a self-criticism, recognizing the mistakes he had made and making clear that he still wished to be useful to his country. In the margin of that letter, Mao wrote on August 14, 1972: "I support the rehabilitation of Deng." But in the Political Bureau, the Gang of Four, led by Jiang Qing, firmly opposed Mao's decision. Not until March 10, 1973, when Zhou Enlai, by then the prime minister, wrote a report for Mao, who approved it, was Deng recalled as vice-premier of the State Council.

It was also in the spring of 1973 that the investigators in charge of my father's case gave their conclusions: after technical verifications, they reported, "the radio set kept by Yan Baohang for his son Yan Mingfu was not a machine designed to send and receive coded messages with the Soviet Union, but an ordinary, Chinese-made radio." Moreover, Mr. Zhu's allegations that Yan Mingfu had committed "treason on behalf of the Soviet Union turned out to be unfounded." Mingfu was asked to sign the report. After that, he had to wait for this document to be submitted to the central government for approval before he could be released.

In Henan, too, there were notable changes from 1973 onward. The "problematic" cadres whose "reeducation" was complete were, one by one, authorized to return to the capital. Keliang was not among them. All the same, she was given another assignment that would completely change the conditions of her exile: she was to be allowed to assist the English teachers at the number one middle school in Shenqiu. Not only that, but she could leave her dormitory and live in one of the Zhangjiawan buildings where I was a boarder. My mother and I were now allowed to live together. As I was now beginning the final year of my secondary education, Mama decided to give me private lessons because I had to prepare as best I could for the degree that I would have to take in Beijing if I wanted it to be nationally recognized. If not, I would be obliged to remain in Henan.

The letters between my mother and her sisters-in-law confirmed an undeniable softening in all areas of the regime. Encouraged, Mama decided to write to the central government about my father. After all those years of uncertainty, we were immensely relieved to find out that he was still alive, held in the special prison in Qincheng, and that my mother could apply for authorization to visit him.

As soon as she received this authorization, Mama left for Beijing. From there, she wrote to me. Then I in turn requested the right to see my father during the school holidays. But where could I stay?

My parents' square courtyard in Weijia Hutong had been confiscated. The same was true for the apartment in the State Council's residence. My first uncle, Daxin, was still exiled in a camp in Ningxia, but his apartment in Beijing was empty, so that was where we stayed.

63

It is hard to meet, but hard to part too,

the east wind languid, hundreds of flowers wasted.

A sprint silkworm may not stop spinning silk after death.

A candle's tears dry

only when it is burned down to ashes.

In the morning's bronze mirror,

you worry about the change in your hair,

and you feel the moonlight cold, reading alone in the night.

Mount Penglai, so celebrated in fairy tales,

cannot be located far away:

O bluebird, please go there kindly, and take a look for me.

> —Li Shang Yin (813–858), "Hard to
> Meet but Hard to Part Too"

In the spring of 1974, after six years of separation, my parents were reunited. As soon as my father saw my mother, he under-

stood how much she had suffered. It was Keliang who stood before him. How could he not recognize her? It was she, but it was
also another woman.

The strangeness was not caused by the coarse cloth of her
peasant clothing, but by the youth that had been erased from
her face, the sparkle that had been extinguished in her eyes. In
spite of her smile, she wore a mask of indelible sadness, a deep
fatigue that had left her features heavy and drawn. Keliang was
only forty-three, but she looked much older.

They did not ask each other how they were. They were alive.
They were in good health. They felt blessed.

She had brought him some books and chocolate. Exactly the
things he had missed most. She told him that his daughter was
working very hard to be the best. Exactly what he had wanted
to hear. She told him she had been afraid for him. Exactly as he
had been for her. She told him: now, everything will be all right.
Exactly what he himself hoped. Mingfu had not slept for several
days, so excited had he been to see her again.

In June, it was my turn to see him. I have an extraordinary
memory of that expedition with my cousin Jiaojiao, the daughter of my uncle Daxin and aunt Shu Ti. We had arranged an
appointment in Beijing at the Ministry of Transport. Two soldiers held books so that we would recognize them. They were
in a jeep. During the journey that took us out of Beijing, I came
to understand that they belonged to the investigation group in
charge of my father's case. One of them talked about how intelligent my father was, and I felt myself swell with pride.

We soon arrived in a steep-sided valley. The special prison, surrounded by barbed wire and watchtowers, was built against a hillside. Outside the gates, the soldier declared: "Your father's situation has been more or less cleared up. It'll be okay."

We went into a large square courtyard, from where we were led to a visiting room containing only one table and a few chairs. The room felt bare and empty, an impression augmented by the echo effect when we spoke. I had the feeling I was being spied on, as if somebody were listening to my words, perhaps recording them.

After about ten minutes, prisoner no. 67124 was announced as being on his way to the waiting room. My father had become a number. There he was in the doorway, escorted by two guards.

He was dressed in prisoner's clothing: black cotton pants and jacket. His head was shaved, and he was very pale, very thin. But he was the same man. I, on the other hand, had changed a lot. For a fraction of a second, I saw his eyes darting from Jiaojiao to me before calling out: "Lan, I hardly recognized you!"

We had agreed not to tell him about the death of his mother and father for the moment. We didn't want to leave him alone in his cell with his grief. He was too weak to bear that. The loving lie we told him was that his parents had moved to Hangzhou, about 120 miles southwest of Shanghai, where they could live in peace. My cousin and I had brought some candies and a box of liqueur chocolates. Having been deprived of alcohol for so long, however, the chocolates had such a powerful effect on him that he started angrily criticizing the injustice he had suffered; after that, I decided not to bring him any more liqueur chocolates.

Back in Henan, Mama allowed me to go in place of her at

the next visit. I saw my father again, in the company of my aunt Mingguang and my cousin Xiaoxin.

Mingzhi, my father's favorite brother, came with his son, Suzhe, who was sixteen. My uncle, who had been his first Russian teacher, feared that Mingfu had lost his ability to speak the language, so he brought him some dictionaries and the Russian translation of Mao's complete works. Mingzhi had been exiled to a reeducation camp in Hunan, but he always saw the funny side of everything, and he joked self-deprecatingly about being "an intellectual who can't tell a cornfield from a field of sorghum." We all laughed, and the visit passed in a flash. As we were leaving, Mingzhi encouraged his brother in a more serious voice to stay optimistic. He assured Mingfu that, as soon as he was released, the two of them would drink a very good bottle of wine together to celebrate the event. Instead of cheering Mingfu up, however, this happy image moved him so deeply that he had to turn away to prevent us seeing his tears.

Mingfu thought he was weeping over the sufferings of his past. He did not know that he had just seen Mingzhi for the last time.

64

Happiness rests on unhappiness. Unhappiness
smolders beneath happiness.

—Laozi (571–471 BCE), *Tao Te Ching:*
The Book of the Way and its Virtue

The reeducation camp was about to close in 1973. The children
of cadres still held in Henan were being gradually sent back to
Beijing on riverboats.

Master Wei at my high school in Beijing imagined that, after I had graduated, I might train as a teacher. Mama and I discussed this and decided that it was a good idea. Now I just had to
submit an application.

In Beijing, the foreign liaison department let us use a room
of about ninety square feet in an apartment where we shared the

kitchen, bathroom, and toilet with two other families. But we were together. We were in the city. And Mingfu was alive.

That year, 1974, a new movement was launched, orchestrated by the still-powerful Gang of Four. This time the criticism was leveled at Lin Biao and Confucius.

Lin Biao may have been dead and buried, but he was accused of having reactionary values, inspired by the philosopher. So it was as a "rightist" that Lin Biao returned to the stage for his posthumous punishment. In reality, however, this campaign "against the reestablishment of capitalism in all its forms" was intended to target Zhou Enlai and his attempt to restart the economy, discreetly helped by Deng Xiaoping.

This resurgence of ideological tension was accompanied by a spate of suicides within the Ministry of Public Safety. One consequence of this was that prison visits were suspended until further notice. This decision was made just after Mingfu had been encouraged by his family to hold firm while he waited to be released, more than a year after the investigation had declared him innocent.

For my father, it was the last straw. The loss of our visits was a huge blow, and he suddenly became very angry. His rage was aimed at the prison, at his guards, at the whole world. He insulted the guards, the investigators, the prison governor, one after another, but his anger seemed inexhaustible.

In late January 1975, he was transferred to a different wing of the prison, where he quickly noticed that his fellow inmates would laugh hysterically or weep for no reason or mumble incoherently. He realized that he had been sent to the section for mad people.

The next day, a doctor spoke to him about his "cerebral dysfunction" and advised him to cooperate with his treatment. My father found it hard to stay calm as he explained that he was not crazy.

He was led to a room. He was tied up. Electrodes were placed on his body. They electrocuted him until his body went into convulsions. "What the hell are you doing?" he yelled. "Are you trying to kill me?" At that moment, Mingfu had the presence of mind to say that he was Mao Zedong's interpreter and that he would write a report on what was happening to him for his investigation group. Was it the power of Mao's name? The fear of reprisals? The "treatment" was momentarily suspended. The patient was told to calm down. He was untied and taken back to his cell.

The next day, two new doctors came to his cell and forced him to swallow a handful of pills. Their effect was powerful. He slept for several days and nights without waking. In addition to this chemical straitjacket, my father was also deprived of his daily walks, newspapers, and books.

Until the morning of his release from prison in April 1975, when, as I woke, Mama told me she had just had an awful nightmare: she dreamed that my father had gone crazy! I reminded her of what Chinese people usually say about dreams: their true meaning is the opposite of their apparent meaning. In which case, I said triumphantly, you can be sure that your dream is good news! In truth, I did not have much faith in this method of dream interpretation; I was really just trying to reassure my mother.

"The Great Leader has decided to free you," the tea-drinking man solemnly announced to Mingfu.

There was no irony in the use of the words "the Great Leader": not for the man who was speaking, nor even for my father, who instantly replied: "The Great Mao has my eternal gratitude!" There was no irony because irony was impossible. Back then, it was literally unthinkable.

The joy of freedom, after seven and a half years of imprisonment, soon turned to sadness. There was no celebratory feast or shared bottle of wine. Mingzhi had died from a heart attack at the age of fifty-one in the labor camp where he had been exiled, far from his family, after being forced to divorce so that his three children could remain in Beijing with their mother. My father's grief was immense. So fragile was his health when he came out of Qincheng that it was agreed we would give him no more bad news until he had recovered his strength.

Mingfu's incarceration had been so long that, to begin with, he had no frame of reference beyond the prison in Qincheng. To our great surprise, the first thing that Mingfu asked for, the only thing that would really bring him any pleasure, was to finally attend a performance of *Shajiabang*.

In a single voice, Mama and I cried out: "*Shajiabang*? Seriously?"

Shajiabang was one of the eight revolutionary artistic works promoted by Jiang Qing, the only eight pieces allowed to be performed during the Cultural Revolution. *Shajiabang* was one of the five Peking operas that, along with two ballets and one symphony—also entitled *Shajiabang*—formed the corpus of the great revolutionary epic in which Mao's philosophy, the People's Liberation Army, the country's proletariat, and the great class struggle had definitively replaced the world of emperors, generals, chamberlains, courtiers, court intrigues, and romantic male leads. In fact, that short list of works known as the "revolutionary canon," chosen by Jiang Qing and published in the *People's Daily* in May 1967, became the staple cultural diet of the people of China for the next ten years. All those works were studied in schools, factories, farms, everywhere. Sometimes performed by traveling companies, sometimes sung by family or friends. Everybody in China knew their most famous songs because they were constantly broadcast on the radio, forever blaring from loudspeakers wherever you want. This phenomenon was summed up in the expression "Eight hundred million people watch eight shows."

And yet there we were, my mother and I, taking my father to the theater, soon after his release from prison. While we were waiting in line to get our tickets, my father suddenly rushed away and embraced another man. When he came back to us, he told us that this man had been his prison guard. "We embraced because he apologized," my father said, "for not having known the identity of this unjustly condemned prisoner."

I also remember a meeting between my father and a former minister who had also been a prisoner. Their conversation was all about where they had been imprisoned. When they discovered that they had been in adjoining cells at Qincheng during the same time period, they were delighted. "Every day, I used to hear my neighbor furiously complaining that he was not being given enough to eat," the former minister declared, laughing. "So that angry whiner with the northeastern accent was you!"

Another time, my father stopped suddenly in front of a man who was concentrating on his *tai-chi-chuan* exercises. He walked up to him because he felt certain this man, almost a hundred years old, was Liu Jianzhang, the former railway minister, who had also been detained in Qincheng and whose wife had courageously written to Mao to complain about the conditions of her husband's incarceration and of the conditions in which political prisoners generally were held. My father asked the man to thank his wife for her courage, which resulted in an improvement of his quality of life in Qincheng. "My wife is dead now," the old man said, moved by my father's words.

Finally, one day Mingfu bumped into an old friend whom he had known before his arrest. Happy to see my father apparently in good health, the man said: "At least you got out alive, Mingfu! But I am always sad when I think about your parents, and particularly your father's undeserved fate."

This was how my father learned the truth about his parents' deaths.

65

Good-bye to the past, welcome the new era!

—Chinese adage

I graduated from high school in the summer of 1974, finishing top of my school year. Despite this, my application to become a teacher was rejected.

Their argument was that, since I came from a "problematic" (i.e., counterrevolutionary) family, they believed that I would have to be reeducated, and that in any case I was not fit to educate others. I was not in any circumstances to be allowed contact with "uncontaminated" children. Consequently, I could not be a teacher. I had not been expecting this outcome, so now I did not know what I was going to do. For the first time, however, I did not feel guilty. Perhaps I had simply grown used to being labeled in that way.

Finally, after my father's release, I found myself among a battalion of new employees in a branch of the Academy of Sciences specializing in the import and export of scientific books. We spent our first three months in the packaging department before joining other departments. I was constantly reminded that I, in particular, had to be very disciplined, very conscientious in learning all of the packaging techniques. That I had to be careful to arrive early so I could clean the offices and that I should stay late every day to make a good impression. That I should always make sure that my superiors had enough hot water, that I should never try to cut in line for the cafeteria, etc. If I did all of that, perhaps they would look more favorably on my application and one day I might hope to be recommended for entry into a university.

Zhou Enlai died on January 8, 1976, in the morning. The prime minister, suffering from cancer, had been conducting all his meetings over the previous few months from his hospital bed, assisted by Deng Xiaoping.

No other Chinese leader of that period commanded as much respect as Zhou Enlai. His personal charisma, his renowned intelligence, his cultured mind, his great generosity, and his absolute faithfulness toward the other leaders, all of this had made him an almost untouchable figure, despite the bitterness of the power struggles going on around him. Despite Mao Zedong's paranoia. Despite the scheming of the Gang of Four, and particularly of Jiang Qing, who did all she could to sow doubt about Zhou in people's minds. But while Jiang Qing was secretly hated by the people, Zhou was perceived as a fair and wise man. He was loved like a family member.

For us in the Yan family, it is impossible to describe how important he was, this "uncle" with his thick black eyebrows, such a familiar figure from my father's childhood, so close to "great sister-in-law Gaosu" and to Baohang, who had worked with him as a secret agent in the years before the revolution.

Why had Zhou, who was so close to my grandfather, so constant and faithful a friend, not been able to save him? Simply because it was impossible. One need think only of Liu Shaoqi, who was found dead in November 1969, abandoned in his isolation cell in Kaifeng, in a state of utter destitution. If Zhou had not been able to do anything for the chairman, then it is no surprise that he could not help my grandfather.

A few days after Zhou's death, Deng Xiaoping paid an emotional and very personal tribute to him while their shared political enemies conspired to denigrate him as a "capitalist infiltrated in the Party." The Gang of Four heaped insults on Zhou. Any public show of grief toward him was outlawed. No armbands, no flowers, no meetings, no displays of any kind were authorized. All attempts at collective mourning were suppressed.

This repression produced a surge of rebellion among the people that foreshadowed the end of a reign. Everybody agreed that these prohibitions underlined the absurdity of the persecutions suffered over the past ten years.

On April 5, the Qingming Festival, when Chinese people revere their ancestors, Tiananmen Square was filled with banners and processions, flowers and photographs, all in tribute to Zhou Enlai. I went there to commemorate this great man. In cities all over China, the people's love of Zhou was made abundantly clear.

And for the first time since the proclamation of the People's Republic, there was a mood of anger.

The consequences were quick to materialize: people were arrested, imprisoned, exiled. And Deng Xiaoping, who had succeeded Zhou, was stripped of all his duties on April 7, 1976.

Five months later, on September 9, Mao Zedong died. Less than a month passed between the death of the leader and the fall of the Gang of Four. Jiang Qing, ironically, found herself imprisoned in Qincheng.

Soon, Deng Xiaoping took over the leadership of the Party again. After ousting Hua Guofeng, he ordered the release of anybody who had been imprisoned or exiled for attending Zhou's commemorations. From that point on, Deng Xiaoping appeared to be the uncontested leader of the "reformists." In July 1977, the tenth congress of the Communist Party of China rubber-stamped his ascension by naming him first vice-premier, vice-chairman of the Central Committee of China's Communist Party, and chief of the People's Liberation Army.

The Cultural Revolution was over.

In August 1977, eleven years after it was abolished, Deng Xiaoping reestablished the *gaokao*, the university entrance exam. Without restrictions. Without any class distinctions. My heart leaped with excitement. I felt as if I had been woken from a long, long sleep. I felt as if I had just caught the last train as it was about to leave the station.

66

The mind is like a clear mirror: you must constantly wipe it, rub its surface, to keep it free from dust.

—Shenxiu (circa 605–705)

For eleven years, the Chinese university system had been in a very strange state. Between 1966 and 1977, only workers, peasants, and soldiers had access to it. Entrance required a recommendation that was based not on intellectual accomplishments, but on the applicant's practical skills and political suitability.

That year, 1977, 5.7 million of us applied. Anybody who had graduated high school between 1966 and 1977 was invited to apply. An entire generation, abandoned to its fate, now saw a chance at redemption. Afterward this was known as the '77 *Ji*: the school year that would rebuild China. The generation that would gradually reform and modernize it, following Deng

Xiaoping's famous injunction to "cross the river by feeling the stones." The generation that would lay down the foundations of public and private enterprise, the foundations of administration and ministers. The country's current premier, Li Keqiang, emerged from this generation.

The official restoration of the university entrance exam changed everything for me. Professor Wei, my former math teacher, got in touch with all his ex-students who wished to take the *gaokao* and offered to help them review for it. Filled with enthusiasm, I went to his apartment every evening. Professor Wei and his wife lived with their two children in a 120-square-foot room. He was not aiming to make money because he did not charge for the classes. He seemed to want to pay us back for our unimaginably huge appetite for knowledge, irrespective of our living conditions.

Wei Lao Shi knew that we had left school two years ago. He knew how difficult it would be to catch up on those lost years in only three months. For each student, he created a special program based on their orientation, whether scientific or literary. I dreamed of becoming a diplomat, simply because that was the model that my parents' careers offered. In that case, my mother suggested, you should apply to the Peking Foreign Languages Institute. This meant passing a very difficult exam.

Although that option was ostensibly literary in orientation, it also included an important math test. More worryingly, my English was substandard, particularly as I would be competing with applicants who were already teaching that language or who had been taught by better teachers than I had. I asked for some time off from work and spent the next few months locked in my small bedroom with a stack of books, emerging only in the evenings to attend Wei Lao Shi's classes.

I remember seeing a contemporary painting back then that really moved me. To me, it seemed emblematic of what the '77 *Ji* was going through. A crowd of people, wearing the famous blue or pea green jacket that was de rigueur under the Cultural Revolution and that many of us still wore, was massed together to look at that same painting through a window. Everybody was staring at that possibility beyond the glass, and for me that symbolized the thirst to learn that drove us forward, a thirst intensified by ten years of frustration.

During the written tests, I had the feeling that everything was going well. But then came the English oral exam. I will never forget the text that I had to discuss. It was an English translation of a speech by Mao Zedong written in Yan'an and given in September 1944, with the title "Serving the People." It was about a poor twenty-nine-year-old man named Zhang Side, from Sichuan. The Kuomintang was blockading communist-held Yan'an at the time, and the region had to be self-sufficient. Zhang Side became famous for his almost superhuman productivity as a charcoal burner. Mao gave this speech only three days after one of the kilns collapsed on the hero:

They say that all men must die one day, but not all deaths have the same meaning. A writer from ancient China, Sima Qian, said, "It is true that men are mortal, but some deaths weigh heavier than Mount Tai while others are lighter than a goose feather." If you work for the fascists and die in service of exploiters and oppressors, your death has less weight than a goose feather. If you die defending the interests of the people, then your death weighs heavier than Mount Tai. From now on, whenever somebody dies in our ranks, whoever they might be, soldier or cook, if he has done useful work, we will organize a funeral in his honor.

"What was your understanding of this text, Miss Yan, and what thoughts does it inspire?" I understood the text, but I did not have the vocabulary to comment on it.

I felt devastated—until the day when I was informed by letter that, when all my grades were added together, my results were among the best of my year. I even got 22/20 in math, by answering two subsidiary questions. Despite this, my average grade in English was insufficient. For that reason, they suggested I join the French or Romanian departments, where I would have to learn the language from scratch.

For me, it was an easy choice, as I had always loved French literature. So I chose the French department, and I could celebrate being chosen among the 273,000 applicants who passed the *gaokao* that year.

67

All rivers run into sea, the tolerance is its greatness.

—Chinese adage

Just before I turned twenty-one, after being accepted at university, I heard the news that my grandfather was to be rehabilitated. Yan Baohang was among the first victims of the Cultural Revolution to be officially exonerated.

Three years after my father's release, nothing could have given us a greater sense that the injustice had been repaired. Yes, things were changing. A new era was beginning. The sufferings of the past would never be erased, but we could hope that honor and dignity would be restored to those who, having been imprisoned for no reason, did not survive. And honor and dignity were the things we needed most of all.

The ceremony took place on January 5, 1978. Hu Yaobang,

on behalf of the central government, gave the eulogy. This man, elected chairman of the Communist Party of China three years later—and its last chairman, since he chose to abolish that title, redolent as it was of the Maoist era—was unstinting in his praise of "Yan Baohang's inestimable contribution to his country and to the world."

Then some ashes, supposedly my grandfather's ashes, were taken to the revolutionary cemetery in Babaoshan, west of Beijing, There, on the "hill of eight treasures," all those who had worked for the good of China were buried together.

We had not managed to find my grandfather's real ashes, despite a great deal of research. During one of those investigations, Mingguang recorded the testimony of an employee at the hospital where prisoner no. 67100 had been taken as he was dying. His condition revealed a complete absence of medical care. This account devastated Mingguang due to certain details that had appeared to her in a dream at the time of her father's death. At the crematorium, his cremation was confirmed, but in accordance with the instructions of Jiang Qing, the ashes of "counterrevolutionaries" were not kept.

At the end of our investigation, Mingguang and my father had found a short note written by Baohang to his wife: "Gaosu, my dear old wife, I would so love to go home . . ." As we no longer had my grandfather's ashes, it seemed natural to substitute my grandmother's so that the two of them would be united in the same memory, the same wreaths of incense smoke, the same offerings of burnt paper.

Before the ceremony, I went to a meeting attended by my

father and his brothers and sisters, along with some of my cousins.

The question of Da Pangzi quickly reared its head. I did not know what to say, nor did my cousins. For the others, however, it was clear: his presence could not be allowed at such a ceremony because it would insult the memory of his grandfather. Da Pangzi had betrayed and dishonored the family; it was because of him that Baohang had been arrested. Everybody agreed that he should not be invited.

Everybody except Yan Mingfu.

The only discordant voice was my father's, a man who had only been freed from prison three years before. He was the only one prepared to forgive. But to my mind, the most important thing was not that my father should forgive Da Pangzi, but that he should explain the reasons for his forgiveness.

He had long championed the idea that, for us Yans, Da Pangzi personified an entire youth driven to its destruction by the Cultural Revolution. That he embodied a lost generation. That he was an emblematic figure of the madness that had seized our children. We could not, my father said, add the insult of missing this ceremony to the injury done to Da Pangzi—and to so many others—by the toxic mirage of the Cultural Revolution. Exclusion, hatred, and reprisals are not the means by which a society moves forward. That is why, he concluded, we must forgive him.

I remember the silence that followed his words.

In fact, the absolution granted him by his own family led to Da Pangzi being ravaged by remorse. He gathered the testimonies of everybody he could think of who had ever known Yan

Baohang and paid for the publication of a collection of these texts. Despite this, Da Pangzi still felt himself in the grip of an indelible sin. In the end, he abandoned his wife and children and went into exile in the United States. He did not even react when we sent him news that his mother, Mingshi, had died, in 2000. And since he was not the only one who had wanted to turn the page, to act as if that page had never been written, I could only conclude that my father had been right when he said that Da Pangzi was an emblematic figure of that lost generation.

68

My beloved gives me a rose;
What should I give her in return? A little red snake.
Since then she turns away and ignores me,
I don't understand why.
Ah, let her go her own way.

—Lu Xun, "My First Lost Love," 1924

Campus life encouraged my total immersion in work. That was true not only for me but also for three other girls in my class, Hirondelle, Zhen, and Si, who were studying French. For four years, we had the same lecturer, Mrs. Dong, a woman who was not much older than we were. Today, my three former classmates all live in France, Mrs. Dong lives in Paris, and we are all still friends.

One of my classmates penned this description of me in my

first year at the Peking Foreign Languages Institute, and I have to admit that it is very lifelike: "Always dressed in that impersonal, asexual blue or green uniform, a long braid of hair falling down her back, a large military-style knapsack filled with books and textbooks, you invariably followed the same itinerary: dormitory, canteen, classrooms—library, canteen, classrooms—classrooms, canteen, dormitory. We saw you from morning to evening, eyes staring straight ahead, nose to the grindstone, and nothing and nobody could break your concentration. Not even . . . boys!"

When I see the lives that students enjoy today, I sometimes regret not having granted myself a little more time for fun.

But having a love life, back in those days, was considered highly inadvisable. The message, repeated and underlined, was always about the necessity of devoting all our energy to our studies. And just in case we might not have understood, there would be an allusion to the married couples among us, "bearing in mind their advanced age and their exceptional admission to the *gaokao*." What our professors meant by this was: that is done, and sadly we can do nothing to undo it, but for those of you who are not yet in that state, we strongly discourage it. In fact, marriage was against the rules while students were still at the university. Which did not stop young people from falling in love, of course.

Mrs. Dong's teaching was excellent. There were also some teachers brought over from France who shared with us examples of the French press and the French cinema. I remember watching Robert Enrico's film *The Old Gun* soon after it was victorious at the César Awards.

During the third year, however, I began to get bored. Or

rather, I became aware that my appetite for knowledge went further than the acquisition of a language, even if that language was French. I opened up about my feelings to a family friend named Yuan Ming.

At that time, Yuan Ming was not yet the international historian and eminent public speaker she has become, but she was already the student of a highly renowned professor of international law, Wang Tieya. This man, who studied at the London School of Economics, became widely known when he was named as a judge on the International Criminal Tribunal for the Former Yugoslavia in the Hague.

Since the end of the Cultural Revolution and the reopening of the law faculty at Peking University, Wang Tieya had been looking to recruit foreign language students—Anglophone or Francophone in particular—so he could train them in international law, since most of the documents in that area of the law are written in one of those two languages.

I asked to meet this famous professor, the dean of the law faculty. He told me that his objective was to train Chinese lawyers in international law, and he insisted on the importance of French, notably because of the "Chronicle of International Developments" published since 1958 in every issue of the *Revue générale de droit international public* (General Review of Public International Law) by the famous French lawyer Charles Rousseau.

Wang Tieya gave a brief outline of this course and provided me with some advice on how to prepare for the exam that would enable me to be admitted into the master's in law. I was mentally dancing with joy before he had even finished speaking. Outside, I got on my bicycle and said to myself: "So that's your next objective!" The thought was as invigorating as the pedal strokes I gave to my old bike as I accelerated along the road.

In 1980, while still studying for my French degree, I began intensely preparing for the admission exam to the master's course, commuting the forty-five-minute bicycle ride between the Peking Foreign Languages Institute and the law faculty.

That year, I spent a lot of time thinking, not only about the various international bodies on the syllabus, but also about the meaning of concepts as abstract and fragile as law and justice and their concrete consequences.

What happened to law and justice during the Cultural Revolution? What was the meaning of *accusation*? What did we mean by the accused person's right to a criminal defense? What was the function of a judge? What was a lawyer? So many questions that partly, if not fully, explain why I was so shaken by the case of Feng Daxing, one of our fellow students.

69

I opened a history book to check; there was no
indication of the chronology, but on every page,
I could read the words: "Humanity, Justice, Way,
Virtue." As I couldn't sleep anyway, I spent most
of the night studying it in minute detail and finally
discerned the characters written between the
lines: the book was full of the words: "eat men!"

—Lu Xun, "A Madman's Diary," 1918

Like me, Feng Daxing was part of the '77 *Ji*. Like me, he joined
the Peking Foreign Language Institute to study French. This
was 1980, he was twenty-five years old, and he, too, would study
at the Peking University Law School. I would often see him there
in the morning, and one day I asked him: "So you're preparing to
do a master's in law, too?"

Feng Daxing was not very handsome. He was quite introverted. He appeared to be either shy or haughty, perhaps both. He communicated very little with his classmates and, indeed, he barely responded to me: just enough for me to understand that the specialty that interested him was the same one that interested me. His reply, laconic without being aggressive, almost kind, in fact, was that we would be rivals. And he was right: of the eighty students who were going to take the exam, Wang Tieya would admit only one or two.

We would often make the same journey between the Peking Foreign Languages Institute and the law faculty, and we would nod at each other.

Then, in the spring of 1981, a few months before our exam—for which I knew Feng Daxing was as well prepared as I was—I heard the unbelievable news: he had been arrested.

We discovered that Feng Daxing had committed two robberies, one week apart. The first, on April 11, in the Xinhua bookstore near the university, where he stole 200 yuan. The second, on April 18, the day of his arrest, in a large store in Xidan, in the center of Beijing, where he stole a radio, some sunglasses, and a police badge. As with the previous robbery in the bookstore, his face was hidden and he was armed with a metal bar and a hammer. This time, however, he was confronted by two guards, and he hit them. One of them died; the other was left paraplegic. The day before this, he and I were sitting in the same classroom.

Everybody was stunned. Feng Daxing did not fit the usual criminal profile. The people who were interviewed about him all mentioned his strong academic performance. They spoke of a reserved boy, with no previous difficulties. In the press and on television, he was described as an elite student.

In July 1981, he was sentenced to death. He was executed by firing squad.

There was an intense wave of emotion throughout China's universities. We were all aware of being survivors of the Cultural Revolution. How was it possible that so much determination devoted to higher education, so much serious study, could end in this tragedy?

It was all the more incomprehensible given all we knew about the extraordinary '77 *Ji*. About those famous 4.8 percent who were admitted after taking the *gaokao*, all of whom had worked so hard, in difficult circumstances, to quench their thirst for knowledge. Who were these supposedly gifted students? What education had they received? What moral values had they been given? People tried desperately to understand what had gone on inside that boy's head.

There were so many questions. But nothing could justify the enormous risk that Feng Daxing took in compromising his future, first by stealing and then by killing. Was he bereft of any morality? Wasn't morality precisely what that generation had lacked during the entire Cultural Revolution? Wasn't morality the first and most important thing that the ideologues of the Cultural Revolution had destroyed, by driving young people to inform on their parents, their grandparents, their teachers? By encouraging denunciation, bullying, and humiliations?

Feng Daxing decided to conduct his own defense. The trial

was very high-profile, with a lot of press and television coverage. Because the prosecution had demanded the death sentence, Feng argued that his crime was not premeditated. According to him, it was an accident. He asked for the verdict to be commuted to life in prison, which would give him the opportunity to repent, and to atone for his crimes through translation work. Our department asked the court to be lenient. We highlighted what a waste his death would be and focused on the idea that his remarkable intellectual abilities could serve the community from behind bars.

But during the trial, Feng Daxing made the mistake of quoting the famous line by the English philosopher Thomas Hobbes, from his book *Leviathan*: "Man is a wolf to man." It was hard not to conclude that this boy had drawn his conception of the world from the works of that pessimistic philosopher, who saw humanity in a perpetual war against itself. The same message emerged from his personal diary, which was mentioned in the verdict and which apparently counted against him since his appeal was rejected.

Some people described Feng Daxing as immature. Personally, I cannot judge him. The question might well have been asked as to whether he was insane.

Deng Xiaoping's analysis at the end of this tragic episode was as follows: the greatest fault, committed over the course of those ten years, concerned education, he said. And by "education," what he meant was moral education. The poison that the Cultural Revolution injected into China's body politic consisted of the destruction of basic moral values in interpersonal relationships. It was the existence of such an environment, cut off from any moral compass, that allowed the creation of a Feng Daxing. In this sense, I believe that Feng Daxing, too, was a victim of the Cultural Revolution. One among many others in a lost generation.

70

Poke a bush, a snake comes out.

—Chinese proverb

Forty years after the end of the Cultural Revolution, we should have enough distance to be able to analyze what made such an episode possible. We should do so to understand how and why the political chaos and economic paralysis endured for an entire decade, creating a society that was profoundly depressed and probably traumatized, and condemning a whole country to poverty.

Just after the end of the Cultural Revolution—and that will remain its name in history, despite the massive destruction of Chinese culture during the ten years that it lasted—I was struck by the doom-laden phrase that my father used to characterize China: "A place weighed down by history." It was as if he were standing in front of one of those traditional Chinese paintings where, in a magnificent, misty landscape, man appears in the form of a humble silhouette, minuscule and fragile, overwhelmed by either the great sky above or the emperor, whose power had grown ever more tyrannical since Confucius, in the fifth century BCE, declared that, in China, the individual was subordinate to the community.

When Deng Xiaoping took center stage again, in 1978, to attempt the reconstruction of a country on the verge of bankruptcy, his first acts were designed to carry out all that had not been done during the Cultural Revolution. There was a development plan for agriculture, for industry, for science and technology, for national defense; for everything, in other words, on which a sovereign state is based. His objective was clear: to enable China to become a great economic power by the beginning of the twenty-first century. It should be noted that there was no mention of ideology in this plan.

The policy of openness that took hold after the Cultural Revolution was founded not only on the determination to reform the country, but also on the pragmatic need to trade with the rest of the world, to allow China to play its part in the international market, and particularly to strengthen its relations with the Western economies.

While this new era inaugurated by Deng was possible only after the death of Mao and the neutralization of the Gang of Four, it was also the result of a lesson drawn from the slump caused by the Cultural Revolution. The proof of this is in the essays Deng wrote on the history of the Communist Party of China since it entered power in 1949.

Deng analyzed what he called the party's "leftist" drift from 1957 onward. This drift was the origin of the Great Leap Forward, which destroyed the country's production capacities. What Deng showed was that all attempts to redress the Chinese economy, from 1962 on, were doomed to failure as long as the ideological drift remained unchecked. Partly because that ideology presupposed the importance of the class struggle over economic development, and partly because it required an isolationist foreign policy.

Finally, one of the main causes of the Cultural Revolution and one of the main reasons for its long duration was the concentration of power in the hands of one man: Mao Zedong. His omnipotence had led to a cult of personality.

This cult manifested itself not only in the Little Red Book, of which everybody had to possess several copies in different formats, and which it was advisable to exhibit in public; at the beginning of the Cutural Revolution, there was also, for example, the insane diktat on how one should answer the telephone. Under Mao, it was not permitted to say simply "*Ni hao*" ("hello" in Mandarin) when you picked up the receiver; you had to say something like "Serving the people!" and the person on the other end would reply with a similar phrase: "History is made by the masses!" Another example: the daily gymnastic movements were replaced by a "dance of loyalty to Mao." Portraits of Mao were hung everywhere, and the idea of displaying a painting of anybody else was blasphemy.

After millennia of feudalism, it was easy for the Chinese to revert back to their reflexive position of venerating the country's leader: What difference was there, really, between an emperor and the "Red Sun"? The failure of the party to draw up any checks and balances, combined with Mao's indulgence toward those idolatrous practices, created the ideal conditions for the exercise of absolute power.

The terror could only end when Mao died because Mao undoubtedly realized the unswerving devotion that the people of China felt for him. How else can you explain the persecution inflicted on the chairman Liu Shaoqi?

The Chinese people put on the blindfolds themselves. They stayed silent out of fear of others' cruelty. These were the toxins that would spread throughout the entirety of the Cultural Revolution. There was also the impossibility, in the end, of distinguishing the persecutor from the persecuted, as in the case of my cousin Da Pangzi. This phenomenon has emerged from the countless confessions, the individual and collective repentances that have been exposed since the end of the terror.

Deng believed that, to turn the page, he had to leave it up to future generations to judge what had happened. Fifty years have passed since the start of the Cultural Revolution. Perhaps it is time to think more deeply about that tragedy in China's contemporary history, and to judge it. Because, as painful as it was, it can also be a useful source of information for the generations to come. It is our duty, as Chinese people, to remember. And to ensure that such events are never repeated.

71

If you want to see farther than a thousand li,
you must climb higher.

—Chinese proverb

The entrance exam for the master's in law took place in June
1981. Yuan Ming knew how fierce the competition would be:
several hundred applicants for only a handful of places. During
the three-day exam, in order to minimize my need to travel, she
let me stay in her little seventy-square-foot bedroom, where she
had two bunk beds. For me, this was incredibly helpful: it meant
I could study between tests, and not waste any time.

Three intense days of exams, three nights spent cramming
instead of sleeping. It is hardly surprising that I passed out almost as soon as the final test was over. At least my efforts were
rewarded: of the three hundred applicants to the international

law course, only two were accepted: one for the English class, and one for the French—me. I felt very proud to be accepted into Peking University, because it was there that my mother had studied in the 1950s. It is the intellectual center of China.

During the Cultural Revolution, China's legal system practically disappeared, except in its most basic form. Society was ruled by man, not by law. So it was understandable that some of my friends and family should wonder just what it meant to be a lawyer, what exactly international law was. It was not until 1978 that Deng Xiaoping and the congress—in other words, the country's parliament—wrote the system of criminal defense into the constitution. The public prosecutor's department and the Beijing Municipal Bureau of Justice were reestablished. Lawyers began to work again, just as the law faculty at Peking University reopened its doors.

The simple fact of being on the master's course gave us the chance to work part-time as court-appointed lawyers in the people's court of Haidian, the Beijing district where the university was located. Even if we were defending petty criminals too poor to pay for a lawyer, on the face of it this seemed a very useful experience. But then we came to realize the state of law in China. We were not allowed to meet our client, to talk with him for even five minutes before the trial began. There was no presumption of innocence: the accused was presumed guilty. So there was no need for the prosecution to produce any evidence; that was our task. Often, the trial would have barely started before the judge announced that the sentence had already been decided. We discovered to our horror the gulf that existed between what we had learned and what was actually happening. We were there only as a kind of security. The reality continued to reflect the absence of any real tradition of law. In fact, the laws relating to the status of lawyers in China were not proclaimed until 1996—and not actually enforced until 1997. In those conditions, I was not interested in working as a lawyer in China, so I concentrated on international law.

Wang Tieya was an English-speaker, so he entrusted the four Francophone students to the care of old Professor Tang, who had studied in France.

The four of us—three boys (Jiang, Lou, Robert) and me—were known as the Gang of Four: a very black joke, considering that Professor Tang had been persecuted as a rightist in the 1950s and banned from teaching.

The problem with Professor Tang was not his ability to teach French, but his grasp of the law itself. Because, after so many years without teaching, he seemed to have forgotten quite a lot of the subject. Consequently, it was up to us to read our law textbooks in French. His classes were the most boring I have ever attended.

Thankfully, the reopening of the university had attracted some other lecturers from prestigious establishments such as Columbia and Harvard who taught us fascinating classes. The only problem: they were in English.

Three years later, at the start of the 1984 academic year, Wang Tieya advised us to go abroad to study. He provided us with his contacts list and gave us all the information we needed about great universities and foundations that offered grants.

When the brochures for those institutions (Harvard, Yale, Princeton, the Ford Foundation) arrived, I was blown away by the perfection of their presentation. From the envelopes stamped with their logos to the registration forms, the photographs of campus, the colors, the smell of that thick, glossy paper (which did not even exist in China at that time) . . . I will never forget my first impression of the smell of that paper. If this was our future, it seemed to me like a dream.

But that dream had a price, and it was exorbitant. Even though our parents were senior civil servants, they would never earn enough to pay the tuition fees. The only solution was a grant, and that would depend on my results.

China had entered a period of openness and reforms, however, and the government was aware of the importance of sending its youth abroad to be educated. So a system of state grants was established for the best students. These grants could be added to the grants offered by the foreign university. At the time, any student who benefited from a Chinese government grant had to return to China afterward, as a sort of "return on investment." But the essential thing for us was to leave in the first place, so we could see the outside world. All the more so since a foreign grant, like the one that I got for my PhD, came with no strings attached.

My first response came from the Ford Foundation, which offered me the chance of taking an LLM at Yale. Soon afterward, Geneva raised the bar by offering me a three-year grant, with the preparation of a PhD thrown in. Geneva also had the advantage of being a Francophone city.

This brought a temporary end to our Gang of Four: Jiang was able to use the Ford Foundation grant that I had declined, while Lou, who spoke Portuguese, left for Rio de Janeiro. Robert, who would become my husband, was sent to Halifax, in Canada, in a university renowned for its international law department.

I traveled to Switzerland in the summer of 1984.

72

The sky is unlimited for birds to fly at liberty, the ocean is boundless for fish to leap at will.

—Chinese proverb

At the airport, I hugged my parents one last time. This was my first time on a plane. At the moment of takeoff, I felt a completely new sensation. Like a kite when a child lets go of the string. A kite swept away by the wind, floating toward an unknown destination, unsure whether I would ever return home and see my loved ones again. I felt overwhelmed by anguish. I cried my eyes out.

That sensation remains vivid in my memory. So much so that, years later, when I saw my own son catch a flight the way I might catch a bus, I wanted to ask my parents what they had felt, watching their only daughter take off.

Mama told me, "After the Cultural Revolution, what we

wanted most of all, despite the sadness of that separation, was for you to leave this place with its dark past."

She added that, for almost her whole life, she had felt an unbearable weight pressing down on her. The unbearable weight of not being able to decide her own fate. Here, even when they don't throw you in prison, they still keep you in a cage.

All of my parent's generation felt the same way. All those who could, despite the sacrifices it required, were desperate to send their children abroad to give them a chance of fulfilling themselves rather than staying and having to submit. This did not alter the fact that my parents believed China would change and that their daughter would come back one day to contribute to her homeland's progress.

73

How can he speak, he who has not studied the odes?

—Confucius (551–479 BCE), *Analects*

The Graduate Institute of International Studies, founded in 1927 in Geneva, was located in the beautiful, tree-filled Parc de la Perle du Lac, by the edge of Lake Geneva.

From our classroom windows in Villa Rose, we could see pairs of swans gliding over the water that reflected the snow-capped Alps. The vision was so spectacular that our lecturers often had to remind us to pay attention.

Professor Lucius Caflisch, who was eminent even then, before he became a judge at the European Court of Human Rights, came to the airport in person to meet me. I owed this privilege to Wang Tieya's warm recommendation. Throughout my stay in Switzerland, I had so many reasons to be grateful for the welcome that I received from Professor Caflisch and his wife.

There were usually no more than twelve students in each class. Lectures were given by guest professors from the most prestigious international law faculties in France and the United States. I must admit that it was hard for me at the beginning. I had a degree in French, but in reality I understood almost nothing during that first semester. The avalanche of words—particularly specialist legal terminology—was so fast that I could not manage to take notes. So I would copy my classmates' notes before heading straight to the library, which was in the basement of the World Trade Organization building. I would stay cloistered there until it closed. It was always dark outside by the time I left.

For the first eighteen months, I did not leave campus, leading an almost monastic life. Although Geneva is actually quite a small city, I didn't even know where the main shopping street was. I knew I had to quickly improve my level of French because if I failed my exams, I wouldn't get my scholarship.

I received 700 Swiss francs per month, and I was housed in a small wooden bungalow located directly opposite the Villa Rose, which certainly simplified my life.

By chance, there was another Chinese student there—Xiao Zhang—and he and I would help each other. He was slightly younger than me, and his French was excellent. For both of us, it was a point of honor to earn the best grades. Never let it be said that Chinese students should be left behind. In fact, by the end of the first semester, we had succeeded: Professor Caflisch declared that, after us, he was ready to accept any Chinese student that Wang Tieya recommended.

The only problem with my bungalow was that it had no kitchen—until the weekend when Xiao Zhang, browsing through a flea market in Geneva, spotted a secondhand electric camping stove. He tried to haggle, but the vendor, touched to see a young Chinese student—rare at that time in Switzerland—ended up giving it to him for free. Xiao Zhang immediately came to see me, with the camping stove under his arm. If I wanted to keep it, he said, he could use it to warm up his lunch, and I would finally be able to do some cooking. That was a deal I was very happy to make!

From then on, I could invite classmates and even sometimes professors to my bungalow to try some Chinese specialties. They were kind enough to say that they enjoyed them. But only Xiao Zhang and I knew that those meals were also a way of soothing our homesickness.

There was one other Chinese man in Geneva. He was finishing his PhD, but he was not from "mainland China," as we called it, to distinguish the People's Republic of China from the island of Taiwan. Having still not fully escaped the propaganda of my youth, I wondered if it was appropriate to speak to this "enemy of the motherland," as Taiwanese people were known in China. In the end, though, I overcame my reservations. And discovered that Lao Zhou was a very nice boy.

There was also an Israeli woman with us. Again, having been primed by my country's propaganda to consider Israelis as "enemies of the Palestinian people," I found it hard to imagine that she might be pleasant company. And when I found out that she had served in the army (because I didn't know that in Israel, military service was obligatory for both sexes), I was practically horrified.

Those experiences taught me that nobody is free from those types of prejudices. It works the other way, too, of course, as when you hear, in Europe, that "the Chinese are taking all our jobs."

As for Lao Zhou, he and I ended up becoming friends. One evening we met for dinner with friends from school, and we were talking about the Kuomintang. Not everybody at the table was familiar with Chinese history, so someone explained that the Kuomintang was the nationalist party founded by Sun Yat-sen in 1912, and that it had been the party of government in China, under Chiang Kai-shek, until 1949, when the "bourgeois republic" retreated to the island of Taiwan, leaving mainland China to the People's Republic, led by Mao Zedong.

There followed a fascinating discussion, during which I stated that the Kuomintang had never fought against the Japanese invaders. Lao Zhou could not believe his ears; he countered by mentioning the Kuomintang's first front against the Japanese . . . In the end, after some raised voices, we managed to calmly exchange our viewpoints and even to see each other's.

Discussions such as that one enabled me to understand how much misinformation I had been fed under the Cultural Revolution, the rewriting of history through a political lens, with little care for objectivity. In this way I learned to distance myself from ideologies; I learned to cherish freedom of information, freedom of knowledge, freedom of debate. By leaving China, I was able to see how the brainwashing of an entire country had been achieved. Because the Chinese were not the only ones concerned, even if China today has begun to unravel its old dogmas and to recognize the role of the Kuomintang in its contemporary history. But, for example, what about Japan? Why is there no mention in any school textbooks of the atrocities committed in China by the Japanese empire between the nineteenth century and the Second World War? There exists irrefutable evidence of those atrocities, and they are comparable to the horrors perpetrated by the Nazis. How will young Japanese people today be able to shape their views without going through the same painful process of remembering that the Germans went through after Nazism? When the Japanese prime minister goes to the temple every year for a military commemoration, we Chinese know that the dead who are buried in that place are, for the most part, war criminals. This is the kind of thing that only fosters anger and causes considerable damage to the relationship between our two countries.

74

Memory of the past can serve as a guide for the future.

—Chinese proverb

I was still in Geneva in 1985 when I heard that my father had been appointed by the party's Central Committee to the position of leader of the United Front Work Department, then to the position of secretary to the Central Committee.

By coincidence, Mikhail Gorbachev became the new secretary-general of the Communist Party of the Soviet Union that year. Soon after starting his new post, Gorbachev stated that he wanted to improve relations with China.

Deng Xiaoping had several reservations regarding this wished-for rapprochement, all of them military. First, there was the presence of Soviet troops in Mongolia, as well as on the Sino-Soviet border. The Soviets were intervening in Afghanistan and supporting the Vietnamese forces in Cambodia, an unacceptable situation in the eyes of Beijing.

Deng Xiaoping was able to lay down a whole set of conditions because China was in a position of strength. The economic reforms implemented by Deng in 1978 were bearing fruit, whereas the Soviet economy, in decline since the late 1970s, was forcing the USSR to give up its arms race with the United States.

After the retreat of Soviet troops from Afghanistan, Deng gave the green light for Gorbachev to make an official visit to China between May 15 and 18, 1989. The symbolism was strong enough that Yan Mingfu—who was, in some way, the living memory of the history of Sino-Soviet relations—took part in the ceremonies in his role as secretary of the Party's Central Committee.

As it happened, Hu Yaobang had died from a heart attack the previous month in Beijing.

As the Party's secretary-general, Hu Yaobang had been a reformist, but he had been dismissed in 1987 following student protests whose democratic aspirations he seemed to share. Hu Yaobang was particularly admired because, in the wake of Mao's death, he accomplished the reintegration of hundreds of intellectuals and leaders fired during the Cultural Revolution, as well as the posthumous rehabilitation of the regime's victims, including my grandfather. Then, in 1979, he had done the same for rightists.

The day after his death, spontaneous protests all over the country forced the government to organize a state funeral on April 22, 1989. In Beijing, however, the fervor did not die down.

In Tiananmen Square, it became impossible to carry out the ceremonies planned for the Soviet leader's official visit. Tiananmen Square was filled with students who had begun a hunger strike, so it was decided to prepare a reception at the airport instead. Gorbachev was welcomed on May 16 by Zhao Ziyang, the party's secretary-general, and by Deng, in the Great Hall of the People. I followed the event on Swiss television.

What the television footage did not show was that the central government had asked my father to negotiate with the students in Tiananmen Square, to convince them to move away after four days of their hunger strike.

One wonders why the government did not send the education minister to Tiananmen Square that afternoon. Particularly since my father had been ill for some time, regularly hospitalized with high fevers. In fact, he left for Tiananmen Square in an ambulance from the hospital where he had been admitted with a temperature of 102.

Barely had my father arrived in the middle of the angry crowd when the leader of the student movement asked everybody to calm down. What happened next was told to me by a friend of mine, Caroline, who was a student at Peking University at the time. At that moment, she was sitting close to my father's feet.

Before passing the megaphone to my father, the movement's leader told the protesters that Comrade Yan Mingfu had come as a friend, that he was a genuine communist. "I can promise you, he is one of us." My father took the megaphone and began speaking: "First of all, your determination and the spirit of your demands has touched the entire country. Be assured that your demands for reform, freedom, and an end to corruption have been heard, and I have no doubt that the Central Committee, as well as the People's Assembly, will take them into account. But those demands are not worth paying for with your lives. As a humanist, let me tell you that you cannot sacrifice yourselves. As the representative of the Central Committee, I can promise you that—once you have suspended your hunger strike and started classes again—there will be no reprisals against you." And to persuade the weakest among them to go to the hospital, and the others to go back to their classrooms as soon as possible, he offered himself as a hostage, as proof of the government's good faith, assuring the students that their demands would be considered and that negotiations would begin. Despite this, the students decided not to vacate the square. My father left.

Later, he would say that it was lucky that Deng was hard of hearing because he would not have been happy to hear the students yelling while he was welcoming Gorbachev in the Great Hall of the People.

While the square was still occupied by protesters and hunger strikers, Gorbachev's official visit continued, notably at the famous Great Wall of China. When a journalist asked him for his impression of this edifice, Gorbachev replied that the wall was magnificent, before adding, "But there are too many walls between people." The journalist took the bait, "Does that mean you would like to bring down the Berlin Wall?" The response was serious: "Why not?" As for the protesters who were still occupying Tiananmen Square, Gorbachev chose his words carefully: "The USSR, too, has certain 'hotheads' who wish to change socialism overnight."

It was from that moment that my father disappeared from television screens, and that the reporting focused less on Gorbachev's visit than on what was happening in Tiananmen Square.

In Geneva, I spent all my free time glued to the television—until June 4, 1989, when I saw the pictures of the tank advancing toward a young man. That image seared itself into my memory.

I followed the events that came next through the young Chinese people who left the country. One year later, in Paris, I saw my friend Hirondelle, who told me that, on that fateful day, she had been walking toward Chang'an Avenue, after leaving the State Council residence where she lived. The avenue was filled with tanks and military trucks. The loudspeakers broadcast the words, "Attention. All rebels will be shot. Stay in your homes." Despite the warlike tone, Hirondelle could not believe this was true. Was it possible that Chinese soldiers would shoot at the crowd? Suddenly, a young man started running toward her. From a nearby tank, a soldier fired. The boy was hit. He collapsed, bleeding. The loudspeaker announced, "Do not remain outside. If you do, you will suffer the consequences." Hirondelle was not sure she had really understood. This is a nightmare, she told herself, and her whole body started trembling. She did not move as the tanks went past. Then, gathering her strength, she ran home and made the decision to leave Beijing.

The day after these events, my father was dismissed. He was not the only one: Zhao Ziyang, too, was dismissed, along with two other Central Committee secretaries.

That November, six months after Gorbachev's visit to Beijing, the Berlin Wall came down.

The next month, in Malta, Mikhail Gorbachev and George H. W. Bush officially proclaimed the end of the Cold War.

By December 1991, the USSR had ceased to exist.

As for my father, his exile would not last long. In 1991, he was appointed vice-minister of civil affairs.

75

Dilligence is the path to the mountain of knowledge,
hardworking is the boat to the endless sea of learning.

—Chinese adage

In Geneva, my PhD thesis grew from many fruitful discussions with Lucius Caflisch and other professors of international law.

Nobody had yet really addressed the issue of arbitration procedures between different states. My thesis director encouraged me to explore this area, where law, international relations, and moral responsibility are interwoven. He suggested I deepen my knowledge of Continental legal systems, including the Anglo-Saxon system.

I compared Romano-Germanic law with the generally

noncodified common law in which, in accordance with Anglo-Saxon tradition, legal precedent prevails.

As common law is broadly applied in the Commonwealth countries and in the United States (with the exception of Louisiana, California, and Puerto Rico), Professor Caflisch encouraged me to take an exam for a grant that would enable me, by studying at the Fletcher School of Law and Diplomacy, to join Harvard as a research associate.

And so, in 1987, I discovered America! For me, it was all completely new. As a research associate in Harvard, I was under no obligation to take classes, so I simply chose the ones that interested me. I did not have to take any exams. I had a small office and, most important, access to the university library, the largest of its kind in the world.

After one year of research, students were advised to find an internship in a large law firm. Three New York–based firms made me an offer, and I chose Baker & McKenzie as the subject for my thesis because at the time this firm was giving legal advice to the US government at the Iran–United States Claims Tribunal. And that tribunal was an arbitration body that had been established following the Iranian Revolution. Arbitration between countries is so rare that I could not miss this opportunity. So I became an intern for a partner who was dealing with that case. There, I discovered the extraordinary efficiency of the American system. For the three months of my internship, I was given great help and support. The firm came up with an extremely elaborate work schedule for me. I was invited to meetings, I went on trips whenever the case required it, I was taken to clubs, etc. The firm did its absolute best to impress and win me over.

At Baker & McKenzie, I was given a very precise case to study concerning an interim protection measure. Essentially, this is a procedure whereby, pending a definitive decision, a judge can decide to sequester an asset with the aim of ensuring the execution of any measures that may be taken in the future. When my internship was over, I gave the results of my research to my boss, who congratulated me three or four years later since my research had contributed to the firm winning one of the arbitration cases in question.

I did my second internship in another American firm with a very different atmosphere. It was a large, well-oiled machine, with thousands of lawyers handling countless cases. But this firm's ambition—to open a branch in China—kept coming up against the eternal problem of the chicken and the egg: Should they invest in the opening of an office in China before they were given a case there? Or should they wait to be given a case before investing in the opening of an office?

When my six-month internship was over, the firm suggested I stay with them in New York, but I had no desire to continue working day and night, and often weekends, too. I had to finish my thesis. And to do that, I needed to return to Geneva, where Lucius Caflisch encouraged me to take another internship with the court of arbitration at the International Chamber of Commerce in Paris. The idea was to thoroughly familiarize me with the private law of arbitration, which would play a fundamental role in my future career.

After that, I went back to the library, where I shut myself away to write my thesis. I dedicated it to Mama, in gratitude for her unswerving support and constant encouragement, and in memory of the dark years we had been through together.

76

Every man has a duty to the rise and the fall
of his country.

—Chinese adage

Studying abroad has been a popular choice for young Chinese
people since the beginning of the twentieth century. It started
after the Boxer Rebellion of 1900–1901, when the United States
decided to retrocede part of the compensation that China owed
the Western powers in the form of scholarships for young Chinese students.

Those first students provided a sort of model for the generations that followed. So it was for both of my grandfathers in the
1920s: on the paternal side, Yan Baohang went to Edinburgh,
and on the maternal side, Wu Zongjie was given a scholarship
to MIT.

Those pioneers, whose ranks included Deng Xiaoping and Zhou Enlai, played a very important role in the modernization of what was, at the time, a semifeudal and semicolonial country, and the phenomenon of studying abroad has only grown since then. For each generation, the question is always the same: How best can they use the knowledge they have gained abroad to serve China?

The name for these Chinese people who study abroad and then return home is *hǎiguī*, which means "return from abroad," the characters pronounced in the same way as those for "sea turtle." The similarity is also metaphorical, since most sea turtles undertake long migrations before returning to lay their eggs on the same beach where they themselves were hatched. So, *hǎiguī* has ended up becoming a play on words: a Chinese person nicknamed a sea turtle is someone who has returned home after studying for a foreign degree. My grandfathers and I are all sea turtles.

After the Cultural Revolution, however, many students who went abroad were unsure about returning to China. Still left with the feeling that they were "survivors," they wondered, as in the ancient *Bamboo Annals*: If a hunted monkey runs toward the forest, does it really have time to choose which branch it likes best?

And besides, how easy was it to return after one had tasted the Western lifestyle? In Geneva, I was surprised to hear my classmate Lao Zhou tell me that he had no doubts about his future: "As soon as I've defended my thesis, I'm going back to Taiwan. There is so much to be done there. It's the right moment!" I could tell that he was animated by enthusiasm, even a feeling of urgency.

Likewise, when I was in New York in 1986–87, there was a group of dynamic young Chinese people, people of my generation whom I met at Harvard, Yale, Columbia, or Princeton. Some were already working, many on Wall Street, and they had only one desire: to return to China and get started. They all wanted me to do the same. There was an association, the China Business Association (CBA), which facilitated meetings and activities. It organized big parties for the Chinese New Year and the Spring Festival. Those who wanted to become sea turtles would invite their compatriots to dinner, and very often, the conversation would turn to what they planned to do once they had gone back to China.

Among them were Gao Xiqing and Wang Boming. I asked them why they wanted to go back. "To create our own stock exchange," they replied. Oh, is that all?

But how could anybody go about creating a stock exchange in China? At the time, nothing of the kind existed. This was 1987. Most of those young, ambitious people joined Zhao Ziyang's group of advisors. Zhao, who was the Chinese premier at the time, was responsible for a number of reforms initially focused on Sichuan and then spread throughout the whole of China. Zhao's reforms created notable advances in the introduction of a market economy through the separation of state and Party, and, in 1990, helped relaunch the Shanghai Stock Exchange in the

Lujiazui business district in Pudong. These early developments were followed by others such as the Shenzhen experimental zone and the eagerly awaited implementation of currency convertibility.

When I think about my close friends, I realize that almost all of them are sea turtles!

Since the opening of China, between 1979 and 2015, more than four million young Chinese have gone abroad to study. Ten years ago, only about 15 percent of those students returned to China; now, the figure is 80 percent.

Of course, this choice is based on mutual benefit. What attracts the *hǎiguī* is the growth of the Chinese market and the many career opportunities it offers. For its part, China sees those sea turtles as hugely important for its economy. For the past century, the successive generations have gone abroad with the conviction that they were serving their country, and that is still true today. As a general rule, young people are happy to contribute to the growth of their homeland, as long as their homeland makes it possible for them to realize their ambitions.

77

By nature, men are similar.

It is only in practice that they diverge.

—Confucius (551–479 BCE), *Analects*

In 1991, I was headhunted by two large international business law firms. One of them, American, wanted me to join their team in charge of arbitration, which had become my specialty. The other, a French firm named Gide Loyrette Nouel, wanted to develop its business in China. I felt immediately enthusiastic about the second project.

All the more so since the 1990s were, in China, a period of prosperity conducive to the constitution and reconstitution of a modern state legal system. It should be said the Chinese legal system was not inspired by common law, as is the case in Great Britain and the United States, but by the Napoleonic code, where written rules have the force of law. The French model left its mark on China by a circuitous route: after the fall of the Chinese Empire in 1911, republicans such as Sun Yat-sen, seeking a new body of laws to replace the traditional system, imported the German legal system, which they had seen implemented in Japan. In 1949, the New China inherited this written codification, also known as the Continental legal system. It has a constitution, a civil and criminal law, but its contents are fairly simplified.

After the Cultural Revolution, China not only had to reconstitute what had been abandoned or abolished by restoring a functioning legal system; it also had to reform and privatize public companies in order to support its badly needed economic expansion. This meant writing new regulations and laws.

In turn, this meant reversing the usual process for producing a law, whereby it is the responsibility of a legislator. Following the "opening" of China, recommended by Deng Xiaoping, foreign investments forced laws to be formulated after the event that they were supposed to legislate. Given that, for a certain category of laws, there is no known precedent to justify their initial drafting, a system of temporary regulations and pilot laws was created to deal with this new problem.

This sort of experimentation was carried out in the free zone in Shanghai. Or in Shenzhen, which was still little more than a fishing village in 1979, when this territory located on the border of Hong Kong acquired the status of a special economic zone, turning a largely rural area into one of the main experimental laboratories of the new policy of openness to foreign investment.

The idea was to test a whole series of laws whose field of application was restricted to Shenzhen. When the test was conclusive or when any possible problems had been solved, the pilot law was extended throughout the country.

This was how China produced regulations for just over thirty years. By the end of that time, the series of codifications required by the ever-increasing foreign investment had produced a fairly complete legal system for that field. This progress was crowned, in 2001, by China's entry into the World Trade Organization.

But let us return to the time when I joined Gide. Back then, it was the Chinese government itself that asked the firm to develop ideas about the reform of public companies. The opening of the Chinese market, as recommended by Deng Xiaoping, led Beijing to formulate a whole host of questions regarding legislation on state assets, and the role and management of the state in the process of privatization. It was natural that France's expertise should be sought in these areas, as both mechanisms had been experienced there.

That was why we organized a series of meetings in Paris for members of the Chinese State Council with the French prime minister's cabinet and various related departments. I remember how surprised the French were by the pertinence of the questions and comments from the Chinese side. After that, the Chinese delegation pursued its legislative inquiries in Italy, Britain, and the United States. Finally, following a typically Chinese method, they synthesized what they had learned in terms of codification. This pragmatic approach led to a composite legislative system that borrowed from both the Continental and the Anglo-Saxon systems and adapted them to the Chinese situation.

With a small group of partners from the firm, Jean Loyrette and I organized a seminar in China on issues of privatization. There was such interest in this subject in Beijing that the seminar was packed with legislators from parliament and the government, as well as from universities and many different Chinese administrations.

Even before the Cultural Revolution, nobody in China would have thought that the country's laws would be a source of pride. Traditionally, it had been a government of men instituted by men and not by law.

Nowadays, the right to a lawyer is widely accepted, even if there are not enough lawyers to go around, particularly away from the large cities. In 2017, a census revealed three hundred thousand Chinese lawyers. I have witnessed this evolution over almost forty years. Today, China has a legal system that can be considered more or less complete, particularly in the economic and financial fields, where nothing at all existed before. There has been considerable progress, but there remains a difficulty with the corruption of judges. The laws exist, but they are not always enforced.

In China, the rule is that foreign lawyers—and I am one, having been a member of the Paris bar since 1994—must partner with a local firm. One day, when I was still working for Gide on an international case that we had to plead, my Chinese colleague informed me that the judge was asking for himself and his family to be "sponsored" on a trip to Thailand! This kind of request was apparently commonplace.

In the first decade of the twenty-first century, two years after my return to Beijing, I was helping a large French group with an arbitration case against a Chinese company. Even though the verdict was in our favor, the opposing side attempted to overturn the verdict by appealing. The local lawyer with whom I was working agreed with me that their arguments were weak, so we were calm about the situation. However, we both noticed that the judges' attitudes were changing. My Chinese colleague suspected a bribe. While the judges discussed the case, I was summoned urgently to the Beijing Municipal Bureau of Justice. Three men interrogated me, attempting to find out whether the firm I represented, Gide, had "violated Chinese law." In China, it is true, the regulations forbid foreign lawyers from practicing Chinese law, or, in other words, from interpreting it. That was why, during the arbitration, I had taken the precaution of summoning lawyers and professors of Chinese law to interpret the Chinese law germane to our case. My interrogators became quite threatening, but I told myself that I had to remain composed, as the honor of my firm was at stake.

After a very long and unpleasant confrontation, I was told that, to maintain my assertion that I had not "violated Chinese law," I would have to sign an affidavit. I did so, with the feeling that they were trying to intimidate me. This feeling intensified when they claimed that it was necessary to fingerprint me. Afterward, with the client's agreement, I wrote to the Chinese Supreme Court, asking them to examine this international arbitration dispute and pointing out the anomalies observed during the appeal process. Six months later, the court in Beijing came down in our favor.

78

Nothing is impossible to a willing man.

—Chinese proverb

When I was starting out at Gide, in Paris, I noticed that the audio message summoning us to important partners' meetings always began with the words: "Gentlemen, would you please go to the meeting room . . ." I asked about the reason for that wording, which made it sound as if there were no women in the firm.

I was told about the existence of an unwritten rule. This firm, founded in 1920, did not have a single female partner. There were female lawyers—"All brilliant in their field," as they took care to point out—but higher up the ladder, only men! I decided that I should get to know the firm better so I could work out what was going on. As a general rule, lawyers become partners in a firm about six or seven years after joining it, and if for any reason that does not happen, you apply elsewhere or start your own firm.

The years passed, and during a discussion with our senior partner, I pointed out my achievements there: "I've been looking after China for six years now. My colleagues tell me that it's about time to ask about becoming a partner. Am I in the frame?"

My senior partner looked deeply embarrassed. He began by congratulating me on my career, but quickly moved on to the fact that I was married and said it was natural that I would want children. "What we observe," he said, "is that men generally devote more time to their cases than women. This is normal, of course, because they have to look after their husband and children . . . And far be it from me to blame them . . ."

I could not listen to this any longer.

"Sir, as a Chinese woman, I am fully prepared to acknowledge that Mao Zedong committed some terrible crimes. But on one point at least, I would like to do him justice: on the emancipation of women, as illustrated by the saying: 'Women hold up half the sky!' Please bear in mind that I grew up in that environment of sexual equality. What does it matter if I am married? For six years, I have proven myself just as invested in my work as any man . . ."

This time, he interrupted me: "You're right! I'm prepared to support your application. But I cannot second-guess what my partners will say. You need more than seventy-five percent of votes in your favor . . . So it is quite . . . difficult. Have you thought, Lan, about what you will do if you are not made a partner?"

"From the foot of the mountain, the cart will find its way round the hill when it gets there."

On the day of the partners' meeting, I was in Beijing for a negotiation. At 3 a.m., the phone rang in my hotel room. I had been made partner!

There is no doubt that women in France are esteemed in a way they are nowhere else. There is no equivalent of "gallantry" in China. No man would give up his seat for a woman, or rush to open a door for her. We have never enjoyed this exquisite form of politeness. But let's not forget that such behavior is essentially superficial. It is true that France has made progress in the last decade in terms of women's social status. The Copé law, adopted in 2011, imposed a quota on the representation of women in boardrooms of companies with more than five hundred employees that grew, year on year, to 40 percent in 2017. This has given companies more diversity, efficiency, and competitiveness. China is behind the times on this point. In 2015, women were represented at boardroom level at only 9.9 percent, and at 17.2 percent on executive committees in 2016.

That is why I personally am in favor of quotas imposed at boardroom level. Put more than three women in any organization, and you have another voice that can make itself heard. Only one woman is not enough—it is an alibi.

79

Any pain that helps nobody is absurd.

—André Malraux, *Man's Fate*, 1933

After spending two years out in the cold, after what happened in Tiananmen Square in 1989, my father was brought back into the government. There were to be no more long days lazing in the house or out fishing. But while everybody could agree that his appointment in 1991 was a sign of the softening political situation, what struck me were the highs and lows that had always punctuated my father's political career.

I asked him, "So what does it cover, this new portfolio of civil affairs?"

"It's whatever the other ministers aren't dealing with," he replied. "Anything to do with the poor and defenseless. From their birth and upbringing—the orphanages—to the end of their lives, with retirement homes . . . and cemeteries. Government aid is primarily aimed at the poorest regions."

In truth, my father could not have imagined, before he took up his new position, that more than forty years after the establishment of New China, there could still exist sections of the Chinese people living in precarious conditions.

Listening to him, I saw clearly that, far from feeling resentful, my father had meditated on the ups and downs of his own fate. He no longer saw in the same way the period when he was working with Mao Zedong and other leaders. "It was like being locked in an ivory tower," he said. "I knew nothing about Chinese society." It was only after being given this new position that he came to believe that it was the most important work he had ever done.

He went out to discover the poorest, most destitute parts of China. He told me about a village, deep in the mountains, in the province of Guizhou, where the families were so poor that they would borrow clothes from one another whenever one of them had to go to the nearest town. The various aid plans that he set up were all based on the philosophy condensed into this Chinese proverb: "Give a man a fish and he'll eat for a day; teach him to fish and he will never go hungry."

During the same period, my father went to the United States. It was a working trip, where he could closely observe the charity and mutual aid work carried out by NGOs. He returned with the idea that civil society, too, should take responsibility and not leave everything to the government. He developed this idea in a book, *An Overview of Philanthropy in the United States*, and began putting it into practice as soon as he retired from public affairs. In 1997, he became president of the China Charity Foundation, an NGO that works on behalf of poor and damaged populations.

80

Women hold up half the sky.

—Chinese adage

I had long been concerned with the cause of women when I met Aude de Thuin. I had been living back in Beijing since 1998 when this businesswoman traveled over from Paris to speak with me about her international organization, the Women's Forum for the Economy and Society.

Founded in France in 2005, with the support of a group of influential women, this organization's primary aim was to promote greater diversity in ruling bodies, opening up the debate on ways of strengthening women's contribution to the world economy. In Deauville, where the meetings took place, I spoke to an audience made up of compatriots and foreigners. I had gone there for a forum in the company of three Chinese friends: Zhang Xin, the CEO of SOHO China, one of the biggest property groups in China; Hung Huang, a high-profile media figure who publishes a Chinese fashion magazine; and Mei Yan, the head of News Corp in China. Each of us spoke about our experiences in China today, and our contributions proved a hit with an audience surprised to see us representing modernity in China. I emphasized the following points: How is it possible that among the most brilliant female students, educated at the best universities, only a tiny percentage find themselves in positions corresponding to their intellectual success, which is often just as remarkable and consistent as that of their male colleagues? Why do so many obstacles appear in their path as they attempt to rise through the hierarchy of an institution or a company? It's a fact: the higher you go up the echelons, the closer you come to executive positions of great responsibility, the fewer women you see. This is the famous "glass ceiling," under which most female careers stagnate. As a senior executive in a large international group, I thought it useful to remind those young women that, if they are given the means, they have everything they need to smash through this unacceptable ceiling, and that we—their elders—are there to help prepare them.

I learned so much in Deauville, if only from the role models provided by women, all over the world, who are a source of inspiration. I think of Tu Youyou, who won a Nobel Prize in medicine for her research on malaria—research in which traditional Chinese medicine played its part. The simple fact that Tu

Youyou acted as a guinea pig herself to test certain experimental medications demands admiration. I was impressed not only by her perseverance, but by her incredible modesty, too.

I changed jobs in 2011, becoming head of the Lazard bank for Greater China (mainland China, Hong Kong, Taiwan). I felt particularly proud that my team of bankers was 45 percent female, all of the women in those positions purely on merit, while in terms of leadership it was 64 percent female.

The world of banking is, just like the legal world, still very misogynistic. No matter how much talk there is about the feminization of certain professions, the fact remains that, beyond a certain level in the hierarchy, the presence of women grows rarer, and a woman having a job like mine is exceptional. That is why I deliberately set out to create a feminine team at Lazard China. Of course, I would not have been able to do that without the constant support of my CEO, Ken Jacobs.

When I say that my teams are predominantly female, that does not mean that I grant women any particular privilege, because that, too, would be a sexist choice. What it means is that being a woman should not be penalized, as happens far too often. There are more women on my team because I chose and promoted them based purely on their abilities.

Over the past year, our CEO has launched a diversity program in the Lazard group to promote female bankers at every level.

Very often, I go to meetings with clients accompanied by a team of female bankers. Facing me will be the CEO of the Chinese company, escorted by his team of men. As I am usually addressed as Yan Zong—a term of respect designating the boss—the CEO will often call out, "Ah, Yan Zong, you came with your red detachment of women!"

I do not take offense. On the contrary, I confirm that I am there "with 'my' detachment of red women." But I can also tell that, while all of this is said in a jokey tone, the men opposite me are nevertheless a little reserved and defensive. After the meeting, it is amusing to see how the tone has changed, because they have been won over by our professional quality. Sometimes, Chinese clients tell us that the Lazard Brothers in China ought to be renamed the Lazard Sisters.

This reminds me that once, at Gide, I had to deal with a case involving a Japanese client who had a reputation for gross misogyny. As luck would have it, at my first meeting with this client, faced with an entirely masculine commando, my two senior lawyers were women. The client dared to ask whether I had "at least one male senior executive!" The case in point was a delicate litigation that ran the risk of serious difficulties for this Japanese company; in fact, if their problem was not resolved correctly, they even risked bankruptcy. Once we had helped the company out of its bind, the Japanese client sent me a card in which he said that I must have been sent by some god to help them, and that I had won their trust so completely that they would send me other clients. Which, in fact, they did.

81

Memory from Heaven, an appellation that had to be used by the Christian missionaries to translate the notion of God. (...) The idea that the one true God finds its counterpart in the universal sovereign of humanity had to remain the basis of China's political philosophy and practice until the beginning of the twentieth century.

—Anne Cheng, *History of Chinese Thought,* 1997

When we returned to China in 1998, my husband, Robert, and I were asked to help with the Beijing Music Festival, which had just been created by its president, Deng Rong, the youngest daughter of Deng Xiaoping, and the conductor and artistic director of the China Philharmonic, Yu Long.

Since my husband is passionate about classical music, we

were happy to be associated with this nonprofit organization, and to help it seek sponsors and patrons.

In the spring of 2008, Deng Rong asked us if we would be available to go to Rome for a couple of days: China and the Vatican had begun a rapprochement, and in a context that was partly cultural and partly diplomatic, the China Philharmonic had been invited to the Vatican for the first time, to perform in honor of Pope Benedict XVI.

Although we are not Catholic, there are millions of that faith in China. But the government counts only "patriotic" Catholics, by which they mean Catholics who belong to the Church of China, which does not recognize the authority of the Holy See. In fact, since 1949, the People's Republic of China has forbidden all foreign interference in the functioning of churches. Their bishops are appointed by the Chinese authorities, and sometimes but not always confirmed by Rome.

But there are also the "clandestine" Catholics, loyal to the Holy See, whose number is, by definition, unknown. This separation between the "two churches of China" was not recognized by the Holy See, which demanded unity among its faithful. The other subject of disagreement between the People's Republic of China and the Vatican concerned Beijing's desire for the Vatican to break off diplomatic relations with Taiwan. That was why our presence in the Vatican was a historic moment, a first step in the relationship between New China and the Holy See. How could we miss this opportunity?

As we knew nothing about the protocol when dealing with

the papacy, I sought the advice of my dear friend Pierre Morel, who was the French ambassador in Beijing until 2002 before being appointed ambassador to the Holy See in Rome. Pierre Morel received us at his home, the Villa Bonaparte, where he taught us what we needed to know for our meeting the next day, May 7, 2008: only the pope wears white. The cardinals and bishops wear black, with a red belt and calotte for the cardinals, purple for the bishops. One must address the pope as "Your Holiness." The cardinals are "Your Eminence," and bishops "Your Excellency." Pierre showed us how to bow to the Holy Father. As nonbelievers, we did not have to kiss the papal ring. We should dress soberly. No bare arms, no flashy jewelry, no makeup. Since the special audience with His Holiness for the thirty or so members of our delegation would take place immediately after the 6 p.m. concert, I opted for a long black Chinese dress and a simple pearl necklace.

Our delegation walked through a guard of honor formed by the Papal Swiss Guard before being welcomed, applauded warmly by pilgrims, in the Paul VI Audience Hall, to the south of St. Peter's Basilica and the Bernini Colonnade. Benedict XVI was sitting between a group of bishops and cardinals and the space reserved for our delegation.

Long Yu gave a speech in English. He expressed his gratitude to everybody who had enabled his orchestra to perform in honor of the pope, then thanked His Holiness for the support he had given to this "message of love and peace."

Mozart's Requiem had been chosen, since Mozart was the pope's favorite composer and the Requiem his favorite piece.

As the first notes were played, I said a prayer, as I had promised my dear friends Catherine and Bertrand Julien-Laferrière that I would; they are Catholic, and they knew that we were in the Vatican. Even though I am not a Catholic, I prayed for that family, whose two daughters had been adopted from the Wuhan orphanage in the Hubei province of China.

The program's finale was a symbolic piece, a small nod to China: Yu Long conducted the famous "Mòlìhuā," or "Jasmine Flower," a traditional Chinese song from the days of the Emperor Qianlong, a piece made famous by the version arranged by Puccini for *Turandot,* and proudly sung now by the Shanghai Opera House Choir. When the concert was over, the Holy Father joined the orchestra on stage and thanked the musicians for their role as ambassadors, as well as our delegation, and for proving that music is a universal language. Finally, he gave his wishes for success to the entire Chinese nation, just a few months before the start of the Olympic Games.

The special audience with the Holy Father began. First he received a dozen people, one after another. When it was my turn to approach him, I noticed that he was slightly taller than me on his rostrum. He had snow-white hair and intensely blue, translucent eyes. What struck me most was his penetrating gaze, filled with wisdom. I told him what an immense honor it was to be able to meet him, and he replied in English, in a very gentle voice: "You are the messenger of peace and love." I was deeply moved by that simple phrase.

As the audience came to an end, a golden late-afternoon light bathed St. Peter's Square. We were all very emotional. My husband and I went with the Morels to have a drink at the home of our friend Paolo Bruni, formerly the Italian ambassador in Beijing, and we all discussed the historic moment we had just lived through, what had been done, and what still remained to be done to bring China and the Vatican closer together.

82

Man moves alive, tree moves dead.

—Chinese adage

In June 2010, I had come to Paris for a series of meetings with Gide, and I was invited to lunch by the president of the Lazard France bank, Bruno Roger. At first sight, there was nothing unusual about this: Bruno Roger and his wife, Martine Aublet, had come to China once after I had met her at the Women's Forum, and we were still in contact. I always let them know whenever I was passing through Paris.

Bruno Roger asked me if I sometimes went to New York. I had not been back since 1988, when I was a student there, but as chance would have it I was due to return there with my son, Martin, to help him organize a summer campus.

"Well, that's perfect! It would be good, Lan, if you could take advantage of your trip to meet up with Ken Jacobs, our CEO, and Alex Stern, the COO of the Lazard group, to talk to them about China."

So a meeting was arranged that summer in New York, during which I did my best to enlighten Ken and Alex about the situation in China in terms of development. I could tell that they were extremely interested in what I had to say about mergers and acquisitions. But what they really wanted to know was how I viewed the Lazard group in China.

The name of that banking group was rarely mentioned in China. However, I did make a suggestion: "If your intention is to develop your business in China, then I think that's a great idea. This is the right time! But the most important thing is to find a local partner." But for Ken Jacobs, what interested Lazard was having its own team in place there. "In fact," he said, "we're looking for someone like you to take the job!" I was very clear in my response: "I'm a lawyer, not a banker! I could think about a suitable applicant, though, and suggest someone to you."

I left New York. But Bruno Roger kept sending me messages, encouraging me to think seriously about their proposal when I was back in Paris. Finally, I was given a firm job offer to run Lazard China.

To be honest, I had never thought about changing my profession—and that was what was being suggested, with an investment bank specializing in asset management and financial advice. Since Gide had expanded into China, I had enjoyed the satisfaction of seeing the firm make a solid contribution to a reliable legal system, and to the promotion of Continental law. With

Gide, I had helped French companies invest in China. I had also launched the Gide Prize, allowing Chinese lawyers to be trained in French law.

But a little voice kept nagging me: "So, what now? What's your next step?"

This was the same little voice that had given me the objective of being named a partner at Gide. Once I had been put in charge of the firm's Chinese business, the same voice had urged me to make a contribution to creating a legal system in China that meant the country was governed by law, not by man. To help my homeland become a truly modern nation. I had learned how important it was to have courageous reformers to change a society where traditions have so much weight.

Luckily, Lazard did not pressure me. Their message was: "There's no hurry. We can wait for you." So I took my time, talking to my friends and family, asking their opinions. They were all favorable to this change, encouraging me to make the leap even while I was still indecisive.

I reflected on my dilemma: there were certain similarities between my job as a lawyer and this new profession of investment banking. Above all, it was about China, which I knew well. I had a network of Chinese clients. And I had plenty of experience forming and managing a team. Essentially, both jobs were about service, advice, human relations. With quality women and men, anything was possible. True, there would undoubtedly be specific elements in the world of banking that I would have to learn about, but wasn't that precisely the kind of challenge I was looking for? New experiences. New ways to succeed.

Deep down, what I had been searching for confusedly from the beginning was a way of making up for those ten lost years, the decade stolen from my life by the Cultural Revolution. I had always had the impression that I was ten years behind. And I had to keep progressing to quell that sense of dissatisfaction.

The next time I was in Paris, Bruno Roger summoned Jean-Louis Beffa, the former president of the French multinational Saint-Gobain, now at Lazard. "Lan," he told me, "you must have the courage to make the leap toward change." In my head, I had already made it. In April 2011, I became Lazard's head of Greater China. The only woman at Lazard responsible for an entire international region.

Experience has enabled me to see how complementary the professions of lawyer and banker really are. Each functions a little like a production line: the investment bank's financial advisors operate upstream, putting together the dossier, inventing and designing the project, building bridges between the parties to reach an agreement. Lawyers intervene downstream of the transaction, helping with negotiation and drafting contracts.

On my first day at Lazard, perhaps noticing the worried look on my face, one of my colleagues said: "Lan, you must have fun with us!" I liked that line. Not for a second have I regretted my choice, despite the scale of the task, the new knowledge I needed to acquire, the inevitable difficulties. And today, I can say unambiguously: it's a lot of fun!

83

When an old monk sees wedding gifts, he thinks:
that will be for a future life.

—Lao She, *Four Generations under One Roof,* 1949

By the late 1990s, China was in full economic expansion and people had only one ambition: to make money. In parallel to this, I could see my parents preoccupied with improving the condition of the poor and helpless, in collaboration with NGOs. I thought to myself: that is the true face of China.

After retiring in 1994, my mother created her own foundation, the Loving Heart Project Committee, a charity based in Beijing that drew inspiration from the agricultural-aid association Kadoorie, which promotes educational systems linked to a respect for and the conservation of nature in poorer regions of Southeast Asia.

On the advice of a professor at Gansu Agricultural University, my mother decided to help with the schooling of poor children, using an ingenious sheep-farming project. She was directed toward a particular breed of sheep that gave birth to three or four lambs and was very easy to raise. This breed did not eat roots, which meant it did not harm the soil, allowing the peasant farmer to use the land for other cultures. The animal's meat, milk, and skin were all good value. And since the province was Muslim, sheep-farming made sense.

The experiment began in Ningxia, close to Gansu, the smallest autonomous region of China, with an elevation of 6,500 feet. The poorest villages were chosen, and from them thirty particularly destitute families. The school drew up a supplementary waiting list of other families. The principle was that each family was given a ewe in return for the obligation of sending their children to school, girls included. As soon as the ewe gave birth, the family had to give one of the lambs to a family on the waiting list. This circuit created connections with the teacher, who checked that the children were going to school, and also between the families: those waiting for the birth of a lamb were interested in the success of those who had already been given a ewe.

My mother was also interested in the issues arising from the one-child policy that had started in 1979 to fight against overpopulation. Because in the countryside, only the birth of a boy was considered good news, guaranteeing extra manpower for the farm and a daughter-in-law to take care of the aged parents. Consequently, infanticide of girls was common. A specific form of aid, given to mothers and their daughters, was aimed to changing this way of life. "If you educate a woman," my mother said, "you educate the whole family."

Mama invested a huge amount of time and energy, so far from Beijing, in this program, which was initially intended for a thousand families, before it doubled, then tripled in size, and spread to other districts. She was very proud of that project, which made her feel useful. It seemed to me that this fulfillment was a form of redemption for all she had suffered.

As for my father, when he was working for the government between 1991 and 1996, his direct superior, the minister of civil affairs, used to work closely with NGOs, particularly ones that helped disabled people. My father grew interested in this subject due to the superstitions attached to disability (whether mental or physical) in China, where almost all disabled children end up in orphanages or are killed.

My father met the American diplomat, politician, and activist Sargent Shriver during his visit to China. Along with his wife, Eunice Kennedy, the sister of JFK, Shriver was behind the launch, in Chicago, in July 1968, of the Special Olympics, the first organization devoted to improving the lives of mentally disabled people through participation in sports. A personal tragedy was at the origin of the couple's involvement in this area: one of the Kennedy sisters, Rosemary, was mentally disabled.

In one of his books, Sargent Shriver reported that, during their meeting in Beijing, my father had assured him that, in five years, they could work together to bring five hundred thousand athletes into the Special Olympics in China. Sargent Shriver had thought this figure was merely wishful thinking, but Yan Mingfu kept his word, he said, and it was wonderful.

At eighty-five, my father still monitors the success of the Special Olympics in China, in which my husband and I are also highly involved on a voluntary basis.

Back in Beijing, I was struck by the contrast between my parents' public and personal commitment to social improvement and the more selfish ambitions that animated Chinese cities at the time. They also managed to keep some time free to have fun, for which nobody could possibly reproach them.

Almost twenty years have passed since my return to China, and I am happy to see how much the awareness of social responsibility has evolved, both from an individual and a societal point of view.

Many of my friends are actively involved in charities, whether they are helping poor people, protecting the environment, or promoting education and culture. We all feel a duty to give back to our society what it gave to us.

In the summer holidays of 2015, my son, who was educated in the United States, left with his cousin Xiting—the son of my cousin Li Lan—to take part in a project aimed at teaching children in Yunnan, a province on the borders of Vietnam, Laos, and Burma. This program was launched by Xiting ten years earlier, while he was still at university. Thanks to his determination and perseverance, thousands of young people now participate in it. My son, Martin, came back deeply moved by the experience. He was amazed by the intelligence of those children in the mountain regions, and particularly by their thirst for knowledge in such difficult conditions. I have the feeling that the Yan family tradition is being carried on.

84

My greatest grief is the tragic sacrifice of my
fellow nations. My greatest joy is the complete
emancipation of my compatriots.

—Yan Baohang 1942

Many of my Western friends who live in Beijing were interested
in finding traditional houses with square courtyards in the center of the city.

Formed by a collection of low houses, the *siheyuan* is arranged on a single story around one or several square-shaped
interior courtyards. Two carved blocks of sandstone or marble
signal the threshold on either side. Outside some *siheyuans*
there is a plank, which you must step over before going inside,
in order to remove any evil spirits that may have attached themselves to you. In the most beautiful of these houses, the main door,

topped with four *zan*—hexagonal wooden patterns—proclaim the owner's status as a mandarin.

The *siheyuan*, which are characteristic of old Peking, first appeared in the thirteenth century. Whether modest, sober, or refined, these houses and their square courtyards are kept closed on the *hutong* side where the little streets that line them are intertwined. The charm of these courtyards lies in their stone ponds, where golden-colored fish swim, and in their fruit trees—pomegranates, barberries, jujubes, and date plums—chosen for the way their flowers and fruit follow each other from spring until fall. Sometimes there will be a vine climbing up a beautiful pergola, at least for the courtyards that were not devastated by the frantic urbanization of the 1990s.

I, too, wanted to live in a *siheyuan* nestled in the heart of the Old City. My husband and I visited dozens of them, until one day in the summer of 2013 when Robert phoned me.

"You have to come here now!"

"Where?"

"Weijia Hutong!"

My God, why would fate draw me back, thirty-five years later, to the saddest place in my childhood? Hearing that name—Weijia Hutong—my heart shrank. I saw again my father and my mother, named as suspects, exiled by orders of the Central Committee, along with other families who were also placed under surveillance. Twenty families all packed into 18 Weijia Hutong. "Counterrevolutionary" families, watched over by "revolutionary" families. My parents were given two small rooms. Then, when we learned that my father had been imprisoned, the searches began. Seven and a half years later, when my father was released, the central bureau sent us back there, to 18 Weijia Hutong, in an even smaller lodging, not much more than a cupboard.

On July 28, 1976, at 3:42 a.m., the walls rumbled and shook: it was the Tangshan earthquake, its epicenter nearly a hundred miles from Beijing. One of the deadliest in history, 8.2 on the Richter scale. But the Chinese authorities underplayed its magnitude as well as the number of deaths. The country, still "closed," refused international aid. All the families in the Weijia Hutong would live for months on end in tents erected in the various courtyards of the *siheyuan*. And so soon after this event, which felt like the end of the world, I was locked in a constant state of study, book after book, in that cramped little space, trying to relearn everything as quickly as I could. With the undying hope that, one day, I would get out of there, because the university entrance exams were once again open to everybody. But stuck to that hope, nestled against it, was the mass of anxiety represented by 18 Weijia Hutong, and for so long afterward I forced myself to keep away from it, to keep the memory at a distance.

Before moving into the house opposite 18 Weijia Hutong, we had some work done, and I would go there to check on its progress at regular intervals. The ghosts had better watch out, I thought, but I could sense them there, prowling around. My father, having discovered that I had decided to live opposite our old address, traveled all the way from the south of China to see it for himself.

I gave him the tour of what would become our house; then he took my hand, looked me in the eye, and said, "And now, shall we go and see our old house over there? What do you think?"

I hesitated, but there was no arguing with my father's stubbornness. In fact, going to our old house, 18 Weijia Hutong, was exactly what I needed. Closure.

As we were walking through one of the courtyards, an old, white-haired lady rushed over to my father: "Are you Yan Mingfu?"

"Oh, Mrs. Wang!" he exclaimed. "It's been so long!" They embraced, and tears ran down Mrs. Wang's cheeks. I thought I remembered that lady being part of the revolutionary family that had watched over us, but I wasn't sure. The only thing I felt sure of was that I did not want to relive that past.

I asked my father how he managed to keep his hope and optimism. He said simply, "Compared to China's long, long history, and all the upheavals it has been through, my suffering counts for nothing."

History of China

1893: Birth of Mao Zedong.

1898: Birth of Zhou Enlai.

1901: Birth of Zhang Xueliang, warlord and son of the fearsome Zhang Zuolin.

1904: Birth of Deng Xiaoping.

1911: Revolution and fall of the Qing dynasty, which had ruled the Empire since 1644.

1912: Proclamation of the Republic of China, which had its capital in Nanjing. Sun Yat-sen, the co-founder (with Chiang Kai-shek) of the Kuomintang nationalist party, becomes the country's first president.

1915: Japan increases its control over China with the Twenty-One Demands, the aim being to establish a protectorate in a country weakened by the revolution and the fall of the Empire.

1917: Revolution in Russia.

1919: Paris Peace Conference, organized by the victors of the First World War. The Treaty of Versailles restores Shandong to Japan and triggers the Chinese nationalist movement in Beijing known as the May Fourth Movement, led by young, intellectual progressives.

History of the Yans

1895: Birth of Yan Baohang.

1907: Yan Baohang, 12, is admitted into the village school in Liaoning, in northeast China.

1909: Baohang, 14, marries Gaosu, 16.

1910: Baohang, 15, goes to school in Shenyang, capital of Liaoning.

1913: Baohang, 18, enters university. Joins the YMCA in Shenyang. Becomes friends with Zhang Xueliang.

1916: Baohang, 21, converts to Protestantism. Birth of his first daughter, Mingshi.

1918: Baohang, 23, completes his education in China. Appointed secretary-general of the Shenyang YMCA. Becomes interested in socialism and communism. Opens the first school for poor children.

1919: Baohang, 24, becomes father to a second daughter, Mingying.

1921, **July:** First secret congress of the Communist Party of China in the French concession of Shanghai. Mao Zedong is among the thirteen founding members. At the start of its existence, the CPC is supported by the Communist International (Comintern) and allied with Sun Yat-sen's Kuomintang.

1923: Sun Yat-sen's government is recognized by the Soviet Union, which encourages CPC members to join the Kuomintang in a united front against the Japanese and the warlords.

1924: First cooperation between the CPC and the Kuomintang.

1925: Death of Sun Yat-sen. Chiang Kai-shek, the new leader of Kuomintang, turns against his communist allies. Start of the Chinese civil war.

1927: With the Shanghai Massacre of communists in April, Chiang Kai-shek's Kuomintang attempts to prevent the CPC from overthrowing his government. Marriage of Chiang Kai-shek to Soong May-ling.

1928: Following a second offensive against the warlords in an attempt to unify China under the Kuomintang, Chiang Kai-shek takes control of the Republic. Zhang Xueliang rallies to the nationalist cause.

1931: Japan invades Manchuria.

1934: Start of the Long March, led by the Red Army and part of the CPC, to escape the Kuomintang forces during the civil war.

1935: At the end of the Long March, surviving communists set up base in Shaanxi and establish their capital in Yan'an.

1936: Xi'an Incident, provoked by Zhang Xueliang's arrest of Chiang Kai-shek. As soon as he is released, Chiang sentences Zhang to life imprisonment. Japan occupies Manchuria.

1922: Baohang, 27, has his first son, Daxin.

1924: Birth of Mingzhi, Baohang's second son.

1927: Baohang goes to London, then to Edinburgh University, to complete his education.
Birth of his third daughter, Mingguang.

1929: Yan Baohang interrupts his studies to return to China via Copenhagen and Moscow.

1931: Birth of Baohang's third son, Mingfu (father of Lan). Baohang organizes the defense of his homeland: from Beijing to Shanghai, passing through Nanjing, he coordinates the anti-Japanese struggle.
Birth of Wu Keliang, Lan's mother.

1937: Second Sino-Japanese War. The Kuomintang government takes refuge in Chongqing.

1939, August 23: Ribbentrop and Molotov sign the Nazi-Soviet nonaggression pact in Moscow.

1941, June 22: The Third Reich invades the Soviet Union.

December 7: Japan attacks Pearl Harbor, causing the United States to enter the Second World War.

1945, August 9: The Soviet Red Army destroys the Japanese army in Guangdong.

China's Red Army takes the name the People's Liberation Army.

1949, October 1: Proclamation of the People's Republic of China by the communist government.

December: Mao's first trip to Moscow.

1953: Death of Stalin.

1937: Zhou Enlai invites Yan Baohang to secretly join the CPC. Baohang starts to work as a secret agent within the nationalist government, in close proximity to Chiang Kai-shek and his wife.

1941: Yan Baohang sets up a spy cell in Chongqing. Obtains the exact date of the German attack on the USSR and immediately transmits it to Moscow.
November: Obtains information on Japan's plan to attack Pearl Harbor.

1944: Interception of complete data about Japanese army stationed in Manchuria.

1946: Yan Baohang is named governor of Liaobei as soon as the territory is liberated by the communists.

1949, October 1: Yan Baohang becomes a permanent member of the Standing Committee of Chinese People's Consultative Conference. He helps Zhou Enlai prepare work on the Chinese Senate. His eldest son, Daxin, is fighting the nationalists in the south. His youngest son, Mingfu, 18, begins a career as a Russian translator and interpreter.

1952: Wu Keliang, a student at Peking University, begins working as an interpreter.

1953: Mingzhi, Yan Baohang's second son, is a diplomat posted to Moscow. Gaosu, 60, joins the CPC. Mingfu meets Wu Keliang.

1954: Wu Keliang joins the Department of International Liaisons.

1955: Mingfu, 24, becomes Mao's personal Russian interpreter. Mingfu and Keliang are married.

1957: Start of campaign against "rightists."

Hundred Flowers Campaign.

Mao's second and final trip to Moscow.

Sino-Soviet relations grow cold.

1958: Launch of the Great Leap Forward.

1959: First of three years of natural disasters, causing the Great Famine that kills thirty million people.

1966: Start of the Cultural Revolution. Mao's cult orchestrated by Lin Biao. Epidemic of "suicides," including those of Lao She and Fu Lei. Creation of the Red Guards. Jiang Qing, Mao's wife, leads the group in charge of the Cultural Revolution.

1967: The chairman, Liu Shaoqi, and his wife, Wang Guangmei, are arrested.

1968, May 22: Deng Pufang, son of Deng Xiaoping, is tortured by Red Guards and throws himself out of a window. His parents are placed under house arrest.

October: Deng Xiaoping stripped of all his duties.

1969: Deng and his wife work in a tractor factory.

Lin Biao is designated Mao's successor.

1971, September 13: Death of Lin Biao in a plane crash in Mongolia.

1973: The Gang of Four, the ringleaders of the Cultural Revolution (including Mao's wife, Jiang Qing), are promoted to positions of greater power.

1976: Zhou Enlai's death, in January, provokes protests against the Gang of Four. Mao dies in September. The Gang of Four are arrested. End of the Cultural Revolution.

1957: Birth of Lan.

Mingshi, an editor, is criticized and condemned as a rightist, and exiled for more than twenty years to Liaoning with her eight children.

Mingfu is in the delegation that goes to Moscow.

1959: At the request of Zhou Enlai, Yan Baohang joins the Archive Research Committee of the Standing Committee of Chinese People's Consultative Conference.

1962, Summer: Lan, 5, stays with her parents in Deng Xiaoping's house in Beidaihe.

1966: Mingfu placed under house arrest in his ministry.

1967, November 6: Arrest of Yan Baohang, 72.

November 17: Arrest of Yan Mingfu, 36.

December: Keliang placed under house arrest in her ministry.

1968, May 22: Death of Yan Baohang, 73, seven months after his arrest.

Summer: Keliang exiled to a labor camp in Heilongjiang, close to the Soviet border.

1969: Keliang sent to a labor camp in Henan, where Lan, 12, is authorized to join her.

1971: Death of Gaosu, 78.

1974: Keliang is allowed to visit her husband, Mingfu, in prison, after seven years of incarceration.

1975: Mingfu is released. Only then does the family learn about the deaths of Baohang and his second son, Mingzhi, 51.

1977: Deng Xiaoping reintroduces university entrance exams after an eleven-year hiatus.

1978, December: New policy of liberal openness led by Deng Xiaoping.

1980: A special court is established to judge the Gang of Four. Jiang Qing is sentenced to death. Three years later, her sentence is commuted to life imprisonment.

1989: Tiananmen Square massacre.

1991: "Suicide" of Mao's widow, Jiang Qing.

1997: Death of Deng Xiaoping.
Hong Kong handed over to China: "one country, two systems."

2001: China enters the World Trade Organization.

2010: China becomes the world's second greatest economic power.

1977: Lan, 20, passes the national exam and is accepted by the Peking Foreign Languages Institute.

1978: January: Rehabilitation of Yan Baohang.

1981: Lan enters the law school of Peking University.

1984: Lan joins the Graduate Institute of International Studies in Geneva.

1985: Mingfu becomes the leader of the United Front Work Department.

1987: Lan becomes a research associate at Harvard.

Mingfu named as secretary to the CPC's Central Committee.

1988: Mingfu named vice president of the Political Consultative Conference.

1989: Mingfu stripped of his duties.

1991: Lan joins the law firm Gide Loyrette Nouel in Paris.

Mingfu named vice-minister of civil affairs.

1995, May 9: Yan Baohang posthumously decorated by Boris Yeltsin during the fiftieth anniversary of the Allied victory over Nazi Germany.

1997: Birth in Paris of Martin Shi, Lan's son.

1998: Lan returns to China as the head of Gide's law office in Beijing.

2000: Death of Mingshi, Lan's first aunt,

2004: Death of Daxin, Lan's first uncle.

2007: Death of Mingying, Lan's second aunt.

2011: Lan named head of Greater China for Lazard.

2015, January: Death of Wu Keliang.

The Yan family is awarded a commemorative medal for Yan Baohang's actions as part of the seventieth anniversary of the victory over Japan.

Acknowledgments

My thanks go to Bertrand and Catherine Julien-Laferrière, who started this whole adventure by encouraging me to write down the story I had told them.

To Christine Ockrent, who arranged a meeting with her editor, and Nicole Lattès for her confidence in me.

To Brigitte Paulino-Neto for her precious help, without which this book would never have seen the light of day.

To Malcy Ozannat, who made this book possible.

To Christine Cayol for her very useful advice.

To Sébastien Rousillat for his translations, from Chinese into French, of certain historical documents.

To Ken Jacobs, who always gave me his support. I asked him

to let me leave Lazard to write, and he replied that he did not know anybody who had written a book after leaving Lazard, only those who had published their book by staying at Lazard!

To Arnaud Michel, my former law partner at Gide Loyrette Nouel, and not only because he specializes in intellectual rights.

To Robert and Martin for their support in every moment, and because they let me use the time that would normally have been spent with them so that I could begin this long, solitary journey of writing and reflection.

To all my friends, who followed every stage in the progress of this writing with great encouragement, interest, and curiosity. "Where are you in your book?" they would ask, every time I met them . . .

Here it is!

About the Author

Lan Yan was not allowed to enter higher education because her Communist family had been designated as counterrevolutionaries. In 1969, she was sent to a reeducation camp in Henan, where she spent more than five years with her mother. In 1977, a year after the Cultural Revolution ended, Lan enrolled at university. Exceptionally motivated, she was awarded grants to study the most prestigious universities in Europe and the United States. She obtained an LLM from Peking University and a doctorate in law from the Graduate Institute of International Studies in Switzerland. Lan joined Gide Loyrette Nouel, a Paris-based law firm, and she became the first foreign-born woman to make partner. After twenty years practicing law in France and China, she joined Lazard, a finance advisory and asset management firm, in 2011. She is the vice chairman of investment banking and chairman and CEO of greater China investment banking.